If You
Could Hear
What I See

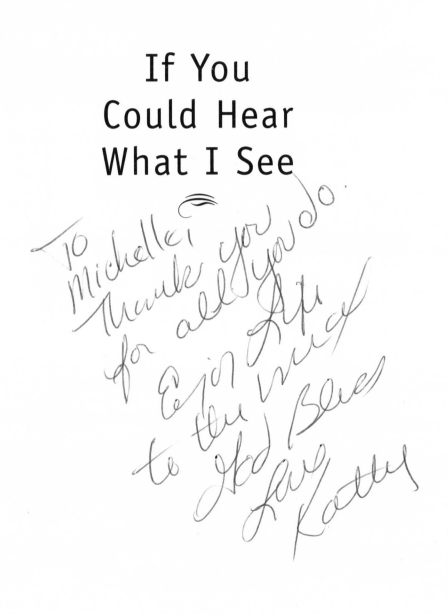

To Michelle,
Thank you
for all you do.
Enjoy Life
to the fullest
God Bless
Love
Kathy

If You Could Hear What I See

Lessons About Life, Luck, and the Choices We Make

KATHY BUCKLEY
WITH LYNETTE PADWA

DUTTON

All the stories and incidents in this book are based on real people and events.
Some names and locations have been changed.

DUTTON
Published by the Penguin Group
Penguin Putnam Inc., 375 Hudson Street, New York, New York 10014, U.S.A.
Penguin Books Ltd, 27 Wrights Lane, London W8 5TZ, England
Penguin Books Australia Ltd, Ringwood, Victoria, Australia
Penguin Books Canada Ltd, 10 Alcorn Avenue, Toronto, Ontario, Canada M4V 3B2
Penguin Books (N.Z.) Ltd, 182–190 Wairau Road, Auckland 10, New Zealand

Penguin Books Ltd, Registered Offices: Harmondsworth, Middlesex, England

First published by Dutton, a member of Penguin Putnam Inc.

First Printing, July, 2001
10 9 8 7 6 5 4 3 2 1

 REGISTERED TRADEMARK—MARCA REGISTRADA

Library of Congress Cataloging-in-Publication Data
Buckley, Kathy.
If you could hear what I see : lessons about life, luck, and the choices we make /
by Kathy Buckley with Lynette Padwa.
p. cm.
ISBN 0-525-94611-X
1. Buckley, Kathy.   2. Comedians—United States—Biography
3. Deaf—United States—Biography.   I. Padwa, Lynette.   II. Title.
PN2287.B745 A3 2001
792.77'028'092—dc21
[B]
2001028719

Printed in the United States of America
Set in Simoncini Garamond
Designed by Leonard Telesca

This book is printed on acid-free paper. ∞

To my family

Contents

Acknowledgments

I would like to acknowledge all those who have crossed my path, whether for five minutes or a lifetime. You were my teachers, and from you I learned to choose the life I now cherish.

Special thanks to—

Lynette Padwa. I know without you I would have written this book with a lisp.

Bonnie Solow, my agent. From the first day we met I knew I couldn't be in better hands.

Suze Orman, who knew that now was the time to put this book together, and who put me on this incredible path to share my light with others.

Brian Tart, my editor at Dutton, for your insight, guidance, and good humor.

Amy Hughes, for your hard work, enthusiasm, and great attitude.

Sioux Saloka, for getting me started on this project eight years ago. Your help was invaluable.

Jerry Washburn, for his mastery of e-mail and my Web site.

Jane West, for always being there when I needed you, even if I didn't know I needed you.

The Bakerink family, because no good work is done without a supportive and loving family.

Mark Buckley, my brother, for being my number-one fan from day one.

Rosemary Meyer, for believing in me and teaching me to take the *t* off my *can't*s.

Roberta Kent, for your love, support, and for the laughter.

My audiences, for allowing me to share my heart with you. In doing so, I hope you too will know just how loved you are.

God, for giving me the choice to live and the wisdom to ask for Your guidance every day.

And to all my friends, who stayed away while I was working on this book . . . I can come out and play now!

If You Could Hear What I See

1

I Can Hear the Laughter

IT WAS THE first time I had played the Hollywood Comedy Room, and I was determined not to be late. It wasn't easy. For once, I could barely tear myself away from my apartment. I had just gotten a new pair of hearing aids that very day, and on the way home from AAA Hearing Service I had stopped at the grocery store. I was listening to things I had never heard before—the signal light in my car beeping, the wheels clicking on the shopping cart. At the checkout counter I kept hearing another strange noise, and I couldn't figure out where it might be coming from. I watched the cashier's face, looking for clues, but she didn't seem to notice anything different. What the heck was that noise? Finally I noticed the young man who was bagging my food. The sound seemed to be coming from his direction.

"What's that?" I asked him.

"What?"

"That."

"That what?"

"I don't know—I'm asking you."

"You mean the food?"

"The food is making noise?"

"No, lady, the paper bag is making noise." He gave me a wary look. "Any other questions?"

I was amazed. Thirty-four years old, and I had never known that paper made noise. I went home as excited as a five-year-old and grabbed every type of paper I could find, laid them all out on the living room floor, then sat in the middle of the floor crumpling up the papers just to hear them crunch. Newspaper, wax paper, tin foil, Kleenex—one by one I'd pick them up and crinkle them next to my ear, saying, "Yes! Yes!" They all had their own sound, until I got to the Kleenex. I crunched it, tore it, waved it by my ear— "Talk to me, baby, talk to me!" Nothing.

I made it to the club with a half hour to spare, keeping a personal vow I had made to myself never to be late for a gig. As usual, I walked onstage with a big plastic hand attached behind my ear in the "Eh? What?" position. Deafness is sometimes known as the invisible disability, and I wanted to make it visible. The plastic hand on my ear made it easier for me to explain my hearing loss and speech impediment right away. Otherwise the audience might think I was just another wise-ass New Yorker, which is exactly what I've been told I sound like. My opening line:

"You would think with today's technology they could come out with a hearing aid that is just a little less obvious than this."

"*AAAAAAAHHHAAAA!*"

The sound hit my ears with the force of a cannon blast. What was *that*? I backed away from the microphone toward the rear of the stage and stared at the faces below me, but they looked normal. Somehow I managed to deliver my next line.

"Yes, I am hearing impaired. No, I am not deaf, I just don't listen."

"*Haraughhh! Ehhhhh! Hehehehehhenck!*"

Laughter! It was the sound of the audience laughing. I stood there in shock and they sat smiling up at me, not knowing why I had frozen. In every performance before this one, I had heard only a muffled rumble when they laughed. I'd wear flat shoes so I could feel the audience's laughter vibrate through the floorboards of the stage. To get the timing, I'd play off the faces I could see, and if I saw a face I didn't like I'd move on to the next one. But I had no idea that laughter could sound like this. Now here it was, coming at me like the big ball in *Indiana Jones*, with hundreds of separate voices chuckling and cackling away.

"I feel like I'm being attacked right now," I blurted out, and the faces shifted from happy to confused. I forgot my rehearsed lines as the tears started welling up. I might as well confess, I figured, or they'll think I'm not just hearing impaired but deranged, too.

"I've just received a new set of hearing aids today. For the first time, I'm hearing laughter without having to feel it. I'm hearing it, feeling it, and seeing it all at once, and it is totally overwhelming! That is your laughter, isn't it? Or are you yelling at me? Because I'm not too sure what's going on up here, but I'm loving it."

While they applauded, I tried to adjust myself to the thick, surreal noise. For the next ten minutes I rushed through the material, standing closer and closer to the edge of the stage, forcing myself to tell the jokes while I stared first at one face, then another, matching the laughs to the people and bracing myself for the bowling ball of noise that rolled at me every time a line connected. I was so awestruck by the fullness of the sound, I wanted to sit in the audience and laugh alongside them. To add to the confusion, I was hearing my own voice in a way I never had before, amplified through the microphone. Damn, I *do* have a speech impediment!

Finally the set was over and I ran to the ladies' room. I locked myself in a stall and let the tears pour out. I didn't know why I was crying—it was a combination of emotions I had never experienced, as if a light went on in a part of my heart I had never seen. A few minutes later the club's manager found me in there.

"Kathy! What's wrong? You killed tonight!"

"Did you hear that?" I asked her. "Because I did! I could hear their laughter."

It wasn't just the laughter, it was what it meant. It was the joy of acceptance. I had been doing comedy for about a year, and this was the first time I had felt the full impact of an audience cheering and applauding. It was a whole new world of communication opening up for me. The audience had been giving me this gift all along, but I had never known about it until now.

When I was little, no one knew I had a hearing loss. I managed to pick up lip-reading at a very young age, and I never realized that other people heard any more than the low rumblings and fuzzy wah-wah noises that I heard. I also had a bad speech impediment. People said I had a "lazy tongue," which made no sense to me. I remember looking in the mirror with my mouth wide open, poking at my tongue as if trying to wake it up. To make matters worse, when I was five years old my two front teeth were knocked out, and my permanent teeth didn't come in until I was about eight. I guess I had lazy teeth to go with my lazy tongue. The only thing I was missing was a lazy eye.

Of course, the main reason for my speech impediment wasn't a lazy tongue or missing teeth, it was that I had no idea how words were supposed to sound because I couldn't hear them. Imagine you're trying to learn Swahili while wearing earplugs and standing beneath Niagara Falls. The language is present, someone's lips are moving, but the only thing that registers is some occasional noise— you have to figure out the meaning without words. It's not easy to understand language that way and nearly impossible to learn to speak it. My voice was very nasal, and I'd drag my words and combine them. I had only a few consonants. In order to tell somebody something I'd stand in front of him or touch him so he would look at me, and then I'd start speaking as well as I was able: "I need some water" might come out as "Iee om aaaher." My facial expressions and miming had to fill in the rest of the story. I could tell if it wasn't working because people would get this constipated look as they struggled to figure out what I meant. When the look eased up a little, I knew I was getting through. I was also very shy and quiet and only tried to communicate when I absolutely had to. Most of my effort went into watching other people and copying the way they acted so I could fit in.

As hard as it was for me to communicate, it didn't stop my parents from enrolling me in our neighborhood school, Hampshire Elementary. I arrived at kindergarten a five-year-old lip-reading mimic with a perm that made me look like one of the Three Stooges. My mom parted my hair in the middle and styled it flat on top and curly on the sides, with bangs—just in case I didn't stand out enough already. I slid through kindergarten, although the teacher noted on my progress report that I wasn't very good at taking directions. She considered me a disruptive child because I made distracting noises in class and seemed to have such a short attention span. I was only paying attention to the people whose lips I could read. These were usually the kids sitting next to me, and they barely made any sense at all. The teacher spent most of her time with her back to the class, explaining the lessons while writing on the chalkboard. Unfortunately, by the time I could find someone's lips to read to figure out what was going on from their answers to her questions, she would be on to another topic. My eyes would ache from all the straining I did looking for some kind of a connection.

Because I was always watching the other kids and making noises without realizing it, I was frequently sent into exile—or as it was known in 1960, the cloakroom. It was supposed to be a punishment, but I kept myself entertained by conducting taste tests of the contents of the brown bag or lunch box I found sitting beneath each coat. Let's just say there weren't any weight problems with the children in that class, thanks to me. After scraping the fillings out of all the Oreo cookies I could find, I'd sample the Twinkies. (To this day Oreo cookies and milk are my comfort food.) Then I'd try on the coats. I remember spending a lot of time in there. Anything was better than having to pretend I understood what the rest of the class was doing.

Despite my "behavior problems," Hampshire Elementary promoted me to first grade and then to second. My talents as a lip-
reader and mimic finally failed me completely in Mrs. Crawford's
second-grade class. She was in her fifties, and I was seven years old.
Neither of us had a clue what the other one needed. It wasn't a fair
fight.

Mrs. Crawford was tall and chunky, with dark, gray-streaked
hair. She wore the standard 1960s teacher's uniform of plain,
straight skirt and pale button-down blouse, with a cardigan sweater
thrown over her shoulders on chilly days. Mrs. Crawford spent a lot
of time walking around the classroom, slowly circling the desks,
watching us. I was always looking to see where she was and praying she wasn't close. Her face was tight, and when she smiled at me
I got scared. She wore glasses but was always peering over them,
and when she focused on me she'd squint so much that I couldn't
tell the color of her eyes. I could barely even see the whites.

I don't know if my other teachers had warned Mrs. Crawford
about me, but she seemed determined not to let me get away with
anything. By mid-November I was terrified. I never felt safe in that
class, not even when we were doing art.

It was just past lunchtime, and Mrs. Crawford was walking
around the classroom passing out sheets of paper. I wasn't sure
what I was supposed to do with the paper because her back had
been turned when she was explaining the assignment. I looked
around to see what the other kids were doing. They were drawing
something on the paper. I didn't know what I was supposed to be
drawing. This made me scared and nervous, and when I got nervous I hummed. *Hmmmmmm.*

I loved humming. I liked the vibration in my throat and chest;
it really helped to calm me. I didn't hear it, I just felt it. I didn't
realize that I was making noise other people could hear. I was
humming and drawing, trying to keep up with the other kids,
when Mrs. Crawford came by and put her hand on top of my
wrist. She seemed to be annoyed with something because she was

giving me The Look. She frowned and shook her head as if to say, "Don't do that."

I was the only one in class she ever did this to and it made me very uncomfortable. I always stopped whatever I was doing when I got The Look, so I put the pencil down. Soon I was bored, so I made my vibration to pass the time. *Hummmmmm, hummmmm.* Mrs. Crawford, who was walking around the room watching the students draw, looked over at me, her expression irritated. I couldn't figure out what she wanted. She returned to my desk, picked the pencil up, and put it back in my hand. She motioned to me as if to say, "Well, go ahead." I started to draw again as she walked up to her desk at the front of the room.

Soon I got engrossed in drawing my picture and was humming away once more. She came back and grabbed my wrist. I put the pencil down. She moved away. *Hmmmm, hummmmm.* My humming was getting more intense—she was really making me nervous now. She looked at me. I picked the pencil up. *Hmmmmm.* What did she want? I put the pencil down. Up, down, up, down, up.

I didn't see her at first. Suddenly she was standing next to my chair. She didn't look good, she looked angry. "Stop it!" I saw her say, so I put the pencil down again. *Hummmmmmm.* Mrs. Crawford grabbed the pencil and paper off my desk, pulled me up out of my chair, pointed at the door, and said, "Take your chair and go sit outside!"

I was horrified but obediently dragged my chair to the cloakroom to get my coat. She shook her head, saying, "Outside, now!" Scared, I did as I was told. I picked up my chair and carried it outside, then out the building to the middle of the schoolyard. I sat there in the snow, with no coat on and tears running down my face, just humming in the wind.

When Mrs. Crawford, Principal Connolly, and Mr. Jake the maintenance man finally found me, they were very angry and I was very cold. I got punished again, and still had no idea what I had done wrong. All I knew was that I was not doing very well in second grade. Later, someone told me that Mrs. Crawford had meant outside the classroom, in the hall. No one explained to me that my humming vibration made noise.

Life continued that way for the rest of the semester. The frustrated school psychologist, Mr. Banks, gave me a series of tests to discover why my ability to keep up with the rest of the class had deteriorated so quickly. Despite the fact that some of these tests revealed a hearing loss, the Hampshire teaching staff never seemed to connect that with my problems in the classroom. They moved me to the front row so I could hear better, but my impairment was far too severe for that. As long as Mrs. Crawford had her back to the class, which she usually did, I was sunk. I was labeled academically slow because I couldn't comprehend the lessons at the same rate as the other students. Mr. Banks plowed on, giving me test after test, determined to get to the bottom of my "disability." Everyone assumed I was slow, the only question was, how slow? Slower than a turtle, or as slow as a snail?

Hampshire Elementary wasn't entirely to blame for overlooking my hearing loss. I masked it well without realizing it. By the age of seven I had become an expert chameleon, since my survival at school depended on how well I could imitate the other kids. Lip-reading was my main source of communication, but with lip-reading I could only decipher 25–30 percent of a conversation, *if* I already had the vocabulary. This is why I hit such a wall in second grade. They increased the vocabulary so that I understood less than I had before, and they started teaching phonics. "Sound it out, Kathy!" I don't think so.

No doubt I had been brilliant at finger painting in kindergarten, and I had even managed to get through first grade on my considerable charm, but this was now The Second Grade and it became painfully obvious that everyone was expecting to see what I had learned. There was one small problem: I hadn't learned anything. The past seven years had not prepared me as it had the other students. I had been busted by the English Language Grammar and Vocabulary Police. "No, sir, it didn't go in one ear and out the other, honest it didn't. It just never made it into one ear in the first place."

By mid-year I was flunking second grade. Here is a copy of my report card:

SECOND GRADE

The REPORT CARD indicate:
1. Poor in accepting responsibility
2. Poor in thinking and working independently
3. Poor in using time profitably
4. Poor in comprehending reading - but improving
5. Poor in attack on new words
6. Poor in increasing vocabulary. Very slow.
7. Poor in expressing ideas in written form correctly.
8. Poor in reading expression.
9. Poor in Spelling.
10. Poor in arithmetical accuracy.
11. Poor in reading problems with understanding.

Cathy had learned to read in spite of a serious speech defect. It is hoped that the speech problem will clear up afther the second teeth come in.

Note that I was judged poor in "using time profitably," which everyone knows is the cornerstone of second grade. My favorite part of that report card is the comments area at the bottom, where the teacher notes that "Cathy had learned to read in spite of a serious speech defect. It is hoped that the speech problem will clear up afther the second teeth come in." I didn't have the heart to tell them I spelled my name with a "K." I didn't want them to feel inadequate. *Afther* all, they were supposed to know more than I did.

One evening, after another long day of testing, Mr. Banks came to my house. I was sitting in my living room looking out the picture window when he drove up. I stayed at my post, staring outside while he explained to my mother that I might have a severe hearing loss. Years later my mom told me what transpired that day.

"She does not have a hearing loss," my mother had insisted.

"Call her name," said Mr. Banks.

"Kathy. Kathy. *Kathy!*"

She came up from behind me and grabbed me by the shoulders, scaring the daylights out of me.

"I've come to the conclusion that Kathy needs a comprehensive hearing exam at the Cleveland Hearing and Speech Center," Mr. Banks told my astonished mother. I stayed frozen in my chair, awash in anxiety. As Mr. Banks got up to leave, my mother barely glanced at him. She was looking at me, and her expression was heartbroken.

2

Confessions of a Deaf Catholic

YES, IT'S TRUE, my mother did not know I had a hearing loss. She was stunned at Mr. Banks's suggestion, and when he left the house that afternoon she still refused to believe him. My father was taken by surprise at the diagnosis, too. How could they have been so oblivious to a child who could barely speak and didn't appear to comprehend what was going on around her? They had low expectations for me, thanks to my mother's doctors.

I was born an RH negative baby, which meant that my mother's and father's blood was incompatible and my own blood was poison to me. Within 15 minutes of birth I was severely anemic and jaundiced and needed a complete transfusion. Unfortunately, they couldn't find any blood for twelve hours. When the doctors released me from the hospital they told my parents that because of the delay in getting the transfusion I might be a slow learner. Back then people didn't think to get a second opinion.

Then, when I was five years old, I contracted aseptic meningitis. The disease is caused by a virus and has many of the same symptoms as bacterial meningitis: fever, headache, stiff neck, lethargy, confusion, and seizures. The longer a person goes without treatment, the greater the risk of permanent neurological damage such as hearing loss, retardation, or blindness. Unfortunately, aseptic meningitis is hard to detect. It is also highly contagious, so when they finally diagnosed me I was put into quarantine in the hospital.

I don't remember being all that sick, but I do remember the hospital room and the cagelike bed I was confined to. I was all by myself—no one was allowed in the room, not even family members. At night it was spooky when the lights went out and all the shadows appeared on the wall. I was so scared and weak from the fever that I'd just lie in the bed whimpering. A nurse would come in from time to time to take my vital statistics, and every time that door opened, I would hope it was my mom. One day the nurse carried me to the window and held me up. Far away on the pavement below, my family was standing and waving. I was so happy to see them that I tried to climb out of the nurse's arms to be with them. When she put me back in the bed I became hysterical. It must have killed my mother to watch her take me away from that window screaming.

When I was finally released my parents got another dose of bad news: due to the delay in treatment, my ability to learn might be affected. I do not believe the doctors mentioned the part about a possible hearing loss. To this day, no one knows whether I had a hearing impairment at birth or if it was caused by the meningitis. In any case, with all those doctors' warnings I can understand how my parents would think I was a slow learner. It would explain so many things, for example, my behavior in church.

My mother is Italian and my father is English, and every Sunday the whole family would get dressed up and go to Our Lady of Mt. Carmel Catholic Church. It was built in a gothic style, with an enormous arched ceiling, stained-glass windows, and plaques showing the stations of the cross. There were statues of the saints and, up front, a huge crucified Christ. The crucifix made me sad, which was one of the reasons I didn't like church. The other was that I never knew what the priest was talking about. Years later I found out that most of the service was held in Latin. I never had a chance!

God moves in mysterious ways, and so did everything else in church. I couldn't keep up with all the standing up, sitting down, kneeling—I guess you could call it Catholic aerobics. I'd look for the oldest lady and try to follow her, but I was always one move behind. The first time they passed the basket for the offering, I thought they were offering it to me. Boy, did my hands get slapped fast! I thought the kneeling pad was a bench for kids. No, I learned, it was for the old ladies' precious knees. When I kneeled on it I couldn't see anything. Was I supposed to be praying now? And I definitely did not understand the communion wafer. It was too bland, and you couldn't go back for seconds. For meager entertainment I'd let it stick to the roof of my mouth and spend five minutes rolling it off with my tongue, as though it were spiritual peanut butter.

When I was eight years old, my mother decided it was time I started going to confession. I had no idea what it was supposed to be about. One day while we were in church she just walked me over to a booth with red curtains and gave me a gentle push. "Go in and tell God your sins," she said.

I thought God Himself was going to be in there. "Hi," I whispered to God as I felt around for a light switch. It was nearly pitch black inside, and I couldn't lip-read in the dark. I sat down carefully and waited, not realizing there was a priest sitting on the other side of the partition. I couldn't see, hear, or even smell him over the musty scent of the confessional. When nothing happened after a few minutes, I figured God wasn't home.

"Did you tell him your sins?" my mother asked when I came out of the booth.

"No." I didn't know what sins were.

"Go back in and tell God you have sins."

From the look on her face, sins were not good things to have. I went in, blurted out, "I have sins," and ducked, certain I was going to be struck by lightning or bonked on the head. I stayed frozen in a crouched position for a few minutes until I realized that God still wasn't there. Outside the confessional, Mom stood waiting for me with a skeptical look on her face.

"What did you say?" she demanded as I came through the curtains.

"I have sins, but I don't know what sins are," I admitted.

"You fight with your brother and argue with your mother. Now get back in there."

Back inside I went. Now that I knew what my sins were, I wasn't going to confess them without offering a defense: "I fight with my brother and argue with my mother, but *you* try living with my mother and not arguing." Silence. I kicked the curtains in front of me for a few minutes, then came out for the third time.

"How many?" my mother asked.

"How many what?" I was totally confused. "I don't even think He was in there. He's not home."

"Go back in and find out what your penance is," my mother was saying, when suddenly the priest appeared from behind the booth. I was flabbergasted and couldn't figure out where he'd come from.

"Don't let her back in here," he said, looking annoyed. My mother blushed deep red.

"What's her penance?" she asked quickly.

"Five Hail Marys and seven Our Fathers."

"Five Hail Marys and seven Our Fathers," she repeated as she pointed me toward a pew. I didn't know what those prayers were, so I knelt down and silently tried to make a deal with God: "I'll quit fighting with my brother if you get him to quit starting it. And my mother—get her to stop talking to me from the other room and I'll stop arguing with her. Hail Mary, Hail Mary, Hail Mary, Hail Mary, Hail Mary. Our Father, Our Father, Our Father, Our Father, Our Father, Our Father, Our Father. Amen."

My first confession pretty well sums up my experiences as a young child. To the casual observer—which is basically what my mother was—I must have come across either as a smart aleck or a very dumb one. In reality, I was isolated and terrified. While everyone else seemed to be gliding through life with no effort at all, I was like a puppy who had been tossed in an icy lake to sink or swim. I treaded water like crazy, trying not to drown or let on how hard it was for me. I had no useful verbal language; I absorbed information through what I saw and sensed. Sometimes I would stare so hard at people that I felt as if my eyes were going to pop out. I had no awareness of my hearing problem and assumed I was dumber than everyone else because I couldn't do what came so naturally to them. If I didn't fully understand something, I just acted as if I did.

There were four other people in the house where I grew up— Mom, Dad, and my brothers Mark and Bret. I loved them because I was taught to, but I didn't know them. My family existed only in the present for me because I couldn't hear the stories that teach a child about the past. I didn't know about my mom or dad's childhood, how they met, what their wedding was like, family traditions or history. I experienced my family the same way a person might experience a TV show with the sound turned off. I recognized the characters, but there was no back story and I only understood the vaguest outline of the plot.

My mother was a petite Italian woman with a 44D chest and dark hair that she wore puffed up into a bouffant French twist. Mom had to quit school in the eighth grade to help support her six siblings. The daughter of immigrants, she worked hard to please other people but didn't know how to give love, probably because she had never received much love herself as a child.

I rarely communicated with her. She always seemed to be *behind* something: a stove, ironing board, mop, or mixing bowl. I would have loved to help her work, but there was no need because she did it all. I didn't even have to clean my room. I had no chores, so there was no way to win her approval. Many times I wished I could talk to her, but I didn't want to interrupt. She was always in motion, and I didn't know how to make her stop. The only time we came together was in the evening when she set my hair. My mother and I both wore curlers covered with a babushka. We wore them to the grocery store, the playground, the drive-in, everywhere but church. I even have in my possession a home movie of Mom and me at the Grand Canyon in curlers.

In those days the man was supposed to bring home the paycheck while the woman tended the hearth, but my mother always did both. When we kids were young, she took in laundry to iron at five dollars a bushel and would spend hours each day at the ironing board. People would take advantage of her by cramming as many dress shirts as they could into the basket. That made me mad. During the rare moments when she wasn't cleaning, cooking, or ironing, she was planning. Holidays and birthdays looked like something out of *Good Housekeeping,* with platter upon platter of food and loads of gifts. The only thing missing was what I craved most—physical affection, hugs, kisses, and communication, some sign that I mattered to her and that she loved me. But she didn't know how to give me that.

My dad was even more aloof. He didn't like to be alone, but that didn't mean he actually wanted to talk to the people who were in the room with him. Dad was six feet tall and very handsome. He was a good provider but had no common sense. (Luckily, my mother had plenty.) Dad was terrible with money but worked very hard selling insurance during the week and taking weekend jobs at liquor or convenience stores to earn extra cash. While I was growing up he never seemed to be home, although we did eat dinner together every night at five o'clock. Then he'd be back out the door again. Often on the weekend he would pick up a case of beer, 24 bottles, and by Monday they would all be gone.

Sitting on the stairs, I used to watch my mom and dad in the living room playing out one of their two standard scenes. In the first, Dad is handing my mom a gigantic chocolate Hershey bar. He was always very sweet to my mother and those big Hershey bars were her favorite treat. In the other scene, Mom is handing

Dad a belt and pointing at one of us. The first thing the poor guy had to do after a hard day at work was drag one of his kids upstairs for a whipping. I don't recall Mom explaining why we were getting the belt, or Dad asking her.

Soon after Dad arrived home we'd all sit down to dinner, which consisted of no conversation, just chewing. Years later I asked my brother Mark about this, wondering if it only seemed as if we weren't talking because I couldn't hear. But he backed me up. "No, we never talked. Except for that time when Bret almost choked on the ham. Then everybody shouted, 'Get it out of him!' and that was our dinner conversation."

No one in my family discussed my hearing impairment, even after it had been diagnosed, but to his credit my father did try to help me. He believed Mr. Banks, whereas my mother could never fully accept the fact that I had a hearing loss and continued to treat me just like my brothers. Dad got me tutors, special schools, and examinations. Like most men of that generation, he was pragmatic and did what he was told, no more, no less: "Okay, she's deaf. We'll get her a hearing aid." Unfortunately, no one told *me* what my problem was. I don't remember having a single conversation with my father when I was a child. He'd just point to the tutor, the therapist, the car door, or the schoolyard, and I'd go.

My ally until I was seven was my brother Mark, who was a year older than me. It seemed to me that Mom was always holding and hugging Mark, which made me envious, but he and I were still buddies. We'd take our piggy banks to the store to buy presents for Mom, which felt very grown-up. I couldn't hear music but I could feel its vibrations and I used to love it when Mark would put on one of my grandma's old swing records and dance with me in the living room.

Then my baby brother Bret came along and Mark and I went our separate ways. Mark, who had always been mischievious, started to pick on us as he got older. It was probably because he was overweight, and other kids were picking on him. I was the perfect foil. Whenever something bad happened Mom would yell downstairs, "Who did this?" and Mark would tap me on the shoulder and say, "Kath, Mom wants you." Upstairs I'd run, like a rabbit into the trap. I got plenty of whippings that rightfully belonged to Mark. His worst offense was thievery. I had an Easy Bake Oven, which used a light bulb to bake a cake about the size of a quarter. I played with it out on the front patio, and every time that cake was nearly done, damn if Mark didn't poke his head out the front door and say, "Kath, Mom wants you." When I came back the cake would be gone and so would Mark.

Mark drifted off with his own friends, and I didn't mind. Now I had Bret to play with, and I cherished him as if he were my own baby. Bret didn't understand my hearing loss, so he didn't make fun of my speech. When he got a little older I taught him crafts, made him costumes, and tried to protect him from our older brother's pranks. Dad was always putting Mark down, so naturally Mark turned around and did the same to us. Bret and I spent hours in the basement plotting ways to get rid of Mark.

There were two bright stars in my small family who made all the difference in those early years. Grandpa Oliver and Grandma Virginia, my dad's parents, were the light of my life. My mother was in love with them, too; she all but admitted to me that the reason she married my father was to get close to his parents. She was right, they were by far the best thing about our family.

Oliver and Virginia were my pride and joy. When I was twelve I used to carry around a picture of Pride furniture polish and Joy dishwashing detergent that I had cut out of a magazine. I'd tell everyone "These are my grandparents, Pride and Joy." My friends thought I was nuts, but Grandpa and Grandma got a big kick out of it. I had no problem lip-reading my grandparents. In fact, I don't even remember not hearing them. It was as if we communicated telepathically. My mother would yell for me over and over again and I wouldn't hear her, but Grandma could be in another room and just say "Kathy" and I'd come running. Later we figured out that when my mom yelled, her voice would go up and out of my hearing range, whereas Grandma had a much deeper voice. She used to call me "Honey Girl," and I loved that.

Grandma gave me the one-on-one attention I craved. Even though she swore she didn't treat me any better than she treated her other grandchildren, I like to believe that she did. It was Grandma who filled me in on the high drama that surrounded my birth. "One doctor was racing around looking for blood while a priest baptized you, just in case you died before the blood came. Then they brought your mother a set of rosary beads and a novena to say for her dying child. After a few hours another priest came to give you last rites. At the end of the day they finally found some blood for the transfusion. The doctor said that because of the delay, you might be a slow learner and that your growth will probably be stunted. He said you'll be lucky to make it to five-feet-two."

By the time I was in sixth grade, I was six feet tall. At that point, maybe I should have started questioning the "slow learner" part, too. Yet despite the doctor's depressing prognosis, I took great comfort in hearing this story from Grandma. I felt especially close to her because she was the only person who would acknowledge that I had a problem and talk to me about it. It meant that she knew me better than anyone and was rooting for me. If I had some type of medical condition, I realized, maybe I could overcome it. Listening to Grandma describe all the turmoil at the hospital gave me a sense of strength. I came into this world fighting and I would continue to challenge anything that came my way. Meanwhile, Grandma kept me busy with craft projects such as making potholders or sewing yarn into pre-punched cardboard pictures. She wasn't sure if there was something wrong with my mind, but at least she could teach me how to use my hands.

Grandpa Oliver was the only person in our family whom I could really understand when I was very young. He was a prankster, and his blue eyes always had a sparkle in them. His face was so expressive that I could always tell what he was trying to say to me, and he was a natural-born clown. When Grandpa was up to something his eyes would start gleaming and you knew his grin was just ready to explode the minute he got you.

Mealtimes were treacherous around Grandpa. I would always eat one thing at a time, saving the best for last, and just as I got to the best he would snatch it up and eat it. One time Grandpa and I were sitting at the counter in the kitchen, and as soon as my mother had her back turned he grabbed my hand and stuck it in a freshly baked pumpkin pie. My mother turned around and there I was, with half the pie on my hand. Grandpa had that "got ya" grin on his face and I looked at my mother, looked at Grandpa, and started to lick my hand as if I had done it on purpose. Grandpa was amazed. My mother yelled at me, of course, but I couldn't hear her.

I learned a lot from Grandpa's joking around. He taught me how to stay one step ahead of the game by keeping my eyes open. Grandpa played with all his grandchildren that way. For them it was entertainment, but for me it was a way of survival. I learned that no matter how much someone loves you, you must always look out for yourself.

Every Sunday we'd have a big family dinner at our house, and afterward Grandpa and I would go upstairs to take a nap, but I wouldn't sleep. Instead, I'd lie with my hand on his throat so that if he woke up and said something I'd feel the vibrations. I used to watch his mustache; I don't know what I expected it to do. I'd lie still as a stone, waiting for his eyes to open.

Grandpa, Grandma, and I called ourselves the Three Muske-teers. We were a team from the moment the doctors first labeled me slow and short, through all my ups and downs at school and home. I don't know how well they understood my voice, but they could always read my face. When I was hurting, Grandma would ask me what was wrong, but I didn't have the words to express my pain. Grandpa would joke with me until I finally smiled. The two of them were my safe place.

I didn't realize it at the time, but the day Mr. Banks came to my house and told my parents I needed a hearing exam marked the end of an era. Kathy the Behavior Problem was gone and a new label was to come. More testing, more schools, teachers, and misdiagnoses lay ahead. For many years, the only part of me that felt real and whole was the part that belonged in the Three Musketeers.

3

Loud Corduroy

ON A COLD day in January, my dad took me for a drive. It was strange, being alone in the car with him for the first time. Where was Mom? Where was Mark? Where were we going? I didn't think to ask my father. We didn't talk, but that was okay with me. I got to sit up front this time. I sat very straight so I could look out the window as we passed by the Cleveland Indians Stadium and frozen Lake Erie. We rarely went to Cleveland, and my eyes drank up the scenery and the elegant brick buildings that lined the city's streets. With their rows of arched windows lit up on this snowy day, they looked like something from a Christmas card.

After a long, happy ride my dad pulled into the driveway of one of the picturesque brick buildings. We walked up the icy driveway to the big double-glass doors and then down a long, dirty yellow hall. Finally my father went into an office where a lady behind a sliding glass window handed him some papers. Maybe this was where Dad worked. I followed him, and he pointed to a hard wooden chair. In a few minutes a man in a long white lab coat entered the room and started talking to my father. I couldn't see all of what they were saying, and what I did see I couldn't understand. My dad touched my shoulder and the three of us started walking down the hall again. Lab Coat took my hand as my father followed behind us.

After leading us down a few more hallways, Lab Coat stopped and opened a door to the weirdest room I had ever seen. It was huge and smelled like a stuffy old closet. The walls were padded with what looked like gray-and-white-striped mattresses. Did people sleep in here standing up? I lifted my eyes to the ceiling and saw that it was punctured with millions of tiny holes. In the middle of the room stood a single metal armchair. Next to the chair was a pair of big earmuffs with wires attached.

Lab Coat kneeled in front of me and spoke: "Uah cawlls araws." I didn't recognize a word. He gently pulled me to the chair and sat me down, placing my arms on the armrests. He lifted an arm up, then put it down again. I managed to grasp that he wanted me to raise my hand, but I didn't know why. Lab Coat placed the earmuffs on my head. They weighed a ton. These were definitely not normal earmuffs. He left the room as I sat there wondering what could possibly be happening.

Mr. Banks had told my parents to take me to the Cleveland Hearing and Speech Center, and my father had obeyed the school official and made the appointment. However, no one had explained any of this to me. So I sat in the metal chair, my stomach in knots, waiting. Moments later Lab Coat surfaced behind a big window. I was so relieved to see him again.

He reached down and turned a knob on a panel in front of him. I heard a beeping sound and tapped on the earmuffs. Now I understood. I was supposed to raise my hand when I heard something. He turned another knob. Nothing. Again. I raised my hand. Suddenly a loud screech pierced my ears—it felt like a knife twisting through my head. I screamed, but Lab Coat just stood there turning the knobs, his eyes on the control panel. I kept shrieking, grabbing the headphones and trying to pull them off. At last he looked up and rushed into the room, while I continued to scream and claw at the headphones.

"Stop!" I saw him say, as he reached to help me get them off. But I was squirming too much for him to grab them. Finally I fell out of the chair and they flew off my head and landed on the floor a few feet away. A look of horror flashed across his face as he realized what I had been hearing. He ran back into his glass booth and turned some knobs again.

Wordlessly, he came back in, set me in the chair again, put the headphones on, and motioned for me to stay still. He left the room and I waited in fear. I had done as I was told, why had he hurt me? I could see my father standing behind the window next to Lab Coat, but he was making no move to come rescue me. Gritting my teeth, I gripped the arms of the chair for dear life. Lab Coat reached for another knob. I held my breath with one eye squinted closed and the other open to see what would happen. This time when I heard the beep I barely raised a finger to motion to him. I was terrified of disturbing the headphones in any way. After what seemed like hours, the session was over and Lab Coat came in to remove the hateful headphones. I felt like I could finally breathe. He reached out for my hand but I refused to take it and ran past him to my father.

There is nothing wrong with having a hearing loss, but there is everything wrong with not being able to communicate. I didn't have the words to tell my father how scared I was or how much the exam had hurt. I didn't know how to ask him what had just happened. All my survival skills, the lip-reading and mimicry, had ultimately isolated me because people assumed I understood more than I did. I left the Cleveland Hearing and Speech Center having no idea that I had just had a hearing exam.

Some good did come from that exam and several other visits to the Center. There was now an official audiological diagnosis: bilateral, non-conductive, neurosensory hearing loss with considerably poorer thresholds in the high frequencies. Cause, unknown. Treatment—ta da—a brand-new set of 1961 Zenith Diplomat hearing aids.

I hated them. The worst part was, after all I had endured for the hearing aids, they improved my speech reception (the ability to understand other people's voices) only a negligible amount and aided in sound discrimination just slightly more than zero. The ear molds must have had a pound of plastic in each ear and the mechanisms behind the ears were as big as earmuffs. It was the only time in my life I was actually top-heavy.

The hearing aids were just one more thing for my mom and me to fight about in our typically uncommunicative fashion.

"Here. Put these on."

"Why?"

"The doctor said so."

"Ma, I don't want—"

"Just put them on."

We never discussed the hearing aids outside of arguing about whether I had them on or not. We never talked about how they really sounded to me, even though I tried.

"Mom, they hurt!" *Swish, swish.*

"The doctor said you have to leave them on."

"But the noise is loud! It hurts. I want them off!" *Swish, swish.*

"Leave them on."

Swish, swish, swish. Every time I walked I heard a loud raspy noise. It had me utterly baffled. I walked, it rasped. I stopped, it stopped. It was enough to drive an eight-year-old insane. Finally I figured it out—I was hearing my corduroy pants! Now that I had hearing aids, all I could hear were my pants and my mother. And the raspy swish wasn't just distracting, it was painful. Either the hearing aids or my pants would have to go, and there was no way I was going to start wearing dresses and exposing my skinny legs.

"I'm taking them off!"

"You will leave them on!"

Through all of this, no one had ever sat me down and explained to me that I had a hearing loss. I still assumed everyone heard the same way I did. Because the hearing aids didn't improve my understanding of anything, I didn't connect wearing them with solving my learning problem, which I still believed was the RH-negative syndrome Grandma had told me about. You could say I was confused. Why did I have to wear hearing aids when my brothers didn't? I felt like I was being branded.

Not surprisingly, the hearing aids didn't help me in the classroom. All the same problems existed: I needed to see Mrs. Crawford's lips, but she spent most of her time at the board. My comprehension didn't improve, and finally Mr. Banks visited my house again to tell my parents that my needs would be best served if I were transferred to an all-deaf school. They wouldn't hear of it. Then he explained to them about a "special school" in East Cleveland called Westfield/Dunbar, which had schoolwork geared toward hearing-impaired students.

I never really understood why I was sent to Westfield/Dunbar, although I sensed there was something broken about me. Most of the time I just edged my way through life, trying to be like everyone else but missing large pieces of vital information. Grown-ups always seemed to be angry at me, no matter how hard I tried to copy the other kids. When Mr. Banks told my parents about Westfield/Dunbar, I thought I knew what must have happened. I was causing trouble and getting bad grades at Hampshire, and he didn't want me in his school anymore.

4

The Boy on the Bus

Hampshire Elementary was a block from our house, and I used to walk there every day with my brother Mark. My new school, Westfield/Dunbar, was a 45-minute bus ride away. On the morning of my first day, my mother and I waited together for the bus at the end of our driveway.

I had never seen a school bus before. When it pulled up it looked to me like some sort of huge, yellow spaceship. I backed away from it, clinging to my mother. As I peered up at it, the doors folded open and I saw the driver, a dark-haired, heavyset man with a kind face. He smiled, and my mother took my hand and led me up the steep metal steps. She sat me down right behind him and they exchanged a few words, but I couldn't see what they were saying. I tried to read the driver's lips in the rearview mirror, but it didn't work. As the doors closed, he turned to me and motioned toward the rear of the bus. "Go back and play," he said.

The bus lurched off and I stood up. Walking while you were riding—cool! As I strolled down the aisle, I noticed for the first time the other children on the bus. I had never seen kids like this before. Some were in wheelchairs, and some had crutches or canes. Others had funny-looking bodies or crossed eyes. One had a really big head.

I don't know why, but none of the crutches, wheelchairs, or funny-shaped bodies fazed me. I just saw a bus full of kids smiling at me and motioning for me to come back and play. The only child who affected me was the one with the big head. I thought he must be *really* smart.

Finally I reached the back of the bus. No one used seat belts in those days, and because the trip was so long the school had removed the last five rows of seats and turned the rear of the bus into a play area. There were boxes of toys and a big dollhouse that I made an immediate beeline for. All the children who could manage it were back there. I sat next to the dollhouse, holding a doll in my hand while my eyes took in all the other kids. A few of the older ones had remained in their seats, and there was one boy, up near the front of the bus, who stayed in his wheelchair the entire trip.

He must have been 11 or 12 years old. The kids told me his name was Kenny. He lived near me and was already on the bus when it got to my house. I didn't see Kenny at school because he was older than me and his classroom was in another part of the building. At the time I didn't know what was wrong with him, but I realized later that he must have had cerebral palsy.

For about a week, I kept my eye on Kenny from my spot in the play area. I noticed that none of the other kids paid attention to him or even said hello. He could barely lift his head and would sit slumped over, drooling. He wore a bib. I never saw him smile or move his mouth. Kenny looked awfully lonely to me, and it didn't seem right. I knew the feeling of isolation and I didn't like it.

One day I walked to the front of the bus with a doll in one hand and a toy airplane in the other. I tapped Kenny on the shoulder. "Hi," I said. He didn't move or respond. I tried again in my best voice: "Airplane." I handed the toy to Kenny, but he didn't take it. I put it on his lap, but it fell to the floor. I put my doll on the floor, picked up the airplane, and held it between my knees. Then I stuck my face under Kenny's drooping head to look him in the eyes, and with both hands I pried open his clenched fingers. I placed the toy in the palm of his hand, and in no time his fingers were wrapped around it so tightly I started feeling sorry for the plane. Then I gave him a kiss on the cheek. It was my first wet kiss, he was such a drooler. As I bent to get my doll and walk to the back of the bus again, I looked up and saw that Kenny was lifting his head. He had a crooked smile on his face. Wow! He could move his mouth—he could smile! I wasn't expecting that.

Kissing Kenny became the highlight of my day and probably of his, too. When I got on the bus I'd plant a kiss on his cheek and wait for him to raise his head and give me that great crooked grin. To me, Kenny's smile was worth a million words. When I got off the bus to go home, I'd give him another kiss. We never spoke a word to each other, but we had some dynamite communication going on.

Trading kisses for Kenny's smiles continued for several weeks. Then one day, as the bus pulled up in front of my house, I saw my mother waiting outside for me. This was unusual. I climbed out of the bus, wondering what the special occasion was. Without warning, she grabbed me by the arm and started spanking me in front of the whole bus full of kids. I was almost too stunned to be humiliated. What had I done now?

"What's wrong with you?" she was shouting. "You can't be kissing that boy!"

How could she know I had been giving Kenny kisses? I turned and looked at the bus driver. He was grinning, but it wasn't his usual kindly smile. It was more of a smirk. I knew at once that he must have told my mother, but what was so wrong about what I had done?

"You are never to kiss that boy again!" she yelled.

That boy's name is *Kenny*.

It was the hardest thing in the world for me to get on the school bus the next day and ignore Kenny the way all the other children did. I walked up the steps and slid into the seat behind the bus driver. Kenny was across the aisle from me and one seat back. I didn't turn to look at him and I didn't go to the play area. I just sat there and stared at the back of the bus driver's neck. If I stayed still enough, maybe Kenny wouldn't realize I was there. I didn't know how to make him understand what had happened and why I couldn't kiss him on the cheek anymore, and I couldn't bear for him to think I had become like all the others.

Not long ago I asked my mother why she told me to stop kissing Kenny. She said she had no memory of the boy on the bus. I believe it was fear that made her react that way, fear of Kenny and his condition. Maybe she thought it was contagious and was trying to protect me. I suppose the bus driver felt like he was just doing his duty, too. Maybe they were even trying to protect Kenny from me, but it didn't feel that way.

Two or three weeks after my mother's punishment, Kenny stopped riding the bus. I didn't know what happened to him, but I never went back to the play area again. I stayed in that same seat behind the bus driver for the rest of the school year, staring out the window. Now the highlight of my trip was when we passed an old cemetery that was filled with carved headstones and elaborate statues. Cemeteries gave me a great sense of peace and comfort, and I'd lean my forehead against the glass, watching until it was out of sight. Once, when I was out with my grandpa and we had driven past a cemetery, he had asked me, "How many dead people do you think are in the cemetery there, Kathy?"

"I don't know. A hundred?"

"No—all of them!"

I thought of that joke every day as the bus drove us back and forth from Westfield/Dunbar school.

I never got to give Kenny a good-bye kiss. I don't know if he passed away or was transferred to another school, but I can still see his lovely crooked smile. All I do is close my eyes and remember the first boy I ever kissed, who taught me that communication doesn't depend on words, it depends on heart.

5

Earning a Dailey Smile

WESTFIELD AND DUNBAR were actually two separate schools situated about a block from each other. Dunbar was primarily a grade school for deaf or mentally retarded children, although kids with physical disabilities were enrolled as well. Most of these children probably didn't belong there, since there was nothing wrong with their minds, they just happened to be minus a few body parts. Westfield was a public school with a half-day program for the hearing impaired. It was a large brick building completely surrounded by a black asphalt playground, without a tree or blade of grass in sight.

"Normal" was not enrolled at Dunbar school, so there was no standard to be compared to. Despite our physical differences—quadriplegic, deaf, blind, or whatever—all the students were equal. To us, Dunbar was like a toy store where you had to figure out how things worked. If we couldn't talk to one another, we'd come up with a different way to communicate. If we couldn't walk, we'd find another way to get to the next room. Dunbar was the first school where I was able to let my guard down a little bit. In this school, no judgments were passed. In this school it wasn't what you couldn't do, but what you could. In this school it wasn't the articulation of your words that mattered, it was the content of your heart. And in this school there was a little boy who pissed me off.

He only had one arm. I didn't know the boy's name; names were hard for me to comprehend, so I just thought of him as "that one-arm boy." For some strange reason, at eight years old I actually believed he left one arm at home on purpose just to make me mad, because I got stuck with him every day for ring-around-the-rosy. It was bad enough that I couldn't hear the music, but now I had nothing to hold on to.

I would get so frustrated with him, thinking he was doing this to annoy me. Each day I'd grab him by his one arm and point at the empty hole in his shirtsleeve, trying to get him to bring in his other arm. He'd glare at me and walk away. The following day he'd return, still without the arm. Finally I got fed up and laid down the law. Miming away to drive home my point, I said, "Bring your arm tomorrow or I'm not your partner anymore!" It came out as a series of angry sounds, but I think he got the gist of it. The next day he didn't bring his arm, he brought his mom. She did her best to try to explain to the irate, half-Italian deaf kid that her son didn't have another arm, he had been born without it. After that sunk in, I realized he wasn't holding out on me.

Now I wanted to save him. That day at lunch, I realized that he didn't have the two hands he needed to put together to make a prayer. How would God know he was here? I gestured for the one-arm boy to come sit next to me. Hiding one of my arms behind my back, I put my other hand up against his. This way I knew God knew he was there. We did this for about a week. I was feeling downright angelic until it dawned on me that if I was only praying with one hand, God was probably only getting half of my prayers. I took my hand back and told the one-arm boy, "I'll pray for you." I was willing to throw in an extra prayer for him in case God couldn't hear his one-armed prayers, but I was not about to jeopardize the clear reception of my own.

My best friend at Dunbar was a little Asian girl who was blind and whose name I never learned how to pronounce. We literally hung on to each other whenever we were together (I didn't realize I was being used as a Seeing Eye dog). Because my life depended on my eyes, the concept of blindness was beyond my comprehension. I never really grasped that my friend could not see. After all, she blinked and had eyeballs, even though they did look different.

Because my eyes were my connection to the world and speech was so difficult for me, I was always "showing" things to my blind friend. She had a bad habit of not responding to these things I was showing her. How rude. Sometimes I would take her hand and point it in the direction I wanted her to look, but that didn't help either. When I picked up some sign language from the other kids at school, I got all excited and ran to show my blind friend. I sat in front of her, running off at the hands, all impressed with myself. To this day I cannot figure out how we communicated. I just remember that every time we got together we hugged, and it felt safe.

Every day my blind friend and I would have lunch together. She had these delicious barbeque beef slices, very much like beef jerky, only better. I had never tasted anything like them. My own lunch was always a boring peanut butter and jelly sandwich, so we would trade. At least, I think she knew we were trading. When I got older I realized that she never saw me exchange those lunches. Then again, I never heard her complain about it.

When I arrived at Dunbar, one of the staff's first goals was to evaluate my IQ. They knew I had a hearing impairment, but because my schoolwork had remained so poor even after I got hearing aids, I had also been labeled *mentally retarded*. They had to determine how retarded I was, and the first tool they used to do this was the block test. They put us in a room with about twelve other children. In front of each boy and girl, the teacher placed a hollow box with different-shaped holes in it, and on the floor next to the box, different-shaped blocks—square, circular, triangular holes; square, circular, triangular blocks.

I saw that most kids didn't know what to do with the blocks. They would wander from box to box with just one block in their hand, pounding the blocks on the boxes to try and make them fit. Then they would hold the block over the wooden box and wait for the teacher to tap their hand to help guide it to the proper hole. When it was my turn I did just what I saw everyone else doing. I held a block above a box and waited for the teacher to tap my hand. "What a goofy game," I remember thinking. "Why don't we just put the blocks in the holes ourselves?"

After a while the teacher got called out of the room. I got bored waiting for her to return so I put all the blocks in their proper holes and went to play with a doll. When the teacher returned and saw that someone had put the blocks away, a strange look came over her face. It was a cross between shock, happiness, and confusion—like someone coming on to drugs. This was a very difficult expression to read, and I didn't trust it. It reminded me too much of The Look.

She pointed to the box as if to say, "Who did this? Who put the blocks in the box?" Oh, no. I was not going to fall for this. I may be deaf, but I'm not stupid. Besides, I'd probably end up out in the cold again. The teacher looked into each of our eyes and asked us one by one, but my face remained as blank as a poker player's.

She left the blocks in the playroom every day after that and watched us through a two-way mirror to see who would put them away. It took me two weeks before I got up the courage to touch the blocks again, and when I did, the staff made a discovery: I might not be retarded after all. They didn't rule it out just yet, of course—the label was already in place, and it's hard to undo labels. I was eight years old when they realized that I only had a hearing loss. And they called *me* slow.

I was at Westfield School for two and a half years, but for the first few months I spent my mornings at Dunbar, where in addition to taking all those psychological and aptitude tests I attended classes with the mentally challenged students. The classes weren't really about learning, they were about taking more tests and being evaluated. Soon Dunbar began to feel like a laboratory where I was the guinea pig. I loved the kids there, it was the constant testing and poking and probing I didn't like. In the afternoons I went to Westfield, where I took classes with Miss Joan Dailey, who taught me how to speak.

I believe in angels because they have touched my life on many occasions. And I believe that some angels are people who just happen to be there when you need them the most. My first angel was Miss Joan Dailey, and I pray that every child meets a teacher like her. She must have been in her early twenties, tall and lanky, with shoulder-length brown hair that was always a little messy. She radiated warmth and energy. Her strong cheekbones and kind eyes made her face glow. Miss Dailey seemed to understand that a smile holds a very special place in a deaf child's heart, that it is so much more than a pleasant expression. It's a visual hug, contact, and approval. The first day I laid eyes on Miss Joan Dailey, I knew I'd like her. I had no choice—her face was always in my face. She knew I was lip-reading and would make sure that I always saw what she was saying. I'd never had that before. It made me feel like she cared.

There was only one other student in Miss Joan Dailey's class with me, a dark-haired boy named Michael. Michael sported a crew cut, heavy black-framed glasses, and a clumsy hearing-aid receiver harness that he wore strapped around his chest. Two thick wires grew out of the receiver, winding up to and around his ears like black, leafless vines. I, meanwhile, was looking lovely in my oh-so-fashionable Zenith Diplomat on-the-ear model hearing aids. Michael was the only other person I had ever met who had a hearing loss. I didn't meet another one until I was 29 years old. It was just Michael, Miss Joan Dailey, and me in class, which was great because it meant fewer lips to read and I could comprehend that much more.

Miss Dailey's room was filled with fun toys and games in every color imaginable. It was like heaven for kids. On Mondays Michael and I would tear into class, throw down our coats, and race to be the first to tell Miss Dailey about our weekends. She always dropped whatever she was doing and gave us her full attention, quizzing us on the details. As we sputtered and struggled to verbalize our adventures, she subtly took notes on our language skills. Careful never to interrupt, she would patiently wait until Michael and I had finished our reports before praising us equally, as if we had just flawlessly performed Shakespeare. With Miss Dailey, I did feel flawless. I still didn't understand that I had a hearing loss or why I had to wear the hearing aids. I didn't care, I just figured I had a lazy tongue and I was here to exercise it, because we were always working on my speech.

My favorite part of the class was when Miss Dailey would tell us stories about her life. No one had ever done this with me before. For the first time, I understood that there was more to a person than the individual standing in front of me at that moment. I realized that my own family must have stories, too, and I began to pry them out of my grandmother. It was the beginning of the world making sense to me.

When it was time for a story, I'd sit as close as I possibly could to Miss Dailey, keeping my hungry eyes glued to her expressive face. I thought it was so cool that an adult would share personal experiences with us. Like all instinctively gifted teachers, she knew how to hold our attention. The more she could shock us, the better.

"I was going on a trip with my mom and dad when I was just about your age," she began one day. "It was summer and it was the middle of a heat wave. We had been driving all day and I was sweating, and my legs were slipping all over the leather seats. The windows were open but it didn't make any difference. It just blew hot air in my face. I finally got so hot that I took off my blouse!"

Oh, my! I couldn't believe my eyes. All I could think of was her father driving the car and her boobies flapping in the wind—as if, at age eight, she had had anything to flap.

"Now, Kathy, please repeat the story." That was part of the lesson, repeating what she had just told us so she could test our lip-reading skills. With my eyes wide open, gasping for the words, I did as I was told. She had a shocked look on her face, too, which turned into a smile as I repeated the scandalous story. I guess you could say I'm not very qualified to gossip—to this day, I'm not a hundred percent sure she took that shirt off!

I was lip-reading long before I attended Westfield, but Miss Dailey taught me how to "listen" and speech-read more effectively. To get an idea how easy it can be to misread lips, watch your mouth in the mirror while silently saying the word *pretty*. Do it again, saying the word *pregnant*. They look the same, but voicing the sentence, "I think your daughter is pretty," is going to produce a much different reaction than, "I think your daughter is pregnant." Miss Dailey would work with me in front of the classroom mirror, tirelessly demonstrating vocabulary words in a context I could understand. She helped me convert the shapes I saw on her lips into shapes I formed with my own. For me, it was a process of physically caressing the words with my lips. I memorized words by how they looked and felt rather than how they sounded.

Every night I would go to bed with a mirror and a flashlight under my covers, remembering everything I had seen Miss Dailey's lips do that day. I'd mimic them in the mirror until either the flashlight grew dim or I did. I had only one goal, and that was to master the correct mouth movements so that the next day I could win Miss Dailey's praise and one of her wonderful smiles. (And maybe piss Michael off, as a bonus.) I knew that if I wanted to be a part of this world I needed to learn how to talk, but most of all I just wanted to please Miss Dailey.

She had lots of techniques to help me and Michael piece together spoken language. She'd light candles to see if we were getting enough air out for the "s" sound—if the flame flickered, we knew we'd done it. She had mirrors so we could watch our lips, and popsicle sticks so she could position our tongues properly. Marbles were put in our mouths for enunciation—I was good at this since I had lots of practice speaking with my mouth full of food. Finally, she used balloons to help us feel for the vibrations in our chest and throat.

It's very difficult for those of us who have not been using our voices correctly to control the muscles in our throat and mouth enough to form intelligible words. I had to rely on sensing the vibrations welling up in my body to know when I had produced the right combination of breath, sound, and articulation. Miss Dailey would often take my hands and place them on her throat, cheek, or nose to help me find the sounds, but my favorite technique was the balloon. She would blow up a balloon, tie the end in a knot, and place it on her throat and chest. I would place my hand on the balloon to feel the vibration in her voice. Then I'd place my hand on my own throat and try to imitate her vibration. (I've often wondered if she was from New York, which would explain my accent.) If I got the word wrong, she'd tap me on the shoulder. Sometimes I'd get the word wrong on purpose just so she'd tap me.

Her patience was remarkable. Once, she spent an entire week working with me just to get me to say a single word correctly.

"Kathy, say A-PPLE." She repeated the word again, slowly: "A-PPLE."

The balloon vibrated and I giggled because it sort of tickled. Then Miss Dailey had me hold the balloon against my chest and motioned me to speak.

"AHPO." The vibration felt strong.

She shook her head and put the balloon back to her chest. "A-PPLE. A-PPLE." The balloon buzzed gently against my fingers. "Your turn," she said, smiling.

"AHPO."

Her lips formed the word, "Again." If I only had a penny for every time I saw that word.

"AHHHHHPO!" I said with extra energy.

Her eyes told me my trick didn't work. We worked on A-PPLE all Monday, all Tuesday, all Wednesday. When on Thursday I still failed to hit the mark, I lost all patience.

"AH-PO!" I spat. The vibrations were still too strong. "I don't unnerstand why your ah-po short and my ahhh-po long," I barked in frustration.

"Because your apple is wrong and my apple is right. You're doing much better, but we still have to work on it until you can say it correctly."

"But you unnerstand my ah-po."

"Yes, I understand you, but maybe someone else won't understand, so you will have to learn to say it right."

"I don't like ah-po. Let's do baaah-naaah." I was mad at her, but she just smiled.

"You still have to learn to say it the right way. Now let's get back to it."

"AH-POL. AH-PULL . . . oh, BAAAAH-NAAAAH! I don't like ah-pos."

Miss Dailey took the balloon, positioned it against her throat, and placed my hand on it. "All right," she agreed. "BAH-NAN-NAH."

I grabbed the balloon and smartly said, "BAAAAAH-NAAAAAH," practically breaking the balloon with the over-pronounced vibrations. Immediately noticing how different—and incorrect—my banana was, I winced. Miss Dailey smiled sweetly.

"Too big, huh? Okay. A-PPLE."

Finally, the day came when I did it. "APPLE." I went into shock. I knew it was right immediately, I could feel it. I looked at Miss Dailey, and there on her face was the biggest smile yet. At that enlightened moment, I realized that I could do it. It was entirely possible. No matter how much I fought her, *it was possible*, and that meant anything could be possible.

The value of this particular lesson went far beyond teaching an impatient child to persevere. Miss Dailey held me to a high standard by insisting that I pronounce the word correctly. She refused to dismiss me with, "That's probably the best you can do, so it will have to be good enough." Instead, my teacher was telling me, "I expect only the best from you. I know it's hard for you, but I also know what you're capable of. You must rise to the challenge because this is important. Because Kathy is important." She believed in me, even when I had no idea what it was to believe in myself.

Michael also adored Miss Dailey and we usually ended up competing for her attention and praise. Every week she'd announce a contest. "Whoever does their very best, at the end of the week I'll take that person out for a hamburger, fries, and a milkshake." You better believe Michael and I were busting lips trying to out-articulate each other. One day we were sitting at the mirror, our tongue depressors in our mouths, working hard on an especially tough word. It must have been a Thursday because Michael was being more competitive than usual, making weird faces at me in the mirror to distract me as I tried to own the word *church*.

"Shursh," I struggled, nearly there.

"That's wrong!" he chided. "You not say that right. You sound stupid."

"What?"

"You. You sound stupid."

"How do you know I sound stupid?" I shouted, stabbing him in the chest harness with my tongue depressor. "You wear glasses!" I thought he had to be able to see me to hear me.

Every Friday, sure enough, both Michael and I would be at the diner with Miss Dailey having a hamburger, fries, and a shake and looking at each other.

"I did better than you."

"No, *I* did better than *you* . . . Hey, what are you doing here?"

Miss Dailey just smiled. Neither one of us ever caught on. She didn't want one to be better than the other, she just wanted each of us to give the best we had to give.

When I began third grade my schedule changed. Now I was at Westfield full time, working with Miss Dailey and Michael in the morning and being "mainstreamed" into regular classes in the afternoon. I hated the afternoon sessions. The idea that the other students were "normal" and I was not made me feel horribly inadequate. The odd thing was, I looked like all the normal kids (except for the Three Stooges perm, which I still wore), but I felt more comfortable with the children at Dunbar. At least there we were all being probed together. At Westfield I was the only one, and every time the door opened I was afraid it was going to be a teacher coming to pull me out of class for yet another test. All the kids would stare as I stood up and left the room.

I kept to myself throughout the year, trying to see what the teacher was saying, restlessly looking around the room for clues about the lessons and to lip-read the other students. I logged more hours in the cloakroom, trying on coats and snow boots. Although my classroom experience at Westfield wasn't all that different than it had been at Hampshire, at least during the morning sessions with Miss Dailey I was learning how to communicate. She also helped me with my schoolwork, so for the first time I was catching up to my grade level.

By the end of third grade I had made great progress with my speech. My teeth had come in normally, and all the hours with Miss Dailey had paid off. People could understand me and I was better at lip-reading. The adults were uncertain about where I should go the following year. Mr. Banks thought I could be completely mainstreamed, but a few teachers, including Miss Dailey, felt I should be sent to a school for the deaf. My parents followed Mr. Banks's advice. They figured I had my hearing aids, I was learning to talk, and I was fixed. All that year they had been building a new house, and when I entered fourth grade they enrolled me in my new neighborhood's grammar school, Lincoln Elementary. My days of special ed were over. Ready or not, I was back in the mainstream.

6

No, Mama, I Ain't Been Hangin'
'Round No Black Kids

THE TOWN WHERE I lived, Wickliffe, Ohio, was as typically American as they come. In many ways it was a great place to grow up, very family oriented, with tree-lined streets, lots of parks, and green lawns everywhere you looked. To me, the smell of Wickliffe is the smell of cut grass. In the fall we'd pick apples to bake pies, and in winter everyone would go sledding down the big hill at Pine Ridge Golf Course. The neighborhoods were full of nice houses that had big backyards where kids could play and have picnics, and the houses were full of kids. It was the 1960s and no one worried about crime.

Like most towns in the '60s, Wickliffe was segregated. The different groups, mainly Jews, blacks, and Italians, had their own sections, and each section was only a few blocks long. The summer we moved, I spent a lot of time driving through town with my mother, ferrying boxes back and forth, checking on the carpenters' progress, or shopping for new stuff to put in the new house. I memorized the different sections of Wickliffe and wondered about the people who lived in them.

On the west side of town were the Orthodox Jewish families, women in long black dresses and men with hats and beards and long, heavy, black coats that they wore even in the summer. I tried to imagine why they always wore black. Perhaps they went to lots of funerals. The Jewish children weren't enrolled at my school, and I wondered what they did all day. If you were Jewish, did you get to skip school altogether? Maybe I could convert. The men never shaved or cut their hair, so I reasoned they must be poor.

"Mom! Let's stop and play. Let's go meet them," I suggested.

"It would be rude to intrude on them, Kathy. They want to be left alone."

I was fascinated. Maybe we had done something to them that my mom didn't want me to know about. Why were they so touchy? What were their beliefs? What did they eat?

That last question was no mystery when we went to the Italian part of Wickliffe, which we did every now and then to visit my mother's family. You could smell the tomato and garlic wafting out of the windows, along with the booming voices of the families inside: "Hey, you, whatta matta for you no passa the pasta down here!" I'm supposed to be deaf, but they must have been too, because they came through loud and clear. My Italian mother was just like them. Of course, now she says she was loud because she was trying to get through to me.

My mother's parents came off the boat from Italy. After my grandmother died giving birth to my mom's brother, my grandfather returned to Italy, married a cousin, and brought her back to the States to raise his family. They all spoke Italian, so I couldn't understand much of what they were saying. I would leave the house cross-eyed from trying to lip-read those people and watching their hands wave all around in some sort of exotic sign language. Food was the only yardstick that mattered to them, and in this respect, they weren't too thrilled with me. A tall, skinny Italian girl? It didn't make sense. "Whatta matta for you, you mother no cooka for you?" It must have stung my mom because every time I walked into my own house she would demand, "When was the last time you ate?"

"The last time I was here!" It was like she wanted to lay me down on a cot in the kitchen with an IV of marinara.

At my grandfather's house we ate in the basement at a long table with food hanging from the ceiling right over our heads—pepperoni, salami, braids of garlic. The step-grandmother would grab my cheeks, the aunts would bite my face (their version of kisses), and one aunt loved to nibble my toes and fingers. I felt like I was the food. But I loved going there and walking down the streets of the Italian section, with all its energy and the loud voices flying all over the place.

Wickliffe also had a black section, which I wasn't very familiar with until fourth grade. All I knew was, when we were getting near that part of town it smelled like barbeque. It seemed to be about three or four blocks long, and while I can recall seeing Italian people all over Wickliffe, I don't remember seeing any black families outside this section. Some of the houses seemed a lot older and smaller than those in other parts of town. Even the streets seemed narrower. It looked as if the people in those houses could see right into one another's living rooms.

Finally, after a summer of preparation, we moved into our new house. My parents were in heaven, but the only thing I could think about was the new school. A week after we moved, the starting bell rang. It was time for fourth grade.

I had no business being in a public school. The first day I walked onto the playground with my Zenith Diplomat hearing aids, I went directly to the classroom and stood by the door. I felt so isolated, as if I had the plague. I was afraid to use my speech because I thought the kids would look at me funny. No one else at the new school had to wear hearing aids. The only other kid I knew who wore them was Michael, and he was no longer with me. I missed him and Miss Joan Dailey and our one-on-one classes. My new class had about 25 kids, and I felt lost in there. I looked around for my familiar sanctuary, the cloakroom, but there wasn't one. The kids at Lincoln Elementary kept their coats and lunches in the hall lockers.

It wasn't likely that I'd be hiding in one of those things to do my taste tests. From now on, I'd have to bring my own Oreos.

My life became focused on getting the other kids to like me and hiding my hearing aids. To win the kids over, I took the most direct route: bribery. I stole candy and money from my parents' house and gave it to my classmates. I don't remember building a friendship out of this caper but I do recall the pressure I put on myself to keep up a supply of cash and goodies. Most of all, I worried about my parents discovering the missing loot. How would I explain why I did it? I couldn't describe my need to fit in when I didn't understand it myself. All I knew was that without the bribes, I wasn't good enough for them to like me. Fourth-graders can be cruel.

Hiding my hearing aids was harder than stealing the money and candy. I wore a thick headband to cover them up, but I doubt I fooled anyone. Think back—can you remember the one kid in your school who was different, who had a hearing aid or another sort of disability? We stand out, no matter how hard we try to blend in. In the 1960s there were very few children like me in public schools. It was a time when people in wheelchairs rarely left the house; when any sort of disability was viewed with fear and suspicion. If I had a hard time fitting in, it wasn't just in my head. Wearing the hearing aids put a wall up between me and the other kids.

My experience in the classroom at Lincoln was exactly the same as it had been since kindergarten, with or without hearing aids. The teacher would write on the chalkboard with her back to the class, and the only way I could get information was to lip-read the students as they answered her questions. It was so hard to keep up. I couldn't understand how everyone else did it. The most I could do was to stay quiet and try not to say anything wrong.

The one and only bright light in that fourth-grade class was Lisa Harrison. Lisa was kind of quiet and shy, and like me she was tall and skinny. But where my skin was pasta pale, hers was deep black. We hit it off right away, probably because we had a lot in common.

We were at least a head taller than everyone else in fourth grade, including all the boys. More important, we had both felt the pain of being rejected from society for something we had no control over— her for being black and me for having a hearing loss. We accepted each other for who we were and never talked about race until much later, in high school.

By sixth grade Lisa and I were both six feet tall—we looked like the number 11 walking down the hall. I was still wearing my hearing aids, fighting with my mother about them, and using a headband to cover them up. Then I met Joey, a boy so cute I knew I had to dump the hearing aids. He was Italian, with thick dark hair and deep brown eyes, and he was cool like only a sixth-grade boy can be cool. I'd quiver when he came into the room. Luckily, Joey sat right next to me. I didn't want him to know I was flawed, so before he came into class I would put my hearing aids in my desk. One day I was running late and Joey was right behind me, so I ripped the hearing aids out of my ears and threw them in my desk, forgetting to turn them off.

When hearing aids are left unattended they make a loud, high-pitched screech that I have been told can be quite annoying to people who can hear it. Naturally, I couldn't. So there I sat, trying to be cool but feeling shy and nervous because for the first time Joey was actually looking my way. I glanced over at him and noticed the teacher standing between us. Suddenly she reached in front of me, opened my desk, and snatched out the hearing aids.

"Put your hands out in front of you," she ordered. *Whack!* came the ruler on the back of my hands. "You put these back on right now, and I don't want to catch you without them again. I will not have you disrupting my class. Do you understand?"

I nodded and put them on while Joey and the whole class watched. Oh yeah, I'm cool. The humiliation was so intense that I might as well have been sitting there naked. All I could do was keep my face to the desk and not look at anyone while I prayed to die.

That was it. I began to leave the hearing aids at home. They didn't help me hear, they were painful and uncomfortable and made me feel broken, so I started "forgetting" them. Then something odd happened. My mother was working at a grocery store at the time and saw a little boy who needed hearing aids, so she gave him mine. I thought it was strange that she didn't even ask me, but—so what! Take them! They were of no use to me. Since she felt I didn't need them anymore, I assumed that I was all better.

I started seventh grade with no hearing device, believing that what I heard was what was being said. I think I was kicked out of every class for not cooperating. I majored in study hall. The only problem was, I had nothing to study.

My favorite class was Home Economics. I loved cooking and crafts; all those punch cards and potholders with Grandma had paid off. But even in Home Ec, things could go wrong. For our first assignment, the teacher gave us a choice either to crochet a doll whose skirt was a toilet paper cover or to knit two place mats by the end of six weeks. I thought she said to make six toilet paper covers by the end of the first week. I was up to the challenge. In fact, for once I was ahead of the game because I'd had a baby-sitter who had taught me how to crochet and knit when I was in grade school. Thanks, Cookie.

I crocheted my butt off that week and made six doll toilet paper covers. When I came in on Friday, I sat there with my toilet paper covers on my desk, noting with satisfaction that none of the other girls had even begun hers. When the teacher came into the room I was beaming from ear to ear. She walked over to my desk and stared down in confusion.

"What is this?"

"My project for the week," I said proudly.

"Do you expect me to believe that you did all six of these in just one week?"

"Yes, I put all of my other work aside to finish them."

"Well, what do you expect to do for the next five weeks?"

"I dunno . . . study hall?"

I kept crocheting for the next five weeks. I had Christmas presents for people I hadn't even met yet. You would see my toilet paper covers in the shopping carts of homeless people.

At the end of the five weeks we started in the kitchen. It was December and we were learning how to make holiday breads. Well, *I* was learning how to make holiday breads; the other students were making holiday bread, singular. Apparently the teacher had said to put a third of a package of yeast in the dough, and I thought she said three packages. We all mixed our bread dough, covered it with a towel, and went to gym. When we returned, my part of the kitchen counter had somehow magically disappeared under bread dough. I didn't have a clue where the towel went.

The teacher was irate. "Kathy, I want you to stay after school and make all this dough into bread." I didn't get it—I had made the most dough, I should get the A. I stayed and baked like an elf on speed, making Christmas wreath bread, candy cane bread, Christmas tree bread, Santa bread, snowman bread, and one little roll with the last of the dough. Between the doll toilet paper covers and the bread, I had Christmas presents for all of Wickliffe.

It sounds like an episode of "I Love Lucy," but at the time I was truly confused. I never thought to question what I *thought* was being said, and the teachers were always exasperated with me. After a while I started to doubt myself and be on guard with everyone, constantly afraid that I'd get into trouble for something I didn't do or something I did too much of. I was even messing up in the one class I was good at, Home Ec.

The only time I didn't feel like an outcast was when I was with Lisa. We were like sisters, and fortunately my sister was an A student. I got Cs, Ds, and mostly Es, and believe me, E didn't stand for Excellent. (For some reason, the Wickliffe School District didn't use Fs.) Lisa saved me on numerous occasions when it came to schoolwork. She'd study with me for hours, but even with Lisa I was sometimes ashamed to admit that I couldn't follow what she was saying. I spent a lot of time nodding.

Not only did I get Lisa as a sister, I also hit the jackpot with her family—Mama, Daddy, four sisters, and one brother. They were every bit as nice as she was and made me feel as if I were one of their own, the white sheep of the family. I went to Lisa's as often as I could, trying to slip under my mother's radar. One Easter I managed to sneak out and walk the twelve blocks to her house so I could celebrate some of the holiday with the Harrisons. When I got there, Lisa took me to the basement where her mom had a second kitchen.

"Kathy, look what Mama's making for Easter dinner," she said eagerly, pulling me over to a pot on the stove. I had been looking forward to eating ham and sweet potatoes, which was what everyone else prepared. Lisa lifted the lid of one of the pots and I peeked in, but I couldn't see much because of all the steam. Then the steam cleared and I stared more closely. Nothing looked familiar.

"Lisa, what is this?"

"Soul food."

"Soul food? What is soul food?"

"Chitlins."

"What is chitlins?"

"The lining of the cow's stomach."

She took a spoon and stirred the pot carefully, closing her eyes and inhaling the steam. I looked over her shoulder into the pot, my stomach lurching a little.

"Whoa. Wait a minute. What is that? It looks like a foot or something in the middle there," I said.

"Oh, that's just pig feet."

"What are you talking about, pig feet? Where is the rest of the pig?"

Lisa grinned and opened the lid to another pot. The contents looked murky.

"What is this?"

"Greens."

"Green what?"

"We just call it greens."

"You don't know what it is, so you just call it by its color?" Lisa's family must be really poor, I realized. All they could afford was the lining of a cow's stomach, the pig's feet, and other leftover animal parts with green stuff they couldn't even identify. I tried to psych myself into being able to eat it because the last thing in the world I wanted to do was to hurt Mama's feelings. She had worked so hard cooking this meal, and this was all they could afford. Out of love for Mama I would hold my nose and eat this stuff. I looked into the pot one more time and caught a glimpse of the pig's toenails. I panicked.

"Lisa, I can't eat this. It will kill me! But I don't want to hurt Mama's feelings." At that moment Mama came down the stairs.

"Lisa, what are you girls doing?"

"Just showing Kathy what's for dinner."

"Oh, girl, you leave her be! Kathy, honey, even Lisa won't eat this. You come on upstairs."

She took me to the upstairs kitchen and in the oven was a golden-brown, clove-studded ham surrounded by sweet potatoes.

"Now, that is what you girls are going to be having for dinner. I cooked up that other stuff for my brothers and sisters."

The smile on Lisa's face just about split it in two. She was basically a shy girl and for her to pull this off must have made her day.

"Hey, Lisa, how do I know that the feet downstairs won't make their way to the pig up here and take off running?"

"You don't. So you better hold on to your sweet potatoes."

I had some incredible times in that home. The parties were the best. All the dancing took place downstairs in the basement, with wall-to-wall people twisting and shaking through the night. Everybody danced, even the grandmother. I didn't do too badly myself, for a white girl. The music was so loud that I could feel the whole house vibrate, and I'd lip-read to learn the Motown songs so that I could sing along. Every once in a while I'd look up and they'd all be staring at me with these disbelieving grins on their faces and I'd realize, "Oops—I must be off key." Okay, the white girl can dance, she just can't sing. One out of two isn't bad.

The parties were a great excuse for everyone to get decked out in their most stylish clothes. One time I made myself a pair of bell-bottom pants with bells so big I kept falling over myself. The guys wore plaid pants and shirts in Day-Glo orange, lime green, or purple—colors so loud I thought I'd go blind from looking at them. In our miniskirts and platform shoes, Lisa and I towered above the others. I probably needed a pilot's license to wear those shoes.

Whenever Lisa'a family had a party I'd spend the night at her house so I wouldn't have to walk home after dark. The next morning Mama would be up before anyone else, preparing a Southern-style breakfast with ham, eggs, biscuits and gravy, and maybe cornbread. I'd pack it away and then walk home rehearsing an alibi for my mother. Less than a mile separated my house from Lisa's, but I rarely brought her home. I didn't like to bring anyone there. We had to take our shoes off when we were inside and I always felt as if my mom was watching us, ready to pounce if we disturbed anything or made a mess. Regarding my black friends, my mother was adamant. They weren't welcome in our house and I certainly wasn't allowed to go to theirs.

My mother understood how much I loved Lisa and she liked her, too, but Mom was a product of the times, and the times were segregated. She was always warning me that I'd better stay away from the black kids, but she wasn't clear about what would happen to me if I did hang out with them, other than getting grounded by her. She seemed genuinely frightened of something, but I never knew what it was. When I was in my twenties, she finally confessed that when she was a little girl, *her* best friend had been black. Black people were not allowed inside my mother's home when she was a girl. Maybe Mom was trying to spare me the pain of prejudice, knowing from her own experience that I'd be in for a lot of hassling from the white kids if I had black friends. At the time, her threats just seemed ignorant.

It became a habit of mine to lie about going to the black neighborhood, but somehow my mother always found out. I'd come home and she'd ask, "Have you been hanging around with those black kids again?" I'd look her right in the eye and say, "No, Mama, I ain't been hangin' 'round no black kids." Then I'd get punished. I could never figure out how she knew until years later, when my brother Mark told me that whenever I had been to Lisa's house I'd come home talking like all the other kids in her neighborhood. I gave myself away every time.

7

Hintz of Greatness

WHEN I TOOK off the hearing aids in sixth grade it was like being released from prison. The only problem was, my schoolwork and comprehension didn't improve. Both my treatment and my cure had been illusions. Miss Dailey had taught me how to speak, but I was still living in a very quiet world. People didn't realize that although I was sending out messages, I was not receiving them accurately.

By the middle of seventh grade it was clear to me that something was still wrong. Instead of hiding my hearing aids in my desk, now I had to hide something invisible deep down inside. I faced the terrifying possibility that I might be retarded after all. Even in Home Ec, where I could knit, crochet, bake, and sew the pants off everyone else, I kept flubbing the assignments. Maybe I did have a slow brain, like the doctors had warned my mother.

Yeast and toilet paper holders weren't the only things I misunderstood in junior high. I also had some big gaps in my knowledge of the facts of life. Health education classes were taught mainly by the use of narrated filmstrips or cartoons. I had no idea what was going on because they weren't close-captioned. It was hard to lip-read a bunch of happy little tadpoles wearing blue baseball caps or pink bows, all swimming through a tunnel trying to break into a wall. When a baby appeared at the end of the movie, I was still looking for the frogs. None of it made sense to me. I was totally unaware that they were trying to teach us about sex.

That was it for my sex education, except for the afternoon Lisa's mother sat the two of us down for a brief chat. We were eleven. "Now, girls," she said, "you don't want nobody touching you. You don't want nobody kissing on you. This is your body. Don't you let anybody do anything you don't want them to do. Just say no." Believe it or not, this talk was very helpful at the time. A little hard to understand, but still helpful.

One day in seventh grade I had borrowed my mother's skirt (or maybe it's called *taking* when you don't ask) and was sitting on the floor in the gym watching a puppet show when I felt wetness on my thighs. I went to the bathroom and saw blood on my underwear, my legs, and the skirt. I thought I was dying. My mind was racing, trying to understand what could possibly be happening to me. I had to hide all the blood before someone found out. I grabbed a long cardigan sweater out of my locker to wear to cover the bloodstain on the skirt while I continued with the rest of my day. With beads of sweat on my forehead, I sat in class praying that the bleeding had stopped.

When I got home that afternoon I sneaked upstairs to the bathroom and stood at the sink with the skirt in my hands, bleeding and scrubbing and crying. You can't get blood out of fabric with hot water, I discovered. It just sets the stain. The green skirt was now purple. Finally I got so scared that I shouted, *"Mom!"* She took one look at the scene, went into the cupboard under the sink, handed me a pad and a belt, and walked out the door. She didn't tell me what to do with them or explain what was happening. Did I mention that our family was not big on communication? On the positive side, she never asked about the skirt.

I thought I was dying for the entire five days of my first period. Every morning when I woke up and saw that I was still alive I thought, *Cool. One more day.* That went on for four or five months, until Lisa got her period. She acted as if someone had just given her a big box of candy. I wanted to slap her upside the head.

"You're happy about this?" I asked. I had been writing my will: *I leave my Operation game to my brother Bret. The school is welcome to have their books back.*

"This is the beginning! We've turned into women," Lisa giggled.

"Well, turn me back into a girl. I don't like this."

"Get used to it, Kathy. This is life."

"How long before it stops for good?"

"Oh, about forty years."

"What?" I thought I might as well cash in my chips then and there. I still had no understanding of the female body and its functions, and I spent a lot of time worrying about what it might spring on me next.

To my amazement, I was allowed to graduate from junior high to high school. Maybe I was likable, or maybe they just didn't know what to do with me and wanted me out of their hair. God knows I was trying.

The older I got, the more aware I became that something about me was different. I didn't think it was a hearing loss. My impairment was never discussed, so I still believed that I heard just as well as anyone else. But I began to realize that I was missing a lot of the basic information that gives people bearings in the world. Everyday facts were like land mines to me—I never knew when I'd trip over one and it would blow up in my face. Like the time in drama class when the teacher told us to pretend we were dogs. When my turn came, I sniffed around for a minute, trotted over to an imaginary fire hydrant, and lifted my leg. I looked up to see everyone laughing. I didn't know that it was only male dogs who lifted their legs. To this day, I don't know how many times people were laughing because of some goof I made or odd answer I gave. True or not, it often felt like they were making fun of me. Maybe they thought I was doing it on purpose to get a laugh.

In high school I developed a new survival technique. I started doing all the talking so I wouldn't have to listen. You could say I was my own one-woman improv group—every time the conversation came my way, I'd take it somewhere else. People tell me I was funny back then, but I wasn't trying to be. I was just trying to stay ahead of the conversation so I wouldn't step on a land mine.

Everyone knew who I was, probably because I towered over them all. My nicknames were Buck, Buckwheat, Daddy Long Legs, and Jolly Green Giant. The names didn't bother me much, in fact I loved being called Buck. It gave me a new identity, a sense of acceptance. What bothered me was bombing out at nearly every school activity or class I tried for. Pass the basketball? I just kept it. I didn't make cheerleader because my legs were too long—I'd do the splits and knock over the girls on either side of me. I got booted out of French class. *Oui, oui,* try lip-reading that! I don't know what I was thinking when I signed up for French. I was asked to leave speech class. I didn't make it in typing, either. I'd sit there at the keyboard with my fingers in the air, ready to go, while everyone else was typing away. Apparently there was a record player going, dictating what we were supposed to type. Music class? I couldn't sing a note. Lisa had a beautiful voice and sang solos in the school choir.

One incident stands out in my mind as typical of all my frustrations and missed cues in high school. It happened early in my freshman year, in health education class. The teacher asked the simple question, "What do we hear with?" My hand shot up: "Our eyes." The other kids' mouths opened in laughter and the teacher sighed. Bewildered, I looked over at Lisa, but she just shook her head as if to say, "Let it go." I slunk down in my chair, ashamed. I rarely raised my hand to begin with and I never would have done it this time if I hadn't been sure I was right. Of course I knew you heard with your ears, but I had blurted out "eyes." My answer was true for me, but if so, why was everyone laughing? I couldn't get even the simplest questions right.

I entered my sophomore year more hesitant than ever. Maybe

things would have been different if I had learned how to ask questions, but words had very little significance for me. My world was visual and emotional. I was tuned in to how I saw people behaving, the expressions on their faces, and the information I could glean from lip-reading. The cafeteria was a very different place for me than it was for the other students because I could lip-read what people were saying from across the room. Most of the time I would have been better off not knowing.

In high school one of my best friends was Darin. He was black but had skin nearly as pale as mine, and he wore his hair in a big Afro. Believe me, he got his share of harassment. One day in the cafeteria Darin was sitting about six tables away from me with some other guys, laughing and occasionally looking at me. I read his lips, and to my horror saw that he was making fun of me. My buddy! I'll never forget the look on his face when he realized I could understand him. His expression mirrored the exact pain that I was feeling. Darin still hasn't forgiven himself for that, but I understood what was going on. He was sitting with a bunch of white guys, and he was trying to fit in.

I saw other things in the cafeteria that disturbed me. Boys would look at girls and their faces would turn smug, as if they had gotten away with something and deserved a big pat on the back for it. I'd lip-read them saying things like, "I got her last night." I knew nothing about sex, so it made no sense to me. Their wolflike expressions reminded me of something, but I couldn't put my finger on it. All I knew was, it made my skin crawl. I never wanted anyone to look at me that way.

I had to repeat Health Science and Biology in my sophomore year. Given my grasp of human biology, I wasn't very hopeful about this class. The teacher was Mr. Hintz, a short man with glasses and a mustache. I had never seen a teacher with a mustache before and thought, *This is going to be great, lip-reading a mustache. Why not just flunk me now and get it over with?* But there was something very familiar about Mr. Hintz. At first I didn't recognize it, but then

I realized what it was. This man was passionate about what he was doing. He loved teaching, he loved his students, and he always made himself available to us. Perhaps he would be my next Miss Joan Dailey.

I got my first taste of Mr. Hintz's kindness the day he brought in the frogs for dissection. He passed them around in these little trays we were supposed to pin them to. Some of the kids were groaning and cringing, others were gingerly pinning the frog's pitiful legs to the tray and testing the tummy with the scalpel. I looked down at my frog and up at Mr. Hintz, cold panic washing over me. I couldn't do it. I couldn't hurt a fly—my brother, yes, but not a fly—much less this frog. It didn't matter that it was dead already. Mr. Hintz watched me for a moment, then pointed at the door and raised his eyebrows as if to say, "Want to get out of here?" I bolted, silently saying, "Thank you, thank you, thank you."

Mr. Hintz went out of his way to help students who were falling behind, and he realized I was one of them. He was in charge of our yearbook, *The Wick,* and one day as I was leaving class, he pulled me aside.

"Have you ever considered working on the yearbook, Kathy?"

"Excuse me, the yearbook? Doing what?"

"Captioning the pictures, writing little blurbs."

"I can't spell very well. By the time I'm done with your book everyone will have a new name and different goals."

"It can't be that bad."

"No, thank you. I'm not interested anyway." Working with other classmates who might make fun of my writing would kill me. Mr. Hintz didn't know that I wasn't up to my grade level in reading and writing, and I was not about to expose it now.

"How about if I start you out as a photographer?" he pressed on.

"But you have a photographer—Darin." I didn't want to push aside my friend.

"We need two photographers."

"Look, I know nothing about taking pictures."

"Darin will teach you. By the way, if you're on the *Wick* staff you get out of study hall."

"Get out of study hall! Why didn't you just say that in the first place? Where do I sign up?"

Working as a photographer for the *Wick* was my passport to popularity. I think Mr. Hintz knew that it would be. Before, most kids had either laughed at me or ignored me. Now everyone wanted to be my friend because they all wanted to get their pictures in the yearbook. I didn't even have film in the camera half the time, but I took it with me everywhere.

With my camera I had access to all the cliques—the jocks, the bad boys with the greasy hair, the nerds, the cheerleaders. Without realizing it, I mimicked the tone and attitude of whomever I was talking to. When I hung around the cheerleaders, I talked like them, in a high-pitched voice: "*Gosh!* Could you believe we lost the game last night? Oh, my God, it was like so not fair." I would act as if nothing were more important to me than putting Kleenex in my bra. Of course, to keep up with them I had to use the whole box.

When I hung around the bad boys, I would roll up my skirt, go a little heavy on the eye shadow, and wear white lipstick. "Hey, Joey!" (Yep, the same Joey from sixth grade.) "So what's happening, man? Heard you might have the hots for Mary Jane."

"Yeah, so what's it to you?"

That ended up being the only and longest conversation I ever had with Joey.

When I hung around the black kids, I talked just like they did: "Don't you be jivin' me, Darin! You best be telling me the truth 'cause I won't be nobody's fool. You hear me?" I had a perm in high school that was so tight I had my own Afro pick. I just didn't leave it in my hair.

I'm sure the black kids noticed my talking like them from time to time, just like my mother always did. I was subconsciously mimicking the vibrations and the shapes people's mouths made when they formed words, but I didn't know I was doing it because I couldn't hear myself. When a chameleon sits on a green leaf and turns green, he's not thinking about turning green, he's just blending in. That's what I was doing. It wasn't until I was in my thirties and got new hearing aids that I heard myself morphing into whomever I was around. I was stunned. I usually sound like a New Yorker, but take me to Alabama and I sound like I'm from the Deep South. Put me with my English friends and I start speaking with a British accent. I still sound like I'm black whenever I get around black people. They probably wonder what the hell I'm doing, but I can't help it. It's a leftover survival technique as ingrained as the way I walk or sleep.

My stint as a *Wick* photographer was fun, but Mr. Hintz had bigger plans for me. My junior year he promoted me to taking the pictures *and* writing captions, and my senior year he made me, of all things, editor-in-chief.

"But I write with a lisp," I objected. It was true, I wrote just like I spoke.

"So you'll get someone to edit your lisp," he said.

Mr. Hintz had figured out that I couldn't read or write very well but was good at putting things together and organizing people. So he instructed me to go out and hire the kids who were the best writers and layout artists. What's more, as editor-in-chief I could give other students passes to come to the Wick Room, which increased my social standing even further. Mr. Hintz knew all the angles.

I'll never forget the weekend he spent in my basement helping me complete the yearbook. Time was running out and I was afraid we wouldn't make the deadline. Late in the afternoon I glanced over at him. He was correcting my lisps, his glasses slipping down his nose. I touched him on the forearm.

"Why?"

"Sorry, what? Why what?"

"Why do you do this?"

"Because I'm a teacher."

"No. Why did you get me involved, why did you pull me in?"

He looked at me for a moment and said, "Because I wanted to teach you to use what you do have instead of worrying about what you don't. Did I succeed?"

"No, you taught me how to manipulate you into checking my spelling."

We both laughed, but hearing him say it so simply caught me by surprise. *Learn to use what you do have instead of worrying about what you don't.* Twenty-some years later, this remains at the heart of everything I teach.

As if handing me the magic ticket to acceptance and teaching me one of the most valuable lessons of my life weren't enough, Mr. Hintz even thought I was beautiful. His whole family encouraged me to try out for Homecoming Queen, but I was too insecure for that. Then he encouraged both me and Lisa to sign up for Teen Board. Two local department stores, JCPenney and the May Company, sponsored one girl per high school to be Teen Board members. This basically meant that we got to do some modeling for the store and work there on the weekends. Tall, black, and gorgeous Lisa got May Company and I got JCPenney.

The two stores were in the same mall, and Lisa and I would work there on Saturdays. We both had uniforms, and although I can't remember a stitch of mine, I can recall every detail of hers. It was in earth tones that I loved, a brown plaid miniskirt with a matching blazer and Roman-style platform sandals with straps that criss-crossed up her legs. I coveted those sandals and somehow they ended up in my closet. In fact, they're still there—I've never found a cooler pair of shoes.

When we were Teen Board members, Lisa and I began to plan for our future. After graduating high school, we'd go directly to New York City, where we would become internationally known models, one black, one white. We were both so tall, and Lisa was so beautiful, that all the magazines would be fighting over us. We'd stride into the modeling agencies dressed in matching hot pants and blow everyone away. I even designed and sewed myself an interview outfit—a skin-tight black bodysuit with black-and-white vinyl snakeskin hot pants, a vest, and a thick black belt.

In senior year it looked like Lisa and I might get a chance to jump-start our modeling careers. The school choir was going to New York; Lisa was in the choir and I would be traveling with them to take pictures for the yearbook. Unfortunately, Lisa's parents wouldn't let her go. I packed up the snakeskin hot pants and ventured into a few agencies alone, where I was told that at six feet I was too tall. Jeez! I didn't care, though, because I knew that when Lisa and I walked in those same doors side by side, we'd knock 'em dead.

Although Lisa was my best friend, I also spent a lot of time moving from group to group taking pictures and organizing yearbook activities. There was a lot of racism in my school, which was about 80 percent white and 20 percent black, but I never focused on it. I was still in a silent world, so the hateful and negative comments that people muttered under their breath rarely reached my ears or consciousness. I saw how people treated me, and that's all that mattered. I didn't care about the color of anybody's skin.

That was a luxury, I found out one February afternoon when Lisa and I walked to the school parking lot to get my car. It was snowing hard, and the car wouldn't start. We both got out to open the hood and saw that someone had snapped off my spark plugs, broken them in half, and left them lying on the engine block.

"Who would do this?" I asked Lisa. I turned to look at her—we were both huddled under the hood to get a little cover from the snow—and saw that her face was full of fear.

"You think the white kids did it?" she asked me.

Her question confused me. "Why would you think something like that?"

"They don't want you hanging out with the black kids, Kathy," she said. "Why do you think they call you NL?"

I was freezing and pulled her away from the hood so I could shut it. We got back in the car.

"I don't know what NL means," I confessed.

"Nigger Lover." She even had to explain to me where the word *nigger* came from and how offensive it was.

I wanted to keep looking at the world through my rose-colored glasses, but when I saw those words coming from Lisa's lips, the glass shattered.

"Let them call me what they want. They don't know you," I told her.

Then she really shocked me: "But it could be the black kids."

"Black kids? Why in the world would they want to hurt me?"

"Because some of them don't want me to have a white friend."

"Who the hell are these people to tell us who we can and cannot be friends with? Lisa, I don't want to hear any more of this black and white stuff. Let's just chalk this up to some random freak out there who doesn't like spark plugs."

"Kathy, this is reality."

"Not my reality."

She saw how upset I was getting, so she let it go. It was the first time in all those years we had talked about race. I realize now that I shouldn't have shut off the conversation, that she might have wanted to tell me some of her feelings about it. But I just closed down. To think that someone would want to hurt us for something so insignificant as the color of our skin? That was beyond my imagination. No, I would not think like this. I didn't want to think like this. I couldn't risk anything that might change our friendship.

8

From the Prom to the Ward

"CHERRIES. NUTS. SCREWS. Balls." Lisa repeated the words slowly, as if they were supposed to mean something. I pictured them laid out on a table: a bowl of cherries, some nuts, a screw, a ball. What did they have to do with guys, with sex?

"The cherry is the hymen," Lisa explained.

"Oh," I said, wondering what a hymen was. I had no clue, but I wasn't about to let Lisa know that. Neither of us knew what the screws, nuts, or balls were for, and there wasn't anyone to tell us. For a long time it didn't matter because no one asked us out. Then Lisa met Norris.

I was staying at Lisa's for the weekend. Her mama and daddy were away, and she had a date with him. All that evening I sat in her living room, waiting for her to return. *She better not do it, she better not do it,* I kept thinking. I didn't know what "it" was, and I didn't know why I was so worried. The minute she walked in the door I saw that she had a beautiful glow on her face. I knew she had kissed him and she was in love and there went our modeling career.

I was a senior and had never been kissed. When I was growing up I was rarely hugged or touched, so I couldn't relate to physical contact. I never felt pretty or acceptable, and my older brother Mark didn't do much to help my self-esteem. He was also an outcast, overweight and cursed with an awful case of acne. To deflect the wrath of the other kids he'd make fun of me, reciting all my bad parts to anyone who'd listen: "She's flat, skinny, ugly, and six feet tall. When she sticks out her tongue, she looks like a zipper. I'll pay you fifty cents to go out with her!" He was more miserable than I was. I knew in my heart that not all the stuff he joked about was true, but somehow it got stuck in my head.

I liked the boys at school but didn't begin to know how to flirt, so I just treated them like pals, joking around and punching them on the shoulder. I didn't know what the next step was. It wasn't as if I had a lot of pent-up desire, but I felt left out. I wanted to know what it felt like to be asked out, to buy a prom dress and get a corsage. At 18, I wanted to go to the prom with a date instead of as the photograper for the yearbook. And I knew who I wanted to ask me: Jimmy.

Jimmy was part of a group I hung out with. He was tall, slim, good looking, and always polite, even a bit shy. He had two sisters, and I used to like watching him when they all got together. The sisters would bug the heck out of him and he seemed to handle it well. Jimmy, a friend of his, and I had spent months fixing up his dune buggy. Every day after school I would go to Jimmy's house. The boys worked on the engine and I did the painting, upholstery, and detailing. Working on a project together made it safe territory, but I had a big crush on Jimmy. As one of the guys I felt comfortable around him, but as girl with a crush I didn't know what to do.

Everyone wanted me to be at the prom, but no one wanted to ask me. Then one day my friend Jennifer pulled me aside and told me that she had heard Jimmy was going to do it—he was actually going to ask me to the prom. Oh, the feelings that swelled up inside. I don't think I had ever been so excited.

"Are you sure? When did he tell you? When is he going to ask?" I practically had a spotlight on Jennifer, drilling her for every crumb of information. Now the four of us could double-date: Jimmy and me, Lisa and Norris.

My fantasies went into overdrive as I planned exactly how my dress would look, how I'd fix my hair, what color my corsage would be, and how we would all spend our last big dance of high school together. I was driving to my job at JCPenney, deep into the fantasy, when I turned left to get on the freeway and a car hit me, smashing into the passenger's side. The windshield caved and glass exploded inward, flying into my face and the right side of my body. It wasn't safety glass like cars have today, just window glass shattering into a thousand shards.

I must have passed out. When I woke a cop was standing outside the car and a crowd of people had gathered. Disoriented, I stepped out of the car and approached the cop, who was trying hard to conceal a horrified expression.

"I have to go," I informed him. "I can't wait here, I've got to get to work."

From behind him I saw a woman say, "Oh, my God, look at her face!" Instinctively I reached up, but the officer pulled my hand back and said, "Keep your hand away from your face."

I could feel wetness, but where was it coming from? I reached up again, but he kept pulling my hands down. There was something on the inside of my cheek, I could touch it with my tongue. I went to look in the car's side-view mirror, but the officer pulled me away, talking to me, trying to keep me distracted until the ambulance arrived. I tried to see myself in his mirrored sunglasses but he caught on and quickly removed them.

At the hospital they put me in a chair to wait for the doctor. When I had the room to myself I got up and looked in the mirror. Something kept cutting at my tongue. It was a two-by-five-inch blade of glass that had sliced all the way through my right cheek to the inside of my mouth. I didn't panic, probably because I was in shock. Dazed, I stood there staring at my bloody mess of a face until the nurse returned, gave a little shriek, and gently steered me back to the chair.

I had shards of glass imbedded all over the right side of my body—
my arm, hip, and leg—which the doctors picked out with tweezers.
But that was nothing compared to the chunk in my face. They were
just getting ready to start removing it when my dad arrived, thank
God. My parents had separated a few months earlier, and I rarely saw
him anymore. But he was always there when a crisis struck, and I
knew he'd make certain I got the best care. Dad came over to the bed-
side, squeezed my shoulder, and said, "Everything's going to be fine,
Kathy. Don't worry." Then he turned to the doctor and asked, "Who's
the best plastic surgeon in town?" Instead of allowing the emergency
room doctor to sew up my face, Dad drove me to Dr. Stengler's office.
As the surgeon worked on me I kept up a steady dialogue.

"I can't have stitches, I can't have stitches."

"Don't move your face. You have to keep still."

"I'm going into modeling! Please don't give me any stitches,
don't give me any stitches."

"Stay still!"

When we were leaving, my dad said, "How many?"

"Thirty-two," answered Dr. Stengler.

"Thirty-two what?" I asked.

"Stitches."

I started crying. The hole in my face had been big enough for
me to put my tongue through. They had to stitch it up in layers
from the inside to the surface of the cheek.

I've always wondered if it was the bandages on my face that
made Jimmy ask Stacy Rhodes to the prom, or if he had never intended to ask me in the first place. I found out about it a week after
the accident. Stacy Rhodes: short and cute, with long, glossy hair. If
I were a guy, I would have asked her out. Kathy Buckley: tall, flat,
with a Frankenstein slash down the side of her face. I felt totally rejected, but how could Jimmy have been rejecting me? He didn't
even know I thought he was going to ask me. I had exaggerated the
whole thing in my mind, based on Jennifer's little piece of information. But fantasy or not, the pain was real.

When I heard the news I went home and climbed into bed, where I started sobbing and didn't stop. I was hysterical, crying and moaning, with my mother sitting next to me looking really scared. Through the haze I realized that I had never seen her look this helpless, and it gave me a pang of satisfaction—she cared!—but not enough to stop the grief. Mom tried to calm me but couldn't, so in the end she called Lisa. I was still wailing when my friend knocked on the bedroom door.

"I wanted to go to the prom with you," I choked out. "I wanted to double-date with you and Norris." Lisa came over to the bed and just held me. Then she sat me up and looked me in the eye and said, "Kathy, nobody white is going to want to double-date with a black couple. So let's not hang out together in school for a while, and that way you'll get a date."

"Forget it. If I have to go with you and Norris alone, I'm going to the prom." Not that Norris would be pleased with that idea.

"It's only for a few weeks, Kathy. I'll bet you can get a date if we just stop hanging around each other."

"Thanks," I said, pulling myself together. "But I don't want to act like I don't like you. I'm not going to lie to get a date."

I ended up getting a date the night before the prom. I told the guy I had free tickets. So I lied. His name was Bob, and he was also friendly with Lisa. He was the only other tall person in the school.

What a nightmare it must have been for poor Bob. It was my first date and I was painfully uncomfortable. The four of us went to the prom, with Norris driving. He and Lisa had been going out for a while by that time and were constantly touching each other. Whenever Norris put his arm around Lisa, Bob thought it was his cue and put his arm around me. I peeled it off. It was like monkey see, monkey do. When Norris leaned over to kiss Lisa, Bob leaned over to try to kiss me. Apparently Bob hadn't dated much himself, because he sure didn't have any of his own moves.

When we got to the prom I pulled Lisa aside.

"Please tell Norris to stop touching you," I begged her. "Because Bob back here is copying everything he does!"

For all my agonizing about the prom, I don't remember much of it, at least not compared to my razor-sharp memory of what went on in the car on the way home. Lisa must have told Norris about Bob's copycat act, because the minute we resumed our positions—Lisa and Norris in the front seat, Bob and me in back—Norris gave me a grin in the rearview mirror as if to say, "Let the games begin!" He held Lisa's hand, Bob held mine. He kissed Lisa, Bob got a dirty look from me. Before every move he made, Norris would give me a big smile in the mirror, then watch the action unfold. He was having a great old time while I was getting more and more tense.

It wasn't Bob's fault. He did nothing wrong, nothing to deserve the feelings of hatred and anger that were welling up inside me that night. I didn't know how to receive touch, all I knew was that I didn't want it, I couldn't stand it. I wasn't hating Bob, but I was hating something.

After the prom I couldn't stop thinking about my reaction to Bob. Why had I responded that way? Girls were supposed to want guys to kiss them, but instead I had recoiled. Would it have been different with Jimmy? Maybe, but I'd never find out. Instead I felt like an alien, repelled by human touch.

I didn't tell Lisa anything about my anxiety with men. She was on another plane anyway. Right after graduation, Norris asked her to marry him. I knew it was coming, had known it since the night he first kissed her. But now that it was a reality, I wanted to protect Lisa. At least, that's the reason I gave myself for constantly questioning her.

Norris gave her a ring: "That's beautiful. Are you sure you want to go through with this?"

Lisa asked me to be her maid of honor: "I'd love to! If you're sure you want to go through with this."

I helped her pick out her gown: "So you're sure you want to go through with this?"

It got to be a joke, but every time I asked her, Lisa said yes. She had no doubts, no questions, no maybes. She knew what she wanted and I admired her for that. I had always liked Norris and I was happy for her, but I still felt left out.

"Just because I'm getting married doesn't mean we can't have our dream," Lisa told me. Yeah, the three of us can go to New York together. Norris will look great in hot pants.

Walking down the aisle in front of Lisa, I wanted so badly to turn around and push her back out the door. As she stood with Norris reciting her wedding vows, I felt myself draining away. Lisa was the only person I had ever connected with—there had been no one else my own age. I can say now that she was my lifeline, but back then I didn't have the words for it. I only knew that when she said "I do," I disappeared. I don't believe God wants any of us to succeed because of someone else; he wants us to succeed within ourselves. We all have to grow up and go our own way. But that day, I got lost.

I tried to continue my dreams of being a model, but instead I felt empty and alone. There were no people to mimic anymore, no high school groups to fall in with, no yearbook to edit, nothing to be. I had no plans to go to college. Just graduating high school had been hard enough. But modeling or no modeling, I had to earn some money, so I took a job at Zayres Department Store. Within weeks I fell down a flight of cement stairs and had to have knee surgery, which kept me out of work, so I lost my job.

I think I actually made myself fall down those stairs. I wanted to hurt myself enough to die. But I recovered, and in a month I was well enough to get a new job in the warehouse at Gold Circle Department Store. It was a good thing I did, because not long afterward Mom kicked me out of the house.

A boy was at the heart of the trouble. He was the best man at Lisa's wedding and his name was Andrew. While we were dancing at the reception, Andrew took a liking to me and asked me out. It was my first official date and my mother had been thrilled to see such a nice, good-looking guy ring the doorbell asking for me.

Andrew and I went bowling, and I creamed him. Not too polite, but as I said, it was my first date. He must have enjoyed the whipping because we had barely gotten back inside his car before Andrew grabbed me and started making out. I pushed him off and told him to stop.

"Mary Beth lets me touch her breasts," he notified me.

Mary Beth HAS breasts, I thought to myself. *If you can find mine, you can touch 'em.* Out loud I said, "So what? If Mary Beth says it's okay, then it's okay? Go call Mary Beth." Pouting, he cranked the car into gear and we headed home. I couldn't wait to get this so-called date over with. All the old feelings of dread and panic had come over me when Andrew was trying to kiss me, and I just wanted to get away from him.

Andrew kept calling me after that night. I guess he saw me as a challenge. I told my mother to brush him off, but instead she somehow struck up a friendship with him. One evening when I got home from work he was sitting in the living room chatting with her. My little brother, Bret, who was twelve, was there, too. I hated what I was feeling when I saw Andrew with my family. Furious, I walked right past them and to the kitchen, where I started making myself dinner. Moments later Mom followed me in.

"Andrew came here to see you," she said.

Rage was bubbling up inside me. "Well, I didn't invite him," I hissed. "I'm making my dinner. He can go home." How dare Mr. I-Want-to-Touch-Your-Breasts come to my home uninvited, invading my private space, my security. My stomach was in knots.

"Don't be rude," my mother whispered.

"He comes by unexpectedly and I'm rude?"

"Go talk to him."

"I will." I stalked into the living room and said, "You can go home now. I don't care to see you."

Andrew calmly got up from the couch.

"Well, okay. Sorry if I disturbed you, Kathy. Bye, Mrs. Buckley."

How could this person act as if everything was all right? Maybe it was fine for him, but waves of uncontrollable feelings were rolling over me, turning me into some sort of monster. I didn't know where they were coming from, I just knew they were there and that I was ready to burst.

"What's wrong with you?" my mother shouted as soon as Andrew's car pulled away. "That's a nice boy! He just wanted to visit with you. What the hell is the matter with you?"

"I don't know what's wrong with me," I shouted back. What was I going to do, tell her he wanted to touch my breasts?

"I want to know what's going on," she demanded. I felt like screaming, *Why would you defend Andrew over me? Who the hell is he? I'm your daughter!* I didn't have the guts to say it, so I slapped her across the face. Voilà—I was out of the house at eighteen. I didn't stop to think what impact my leaving might have on Bret, who had already been crushed by my parents' divorce the previous year. Later I felt terrible about abandoning the brother who still meant the world to me, but I had no choice.

I packed my things that night and slept in my Cutlass Supreme. I had nowhere to go. Lisa was married now and she and Norris had moved to California. I didn't want to knock on her parents' door after being kicked out of my own house; I was too ashamed. Then I thought of Miss Joan Dailey. She had been the only person I could communicate with for two years of my life, and I had always wanted to tell her how much she meant to me and to thank her for all she had done. I drove to Cleveland, only to find out she had been killed in a car accident a few years earlier. I never got to say thank you.

My brother Mark and his wife, Debbie, took pity on me and let me move in with them for a while, and I kept up my schedule at Gold Circle. Then a 150-pound box fell on my head. Back I went to the hospital. People would take care of me there, and they were always so nice. They'd say hello, good morning, good night. Can I help you? Do you need anything? Friends would come and visit me. It was only when I was in the hospital that I felt safe from the monster inside myself.

Shortly after the box fell on my head I passed out on the bathroom floor at Gold Circle. I spent more time in the hospital taking tests—spinal taps, brain dyes. My grandmother said, "There's nothing wrong with you. Stop doing this to yourself," but I really believed I was broken. There was something wrong inside my body and I wanted to get rid of it. "Fix me!" I wanted to cry. "Tell me I'm okay, tell me I'm not broken, or just let me die." I had no way to describe the problem. Why couldn't I connect? Why couldn't I feel love? I was numb to the world.

Looking back, I'm sure that most of my accidents were half-hearted attempts at suicide designed to get my mother's attention. *She should have helped me,* I found myself thinking. *How could she kick me out of the house for not dating when it's her fault I'm so messed up?* I wasn't sure why I was so furious with her and longed to talk to her about it, but we had never once had a decent conversation and now we weren't speaking at all. So I continued to hurt myself, check into the hospital for severe headaches and more tests, and lie on my bed on the front porch of my brother's house letting my mind take me to dark places. I kept visualizing cutting my arm off and watching myself bleed to death. With a little blade, I started scratching things into my arm.

After a month or so of this, I became really frightened. I didn't know what I was doing anymore, and my thoughts were so repulsive that they didn't seem like they could belong to me. I felt possessed. When the thoughts didn't go away I began to worry that I wasn't going to be able to control my actions, either. Maybe I was even capable of hurting Debbie or Mark. I had to leave their house before something terrible happened.

The fear finally sent me to another doctor, but this time I didn't go into the lobby. Instead I sat on the ground near a little pond in front of the building and scratched in the dirt, "I want to die. I have to kill." When the doctor came out and saw what I was doing, he urged me to check myself into Holloway Mental Hospital right away. I went directly from his office to the institution that afternoon.

I had never heard of a mental institution, but if it could help me make my bad thoughts go away, I was willing to give it a try. Holloway looked just like the "madhouses" you see in the movies. It was a hulking brick building set at the top of a hill, with a long driveway leading up to the oversized doors. Inside there was no lobby, just a window with a lady sitting behind it.

"Leave your belongings with me," she said briskly. The doctor must have told her I would be coming. I passed my purse through the window and she beeped me in. The inner door opened and clicked shut behind me. *Wait a minute,* I realized. *They took my purse and now I'm going to be locked inside this place.*

A nurse guided me down a few hallways and into a plush office with wood paneling, deep green carpet, and burgundy chairs.

"Wait right here," she said kindly. "The doctor will be here in just a few moments." I started to feel a little better. Maybe I was going to get some help after all. Finally I wouldn't be alone.

About a half-hour later the doctor showed up. He came on like a storm, running off at the mouth so quickly that I had no idea what he was saying. Then he sat down and scribbled something on a piece of paper and handed it to me. The nurse touched my shoulder and led me out of the room.

My eyes were bigger than an owl's trying to figure out what was going on. The nurse took me over to another window where a second nurse took my piece of paper. She studied it and passed me a cup containing eight pills. I'm not a big pill person, so I asked her what they were for.

"This is what the doctor ordered," she replied.

"Why? He didn't even ask what was wrong with me."

"He'll talk with you again tomorrow," she said, all business. "In the meantime, you are to take these pills for the night."

I don't know who was with me at that moment, but somehow I

knew not to do it. One by one, I put the pills under my tongue and pretended to take them in front of her. Then I followed the other nurse down the hall to my room, where I went in the bathroom and spit them all in the toilet. The colors looked pretty as I flushed them down.

A woman was lying on one of the room's twin beds. "This is Dora. She'll be your roommate," said the nurse.

"I'm not crazy, I'm here because I'm an alcoholic," Dora told me as I sat down on the bed opposite hers. The poor woman looked so defeated.

"The next time you get a craving for a drink, why don't you just drink orange juice?" I suggested, helpful as always.

"I drink it all the time," she replied, deadpan. "With vodka." She turned her back to me.

Left on my own, I wandered into a big lobby that was called the day room. The people looked sloppy and strange. About twelve of them sat in front of a TV set while another guy stood next to it flipping the channels, round and round the dial without stopping. Some people were yelling at him, others just sat and watched the stations change.

There were folks rocking back and forth, staring, and folks sitting and talking to themselves. I tried to join in one man's solo conversation but I don't think he appreciated it. The screaming was my first clue. Still, I was determined to help these people—I didn't want to see anyone suffering, and most of them looked unhappy. I noticed a lady rocking away on a couch. She'd probably be more comfortable in a rocking chair, I thought, so I lifted her up and put her in a nearby rocker. I guess I threw her rhythm off because she started screaming, too, and wouldn't stop until I put her back on the couch. There was an awful lot of screaming going on around here.

By now these people were beginning to scare me. I was ready to go down the toilet looking for the drugs I had thrown out—maybe they were meant to help you cope with whatever the hell was happening here. Looking around the room for anyone normal, I spied a cute old lady with her hair in pigtails sitting by a window. She grinned at me and crooked her index finger, motioning me to sit next to her. We started chatting and I was just beginning to relax when her expression changed. A five-year-old's smile spread over her face and I saw her say, "If I'm a really good girl today my daddy is going to take me roller skating and we're going to get ice cream." She prattled on and I edged away from her, escaping down the hall to my room.

It was empty. I curled up on the bed and cried silently, overwhelmed by this hospital and the people in it. What on earth had happened to them? By now I had pretty much forgotten why I had come here in the first place.

I pulled on my institutional pajamas and crawled under the blanket. I must have cried myself to sleep, because the next thing I knew it was 4:00 A.M. and someone was shaking me. Looking up, I was amazed to see the mother of a schoolmate leaning over me.

"Mrs. Randall! What are you doing here?" I asked.

"I work here," she whispered. "And you do not belong here. You have to leave."

"I can't. I'm not feeling well, I need help."

"Get your stuff!" The look of fear on her face snapped me to attention and I sat up. "Put on your clothes and come with me," she ordered.

I don't think I've ever dressed so quickly in my life. Mrs. Randall had somehow retrieved my purse from the front desk, and now she was shoving it into my arms. Together we hurried down the dim halls to the front door of Holloway. She unlocked it, gave me a big kiss and hug, and pushed me out. I felt the vibration of the metal door slamming shut behind me, a deep *clang* that kept on reverberating as I stood there in the dark.

Now I realized what had happened. I was out, and I wasn't supposed to be. They were going to be looking for me. I ran like hell down the hill, clutching my purse. There was no way I was going to end up in one of those rockers. When I got to the bottom of the driveway I looked back, thinking Mrs. Randall might be standing at a window waving to me, but there was no sign of her. Only later did I realize she had risked her job to sneak me out of there.

9

Porch Smarts

My night in Holloway convinced me that I wasn't nearly as bad off as I had thought. The experience had scared me, but I didn't have time to think about it much because I needed to find somewhere to live. Mark and Debbie were going to be moving soon, so I couldn't go back to their place. In a near panic I rented the first room I could get, in a big gray Victorian house in Willoughby, Ohio, one town over from Wickliffe. The house, which had been converted into eleven single apartments, was managed by a lady named Mrs. Lang. She seemed skeptical about renting to me.

"It's a house where mostly senior citizens live," she explained. "You may not be comfortable there, you being younger and all."

"That's okay," I said, thinking to myself, *Great. I just got away from the loony bin and now I'm settling for the Happy Trails Retirement Home.* On the bright side, the rent was only 80 dollars a month. I told Mrs. Lang how badly I wanted the place and gave her a little of my background, leaving out the part about escaping from Holloway. No matter how clearly I spoke, she probably wouldn't understand that one. Instead, I told her about having to leave my mom's house. Since my parents had split up a year earlier my dad, never a constant presence in my life, had been fading even further into the background. Living with him was out of the question, and now my brother was moving, too.

"All right, you can have it," she finally agreed. "But you'll have to deal with the consequences."

"What do you mean?"

"The old ladies, they're very protective of the house."

"Don't worry, I won't sell it," I said.

The next day I drove to the house to move in. I pulled up to see a row of about a half-dozen old ladies sitting in white wicker rockers on the home's wide front porch, just rocking and staring at me. Obviously, word about the new tenant had spread. With a plastic bag full of clothes in each hand, I walked up the stairs. No one smiled at me, no one spoke. It was like crossing a picket line.

"Hello," I said loudly.

They all ignored me, except for the little one with the white spit curls, who said, "Hi!" and went back to her crocheting.

For the rest of the afternoon they watched me move my stuff into the apartment, and not another word passed between us. I glanced at the group every so often, and I noticed that one of the ladies seemed unusually large, even sitting down. She glared at me whenever I looked at her, so I stopped looking.

My apartment, up a flight of steps and toward the back of the house, was tiny. The front door opened into a hallway that was also used as the closet, and I'd have to push past my clothes to get to the main room, which barely held a bed and dresser. Behind the so-called kitchen was a very small bathroom that had a miniature bear-claw tub about one-third the size of a regular tub. I couldn't even sit in it. A shower head had been attached over the tub, and the diameter of the circular shower rod was so small that the curtain would stick to me as I showered. It was a clean-and-peel type of thing, like showering in a body bag. But I was in my own place at last, and I loved it.

As the days went by, the old ladies continued to snub me. They spent most of their time on the porch, and I knew I had to some-how get in good with them. Otherwise, I was always going to be the subject of their gossip. I hated being snubbed, especially since I had to pass by them several times a day. Finally I couldn't stand it anymore, so I walked over and said, "Is it okay if I sit here, too?"

They all mumbled some version of "All right," except for the large one, who bellowed, "No!" I had felt her voice booming through the house—she was as loud as she was big. But I wanted on that porch, so I ignored her.

I found a rocker and sat down. No one said anything. After five minutes of silence I ventured a few words, thinking that if I told them something personal it might break the ice. I mentioned that the shower situation in my apartment was a challenge. "Every time I go in there it's a toss-up whether I'll hit my head on the rod or get the shower curtain stuck in my butt." It got a few giggles, and I convinced myself that the big woman's lips twitched a little.

The real breakthrough came after I had been at the house for about a month. I had done modeling for local newspapers and mag-azines ever since the JCPenney job in high school, and one week my face was on the cover of the paper's Sunday magazine. All of a sud-den I was a celebrity. That morning when I walked past the porch, a few of the ladies said hello and smiled.

"Is this you?" the little one with the spit curls asked, holding up the magazine.

"Yep," I said.

The big one was not convinced. "Are you sure? How come you never look like that around here?"

"Because I didn't think full makeup was a requirement here."

"We didn't know you were famous!" piped up another lady. At last I was welcome on the porch.

I was 19 years old and the youngest person ever to live in that house. The old ladies—I was soon calling them *my* old ladies, but not to their faces—ranged in age from 57 to 92. The 57-year-old was Betty, who liked to brag that she was a full-blooded hillbilly. I didn't know at first what *hillbilly* meant, but I'd soon find out. Betty was also a tomboy and the handyman of the house. The oldest old lady was the big, loud one. Her name was Hayworth, but because she lorded it over everyone else I took to calling her Ma.

Ma Hayworth was at least 5'10" tall and reminded me of one of those opera singers with the horned helmets. She wasn't fat, just "big-boned," in her words. With her big-boned frame draped in a muumuu, she looked like a billboard moving around the house. I had never seen an old woman that big. She actually scared me, and everyone else too. Ma had a mouth on her and was never afraid to speak her mind. And boy, did her mind speak!

Then there was little Mika, 89 and sweet as pie. Mika was the one with the white spit curls who had said hello that first day. She must have been somewhat blind, because her glasses were so thick that they made her eyes look about four inches in diameter. All day long Mika crocheted these amazing, intricate doilies. No wonder she was going blind. Mika was best friends with 74-year-old Carrie, a chain-smoker and neat freak. She'd walk around the house holding the lid to a jar under her chin to catch the ashes.

When I first moved in, I asked Betty if there was a Laundromat around. "Use the washer in the basement," she told me. I got my clothes together and went downstairs. The place looked like a dungeon, clean but very spooky. There, standing all by itself in the middle of the floor, was a little old tub with four legs on wheels. It must have been one of the first electric washing machines ever made, complete with a hand-cranked wringer on top. By the light of a 25-watt bulb, I filled the tub with water, put in my clothes, added detergent, and switched it on. It jolted to life and started jumping all over the floor, scaring the hell out of me. I darted back upstairs, dreading my next confrontation with it, only to find my old ladies enjoying my journey to the dungeon. "Nice machine, huh?" said Ma.

When the washer was finished I had to hand crank my clothes through the wringer. That's when I realized we had no dryer. Everyone hung their clothes to dry in the cold basement, which took forever. Unfortunately, I didn't know about fabric softener or that I had to refill the tub with clean water to rinse my laundry. Two days later when I took the clothes down from the line, they were stiff as cardboard. When I tried to fold them they felt like they were going to break.

Not long after I moved in, Mrs. Lang said we could have a new washing machine. Betty the handyman was in charge of selecting it. When the new machine arrived I ran down to the basement to try it out, only to find that Betty had purchased the identical machine but with a *push-button* wringer. That was the big advancement in the household! Now I understood the meaning of hillbilly.

Every day when I came home from my job at Gold Circle Department Store the old ladies would be lined up in their rockers, gossiping and carrying on. The stories I heard on that porch! Nobody was old out there, we were all teenagers. When the weather got warmer we'd all congregate there after dinner and chat until we started nodding off, or at least until they did.

One night I noticed that a house down the street had a red light on in the window.

"How could anybody read by that red light?" I commented idly.

"It's a whorehouse!" Ma boomed in her typically gentle way.

"There aren't any horses down there," I said.

"Not a horse house, *a whorehouse*."

"What's a whorehouse?"

"It's where women sell their bodies."

"What do you mean, sell their bodies? Like arms and legs? What for?"

They hooted with laughter, rocking away furiously. To say I had been sheltered all my life would be an understatement.

"They're whores, honey," Mika said, wiping tears from her eyes. "They sleep with men for money."

I still didn't know much about sex. In fact, I didn't know any more than I had after Lisa's cherries-and-nuts lesson. When the old ladies realized how naive I was, they all pitched in to explain prostitutes to me. I felt like I was lip-reading a tennis match—they were all chattering at the same time, and I only understood bits and pieces of it.

"Those women used to go into the beauty salon with their dog and they'd have their hair and their petunias and their dog all dyed the same color," Ma said.

I tried to visualize women lined up outside a beauty parlor with their dog under one arm and a pot of petunias under the other. Why would they want to change the color of their flowers? A brown petunia didn't sound very pretty.

"Respectable women couldn't even show an ankle back then," Carrie told me. "If you showed an ankle or a bare foot, it would get the men excited. And you had to wear big bloomers instead of underwear."

"Of course, the bloomers had to be big so they could hide the chastity belts," Mika reminded her.

"What's a chastity belt?" I asked.

"My sister had to wear one of those," Ma recalled. "We couldn't keep her in the house, we couldn't control her. She was always out wandering. So they put a chastity belt on her. It was a heavy metal belt that had a piece for between your legs, and it locked in front with a padlock. You could hear her clanking as she walked. She hated that."

"What?!" I was stunned.

I can still see Ma's satisfied smile as she watched my eyes popping out of my head. I'd practically be climbing into her mouth to lip-read those stories. I believed every word, no matter how farfetched. I'm sure the temptation to amaze me got the better of them more than once.

"Remember the movie starlet who had sex with her dogs?" Carrie asked the group.

They all nodded and said, "Tell her!"

"I'm not too sure if I'm ready for this one."

"Oh, yes you are. Go ahead and tell her," Ma said, grinning.

When Carrie told a story she would tell it real quietly, puffing intently on her cigarette. We all had to huddle around her to hear it, in between her wheezing coughs and billows of smoke. I'd huddle along with the rest of them to get a closer look at her lips. Talk about your secondhand smoke.

"Well, she had two Great Danes and she liked to have sex with them. One day she had a headache. The dogs wanted to do it and she didn't." She paused.

"So, what happened?" I asked.

"So they killed her."

"No!"

"And ate her."

I looked at Ma and she nodded, happy as a kid on the Fourth of July.

The old ladies taught me more than just their version of the facts of life. They educated me, making up for a lot of what I'd missed in school. On the front porch I learned about horse-and-buggies, the Wright Brothers' first flight, the first automobile, the first television set, and both World Wars. These ladies had been through it all. Ma was born in 1882, just 17 years after the Civil War, and remembered tales from when she was a little girl. Living in that house was like living in a library of life. Some people had street smarts, I was getting porch smarts.

In return for the stories, I helped the ladies by taking them to the doctor's office and grocery store. I was the only one whose driver's license hadn't expired, and they couldn't believe their good luck in having me right there and willing to drive them around. But I didn't mind; I needed to be a part of something. We all depended on one another without having to ask, because if any of us had had to ask, we wouldn't have. We were all too prideful.

Taking a group of eighty-somethings to the grocery store did have its drawbacks, though. For one thing, even though they went every week, they were always astounded at the prices. They'd stand there and yell at the merchandise—not the clerk, not the manager, the merchandise.

"A dollar-fifty for a loaf of bread! A dollar-fifty!" they'd screech at the bakery aisle. Then they'd turn to me: "When I was young, a loaf of bread was five cents!"

"Well, how long did it last?" I'd ask them. "I'll bet it lasted one day before it started to get moldy. It costs at least a dollar to add all those preservatives, so it's really only gone up forty-five cents." I'd try any kind of twisted logic to get them out of there with a full basket.

"I'm not buying it. It's the principle," they'd huff.

"What principle?" I'd demand, pointing to their basket. "What are you going to put your cheese and bologna on? You don't buy it, you don't eat." But there was no convincing them. That is, until the middle of the following week, when they'd send me back to get the stuff they had refused to buy. I'd go alone, return with the groceries, and lie about the prices: "It was on sale!" After a while I noticed that they sent me back more and more often. They knew a good deal when they had one.

We went to the doctor's office nearly as often as we went to the grocery store. All the ladies insisted on arriving for their appointments a half-hour early.

"Why?" I'd ask. "The doctor is always late."

"Maybe this time he'll be early. Then we'll get out early."

Ma hated young doctors, and naturally the older she got, the younger they seemed. I remember when her longtime doctor passed away and we didn't find out until we went in for her regular visit. The receptionist told us that a young doctor had taken over the practice.

"I want to see my old doctor," Ma roared.

"Look, just try this guy," I reasoned. "Maybe a young doctor is up on the new things."

"What does it matter? I have the old things."

"Please, Ma. Just give him a chance."

"I want to see my old doctor," she repeated. I walked over to the receptionist and asked her, "What cemetery is he at?" Then I turned back to Ma: "It's going to be a long wait. Still want to go early?"

Finally she relented. "I don't like young people seeing my body," Ma growled at me as she followed the nurse down the hall.

"If he can handle it, I'm sure you can," I replied.

Living with the old ladies suited me fine. For the first time in my life, I was needed. And to show their appreciation for my help, they competed with one another to take care of me. One day I got sick with the flu. That was the last thing you ever wanted those ladies to know about. Each of them had a remedy that was a sure cure, or kill. I was trying to get some rest when I heard a knock at my door.

"I made you some delicious soup," said Mika, handing me a big bowl.

"Mmmm, thank you!" I took a sip and fell back on my pillow. Twenty minutes later, another knock. I placed Mika's bowl under my bed, and Carrie came in.

"This soup will cure you in a jiffy!"

"Mmmm, thank you!"

Mika brought chicken soup, Carrie brought oxtail soup, Betty brought corned beef and cabbage (that was the sure kill), and Ma brought vegetable stew. By the end of the day, there were four bowls under the bed and it smelled like a toxic dump. Cleared up my sinuses, but my stomach was another story.

After a few months living with a houseful of surrogate mothers, I began to feel my life moving back on track. I was still getting the severe headaches that had put me in the hospital several times over the previous year, but Gold Circle was paying for a company therapist to help with those. I'm sure my strange behavior was the real reason they insisted I go. My accidents, fainting, and headaches must have kept the manager up at night wondering when the next box was going to fall.

As summer heated up I began spending my days off at my favorite sanctuary, the beach at Lake Erie. Water soothed my soul much more than the therapist, and all week long I looked forward to my beach day. One morning in June of 1974, I packed up my blue Delta 88 and drove to the beach. I was wearing a two-piece bathing suit with a red, white, and blue wavy print. It was the first swimsuit I had made and actually worn in public, and I was proud of it. I figured I'd work on my tan, watch the waves, and be back home in time for a late lunch.

10

Let There Be Light

I JUST WANTED to lie in the sun by myself and relax. It was a little cloudy that morning, but someone had told me you could still get a tan through the clouds, so I lay down and greased up. I had my radio, and although I couldn't hear what it was saying I could feel the vibrations of the music and recognize some of the songs. My friend April loved music and listened to it a lot, especially Barbra Streisand. I would lip-read April and feel the music at the same time, to the point where I could actually sing a few verses along with her. It was fun and made me feel accepted in a part of the world that otherwise would have been unattainable for me.

The sun kept peeking in and out of the clouds as I lay on my blanket with my head pressed up against the radio speaker. Now and then I'd sit up and watch the other people on the beach and the kids playing, but after a while I got bored. I was contemplating leaving when I sat up to look around one more time. I saw a lifeguard Jeep driving down the beach and thought to myself, *My God, the way that Jeep is tearing around on the sand someone is liable to get run over.* I never thought it would be me.

It was as if something out there kept telling me to leave, get out of there, and that's exactly what I was getting ready to do when a song that April had just taught me came on the radio. I remembered the syllables to the words. I lay back down and closed my eyes, singing along, thinking, *I'll leave right after this song.* "Billy don't be a hero, don't be a fool with your life."

Out of nowhere I felt my head being pressed down into the sand and a terrible pressure on my face, the warm wetness of blood and then more pressure on my stomach and hips. I opened my eyes and saw the bottom of the Jeep. I don't know what happened with time but it went by s-o s-l-o-w-l-y, almost as if it had stopped. I had enough time to realize that I was under the Jeep and that if the first two wheels made it over me I needed to protect my head from the second two. I managed to drag my right arm close to my body, trying to put it up over my head, but when I did that the rear wheel grabbed my elbow and twisted me and the Jeep drove over my side and back.

As I lay there wrenched to the side I could see the Jeep continuing on down the beach. The driver didn't even know she had run me over! I guess she didn't see my speed bumps. Later I was told that someone had to yell at her to stop. I had been run over by a lifeguard—talk about not knowing what your job description is.

I tried to shout at the Jeep, but nothing would come out of my mouth. Part of me was in my body and part was floating over it. I couldn't feel any pain, but I couldn't move, either—it was as if something were pinning me to the sand. I was just lying there, not knowing if I was dead or alive, when out of nowhere I was watching a little old man in an ivory-colored robe walking along the water's edge. He had a wonderful, gentle face and a long white beard that went down to his chest but looked light and feathery. As he turned and walked toward me I could see his calm smile through the beard and feel the compassion that beamed from his eyes.

Transfixed, I watched him approach me, feeling totally at ease and content. I forgot all about the fact that I had just been run over by a Jeep. Before I knew it he had walked right up to me and was sitting on my stomach. "Katherine, this isn't going to hurt," he said. "You are going to hear a loud *pop*."

Doesn't he know I can't hear? I wondered. For the first time, I clearly understood that I had a hearing loss. There was no emotion, no denial, it was a simple fact. He took both his hands, cupped them over my broken nose, and pulled. It popped and I heard it. Then he looked me in the eyes and said, "Everything is going to be all right."

He got up to walk away, and as he did I was surrounded by an incredible intense blue, a blue I have yet to see on this earth. I was completely enveloped by it and so at peace that I couldn't feel anything except my own existence. A magnificently bright white cloud came toward me and out of the cloud came a beautiful hand. At first I thought it belonged to my cousin Marylou, who had been killed in a hit-and-run accident and whose hands had been lovely. As I reached for the hand it started changing ever so slowly, becoming even more exquisite. I couldn't tell if it belonged to a man or a woman, all I knew was that I had never before felt so safe.

I had spent my whole life looking for three things: love, warmth, and acceptance. Reaching out for that hand, I felt perfect, unconditional love; a warmth in knowing that I was totally protected; and complete acceptance of me just as I was. Then I was given a fourth gift, an incredible gift that I didn't recognize until much later in life.

I felt as though I were floating. It wasn't like I was having a conversation—"Yo, God, nice robe, lose the sandals." There was some kind of communication, but not in words. It was more like telepathy. I was just feeling it, absorbing it, consuming it.

Then suddenly I decided, "No. I'm not ready."

Instantly it all vanished. When I opened my eyes I saw that my left hand was reaching up. A young paramedic was trying to get it down but couldn't, so I slowly brought it down over my heart. He grabbed it and put it by my side in order to strap me onto a board they had slid under me. They put a big brace around my neck to keep me from moving my head. Then they carried me to an ambulance.

"You have to tape my nose! Please, my nose is broken." I thought I had been pleading with them, but when they put me in the ambulance I must have gone into shock because I grew quiet. I felt something cold under my nose and was dimly aware of someone trying to take my pulse.

"Three forty-five. Dead on arrival," the young paramedic announced. A sheet was pulled over my face. *Wow, three forty-five, dead . . . Whoa! Dead? Hey, wait a minute!* I couldn't move, strapped to a board and wearing a neck brace. Talk about coming back to earth! With all the effort I had inside me I started blowing on the sheet.

"Excuse me, can you get this off my face, please?" I managed to croak.

The young paramedic threw himself up against the back of the ambulance, shouting, "I'm so sorry, I'm so sorry!" While all of this was going on an older paramedic was squeezing my right hand to let me know that he knew I was alive. All the way to the hospital I kept seeing the young paramedic saying, "I'm so sorry, I'm so sorry." I think he was in shock, too.

"It's all right," I murmured.

He followed me around on the gurney: "I'm so sorry, I'm so sorry!"

"It's okay."

He was in the emergency room: "I'm so sorry, I'm so sorry."

"Don't worry about it."

I was lying in intensive care and all I could see was his face pressed up against the window mouthing, "I yamm sooo sorrry, I yamm sooo sorrry."

"So am I. Now look, you're really starting to get on my nerves," I mouthed back.

While all this was going on, I kept telling the ER staff, "My nose is broken, you have to fix it." But they weren't concerned about my nose. They were more worried about the internal injuries and my back. I was hyperconscious of what was happening around me, watching and listening to as much as I could, but I didn't feel any pain until the ER doctor came on the scene. He must have been 78 years old, with three-inch-thick, black-rimmed glasses. In no special hurry, he started poking at me.

"Does this hurt?"

"Yeoowww!"

"So tell me, what brought you in today?"

Was he kidding? I had tire tracks across my face, stomach, chest, side, and back. He viewed my wrecked body with detached interest, like someone judging a project at the science fair. In his left breast pocket was a little black book that kept falling out.

"I believe that is your book on my stomach," I told him.

"Hey, you're right."

"Doctor, is that your book on the floor?"

"Yep, that's mine," he said, unaware that it had just dropped out a moment earlier.

When he left I called the nurse over.

"Is he legit?" I asked her. All she would say was, "I'm so sorry, but I cannot give out that information." Now I was scared.

Getting more nervous by the second, I started in about my nose again: "My nose is broken. You gotta fix my nose!" The nurse said there was nothing wrong with my nose, but when they gave me a total body X ray they found out my nose *was* broken. "Whoever fixed it did a perfect job," said the radiologist. I told him that an old man on the beach had popped it back into place. Later I asked everyone who had witnessed the accident if they knew who the old man was. I was told that no one on the beach had touched me except the paramedics.

I had been in the ER for what seemed like hours when at last I saw my father's face at the window. I went cold with relief. One thing I can say for my dad, whenever I was in trouble he was the first person there for me. Just as he had done when I got hit by the car the previous year, Dad immediately asked for an internal spe-

cialist and a legitimate doctor. The next day I was transferred to
West End Hospital and put into the hands of the experts.

At the end of that first afternoon, my mother arrived. Later she
told me that when the hospital had called her at work, they made
the accident sound like a minor injury. She waited until five o'clock
to come to the hospital, and when she saw me lying in the ER with
tubes hanging everywhere, she panicked. I saw her shout, "No, this
can't be true!" In seconds she was at the bed, trying to tear the
tubes out of my arms.

"Mom! I need those," I cried, as the nurse rushed over to re-
strain her. Once they got her away from the tubes, I was glad she
was there. As usual, my father had left after making sure I was set
up with the best doctors and specialists. He was like Superman,
swooping down to save me and then disappearing until the next ca-
tastrophe. Dad didn't return to the hospital, but Mom stayed by my
side.

There was no ambulance available the day I was transferred to
West End. Groggy, with about four sets of tubes draped from my
arms to various poles, I lay in the back of a long vehicle. The window next to me had frosted letters on it with some kind of design . . . the letters were backward . . . S-P-E-A-R-S F-U-N-E-R-A-L
H-O-M-E. I was in a hearse. Hey, doesn't this come with a box? No
one had warned me because they hadn't wanted to alarm me. They
thought I wouldn't notice. But how many ambulances come with
little velvet curtains hanging on the back window? Now, *this* would
have been a good time to hear someone say, "I am so sorry."

When I got to West End Hospital they put me in a room with a
dying man. Not the incentive I needed for a speedy recovery. But I
was kept entertained by med students who filed into my room,
lifted my robe, and checked out my tire tracks, which stayed bright
red for about a week. Poking and probing at me, "Seeing how
you're doing" (fine until you got here), they examined me several
times a day. The ICU had strict rules stating that only immediate

family members could visit. I didn't remember these pokey probey people from any of my family reunions.

After a week of tests, the experts cataloged the damage. Lower back and leg injuries, stomach problems, intestinal problems, internal bleeding, and mental somatic paralysis. My major source of pain, after my stomach healed, would be from severely damaged nerves in my back and legs. It was unbearable, so excruciating that at times I stopped feeling my legs altogether. That automatic shut-off was the mental somatic paralysis, a way for the brain to protect the body from intense pain. I could walk, thank God, and my spinal cord was intact, but the paralysis would cause my body to go numb from the waist down and my legs to collapse. This could happen without warning at any time. They didn't know how long the condition would last.

I was released from the ICU after six days and taken to a regular room, where I remained on my back for another week. I'll never forget the first day they sat me up in a wheelchair and took me in for a shower. It was heaven to finally wash my hair. I could feel the warmth of the water covering me as I slumped over in the chair. I still had some sand on me. The nurse was in the bathroom with me and must have asked a dozen times if I was finished. "Please don't turn the water off," I begged her. I didn't want it to end. It was the first time since the accident that I had felt some kind of comfort.

I was exhausted after that shower. The nurse helped get me into a clean hospital gown and pushed me over to the window while she changed the bed. I sat in the wheelchair looking out at the clouds, and suddenly I was pleading with God: "Please don't forsake me. I cannot live like this. I don't want to end up in a wheelchair for the rest of my life, lip-reading nose hair. Remember when I said I wasn't ready yet? Well, maybe I wasn't thinking too well. I had just been run over by a 3600-pound Jeep. Could we reschedule this question again?"

The day before I was released from West End, my doctor came

to see me. I sat in my wheelchair, again stationed by the window. He stood across the room from me.

"We're recommending that you use a walker from now on, Kathy," he said. "And a wheelchair for whenever you're at the mall or somewhere that would require you to walk for more than a few steps."

"I'm not using a wheelchair."

"Kathy. I know this is hard to accept, but you may never walk normally again. The best thing you can do is to help yourself by using the chair and the walker."

"No."

"Then we'll issue you some crutches. You need something. You can't walk by yourself."

"No crutches."

"A cane?"

"No."

I refused to buy into the idea that this was permanent. As he stood stiffly by the bed, I made a vow that I was not going to live like this. If I used anything at all, even a cane, it would prove that I believed I was weak and would remain weak. The doctor probably made more suggestions, but I turned and looked out the window again. Finally it was my turn to say, *I am so sorry, but I am not accepting this.*

My mother was waiting for me as the nurse wheeled me out of West End—hospital rules, you must leave in a wheelchair. Yeah, well, I am out of it when I hit the door. She wanted me to stay at her house, on doctor's orders. Dosed with painkillers, taking baby steps from the bed in my old room to the bathroom, I survived the first few days at home. But then my legs gave out on me and my mother panicked. She started pinching them, saying, "You can feel that, can't you? You can feel that!" I couldn't feel anything.

The paralysis was brutal. It was literally like having the rug pulled out from under you. I would be walking, poking along clinging to a wall, and without warning my legs would collapse and I'd be numb from the waist down. I couldn't even tell if I was urinating. This time I was really broken, hurt in a way I couldn't control and didn't plan, even subconsciously. Not knowing what was happening to my body made every day terrifying. *I think I can move— I feel like I'll be able to.* But my body wouldn't react.

Mom hadn't believed any of the other accidents. She must have known that in the past I was crying for her attention. This was different. For the two weeks that I stayed with her, I spent more time trying to convince her the paralysis was real than I did actually hurting. In the end I had to leave my mother's house and go back to my apartment in Willoughby. If I were going to heal, I would have to do it on my own.

11

Swimming Back

MY BROTHER MARK drove me to Willoughby. I had been gone for more than a month and wasn't sure the apartment would still be there for me, but it was. So were my old ladies, gathered on the porch as usual. Only one thing was different: someone had painted the white rockers a bright Christmas red. My eyes throbbed just looking at them. No question what had happened—Hillbilly Betty had been making improvements again. I'm surprised the chairs weren't plaid. When Betty saw the car pull up she jumped to help Mark and thumped me on the back (*ouch!*) shouting, "The girl's alive!" Ma didn't budge, but yelled, "What did you go and get yourself run over for?"

"I had nothing better to do."

"We saw the story in the newspaper," Mika said, coming over to hug me. "We weren't too sure if it was you, but then you never came home."

"You let me know if you need anything," Carrie chimed in, flicking her ashes in her jar lid and surveying me with her eagle eye.

The next day I struggled downstairs to the porch. The ladies were eager to hear every last detail of the accident, and I didn't want to disappoint them. They sat like little children waiting for the teacher to open the storybook, and I told them all I could remember, dragging out the good parts like seeing the bottom of the Jeep and riding in the hearse. The other stuff that had happened—the old man and the strange, life-after-death experience—I kept to myself. I didn't know what to make of any of that, and I wasn't ready to share it.

I never let on to the ladies how much pain I was in. After that first afternoon, I went to my room and pretty much stayed there. My condition changed every day. Sometimes I'd be okay, able to baby-step down the stairs, but many days the pain was so intense that I couldn't get out of bed. The burning, tingling sensation in my back and legs was overwhelming, and the lightest touch from the sheets or the waistband of my pajamas was unbearable. When I first returned to the house I wanted to be left alone, and the ladies understood. As a result I lay in bed for three days unable to move or get up. I had no phone, so I couldn't call anyone for help, and my voice was too weak to shout. I just lay there in my own urine, crying not because of the pain but because I was so afraid of what was happening to me.

After a while the ladies caught on to my situation. They insisted I put a phone in my apartment and started checking up on me more often. Ma was the most concerned, but naturally she didn't want to admit it. She had only been up to my room once before, to deliver her vegetable stew when I had the flu. The steep, narrow stairs were too much for her. She could handle coming up them, but not going down. Now she kept tabs on me through her spy, Betty.

"Kathy asked for this magazine," she'd say. "Go up and give it to her. Pain-in-the-ass kid."

Like the others, Betty was used to taking orders from Ma. Up she'd trot with the magazine: "Ma said you asked for this."

"She did? Well, I guess I must have asked for it, then."

If Ma couldn't think of anything to send, she'd develop a need for something of mine. "Betty, go get a cup of sugar from Kathy."

"I have a cup you can borrow."

"I said get it from Kathy! I like her sugar better."

There was a wheelchair in the downstairs hallway, which I supposed was the "house" wheelchair. I used it when I had no other choice. I hated to, because it meant violating the promise I had made to myself not to accept the doctor's verdict. But my body was a stranger to me, and I never knew when I'd fall over. When I was hurting really badly I would move my feet inch by inch, always careful to be next to a wall or chair in case I collapsed. Some days, though, I just gave in and used the wheelchair rather than stay confined to the house.

Unable to work, I applied for welfare and was granted a hundred dollars a month. My rent was 80 dollars, which left me with 20 dollars for food, gas, electricity, and maxi pads. I received food stamps, but the hospitals kept sending me threatening letters demanding that I pay my bills, and I was so scared that I'd sell the food stamps for money to pay the hospitals.

Somewhere along the line I had heard that fish was brain food. Even though my legs weren't working, I figured if I could just keep my brain alive long enough, sooner or later my body would follow through. For the sake of my brain, I sewed pockets inside my jacket so that when I went to the store I could put cans of tuna fish in them, three cans in each pocket. This went on for several weeks, until the day one of my pockets tore and the cans of tuna fell out. I didn't hear them. There I was, wheeling the chair down the aisle with three cans of tuna rolling right alongside me. The store manger stopped me. Pointing to the cans, he asked, "Are those yours?"

"Yes, sir." I opened my jacket. "And so are these." So much for fish being brain food.

I got arrested and taken to the police station. The policeman, Kevin, asked what my situation was. I told him about the accident and he recalled reading about it in the local newspaper ("Jeep Runs Over Area Woman While She Lays Sunbathing"—my very first press). Kevin guessed I was hungry, so he ordered me pizza and milk before booking me. I had mug shots with mozzarella cheese hanging from the side of my mouth and a milk mustache. That was my one and only brush with the law.

After a few months struggling with my legs and the wheelchair and spending a lot of time on the front porch with the ladies, I thought I was well enough to start driving again. Driving was basically the same as sitting, and it didn't take much strength just to push the pedals. Late one night, while driving home from some friends' house in the rain, a dog ran in front of my car just as I was coming to a low bridge. My legs went out on me and I could not move my foot from the gas pedal to the brakes, so the car skidded off the bridge into the creek. It was just like the Jeep accident— time slowed down and I went into some sort of suspended terror, not believing what was happening to me. *After all this, I'm going to drown?*

But although the churning, muddy water looked dangerous, the creek was shallow. I pushed open the door as the car started to sink, lifting myself out by my arms and pulling my dead legs along. The water only came up to my shoulders and I hauled my body up and out of the creek, my hands slipping and scraping on the rocks.

Covered in mud, I scooted back down the street to my friends' house. They cleaned me up and let me sleep there for the night. In the morning I called my mother to let her know I was okay. There are some voices I can hear over the phone and others I am helpless with, but if I can hear anyone, it's my mother. When she's upset with me, she doesn't even need the phone.

"What the hell's the matter with you?" she shouted. "The police called me last night and said they found your car with your purse and ID but they couldn't find a body in the river!"

"I'm calling you to let you know I'm okay, Mom. Can't we be happy about that?" I hung up and my friends drove me back to Willoughby.

My experiment with driving had failed, to put it mildly. It also scared the heck out of me. I was determined never to be that helpless again, and I had no intention of leaving my apartment unless it was absolutely necessary. My life reverted back to basics: my room, the porch, and constant pain. I could not trust my body. My old familiar fear of being broken and not understanding what was wrong with me was not just a theme in my life anymore, now it was my whole life. I had no ambition, no goals, no dreams, only the soap operas on TV.

For months I was in and out of hospitals, taking every test imaginable. I would be in traction for weeks on end, willing to try anything any doctor suggested. And there was never a lack of doctors—my lawyers saw to that. They gave me the names of all the specialists in the area, the better to supply ammunition for the lawsuit they were launching on my behalf. It's a wonder they didn't send me to a vet. I understood very little of this, but I was desperate to find a cure. Each time I visited a new specialist I would repeat my mantra: *Please stop the pain. Please stop the numbness. Please stop the fear of not knowing. Please explain what is happening to me.*

"Apparently your sciatic nerve is getting caught between your vertebras, which could be causing your paralysis."

"Your vertebras have been damaged, which could be causing the pain and paralysis."

"You have nerve damage and there is nothing you can do but take anti-inflammatory drugs."

As doctor after doctor failed to help me, I began to doubt my own perceptions. Was the pain real, or was I imagining it out of fear? Perhaps I was crazy and just looking for attention. Were the doctors and lawyers feeding me this fear? I wanted to believe they were on my side, but maybe I was trusting the wrong people. *God help me, I am all alone with this.*

The doctors, the lawyers, and the hospitals were all so overwhelming. It was like lip-reading a different language. At one point

I was seeing four different doctors and taking four different med-ications three times a day. I was following all the doctors' orders, in-advertently mixing drugs. I just wanted to be pain free, but after a few weeks of multiple drug doses something frightening began to happen. I was in bed most of the time now, and outside my small window I could see an old man being buried alive in a cemetery, with one hand reaching out of the grave. I heard him calling out, "Help me! Pull me out! Stop me from going under!" I needed to save him, and I could see him as clear as day, but I didn't know where he was. I called the police, who came and took a report.

The next day, the same thing happened. The old man was cry-ing out to me, his arm stretching from the hole in the ground, pleading with me to help. I had to find him, but I couldn't leave my room, my legs weren't working. *I had to save him!* Three days in a row, the police came to my apartment. By the third day I could rec-ognize their patronizing tone even through my hallucinations. After they calmed me down and left, I sat there in bed, furious at them for deserting me. I begged the old man, "If you can just tell me where you are, I can tell the police to come for you. I don't know how to help you!" That night I woke up sweating and scared. I reached for my medications, and for the first time I saw them clearly: seven bottles of painkillers and muscle relaxers. I emptied them all into the toilet.

Years later I made the connection that the old man in the grave was the same one who had fixed my nose on the beach. It was *me* who had been going under, and he had saved me a second time. I gave my angel a name, David.

A week or so before the hallucinations, I had joined the YMCA, thinking that maybe I could swim my way back to health. Water was the only element that didn't hurt my back and legs, and on the days my legs were numb I could just put a ring float around my calves and swim with my upper body. I returned to the Y the morn-ing after I had tossed out the pills, and right there in the pool I went into some sort of withdrawal convulsion. The lifeguard pulled me out, and once again paramedics rushed me to the hospital. (I think the paramedics were starting to take out life insurance on me. They knew me by name. It was scary.) The ER doctor found out what I had been taking and hit the roof. "You are never to mix medications again! Every time you see a new doctor you must tell him everything you're taking!"

But I was through with drugs and, for the most part, with doctors. It was going to be up to me to save myself. I did the only thing I knew how to do, which was to swim my butt off at the Y every day. I believed with all my heart that if I could just keep swimming eventually everything would fall into place, and after about a year, it did. I still had pain, but my legs no longer gave out on me. I could walk with less fear, and if it felt like hell, at least it looked all right from the outside.

Throughout all my ups and downs, the old ladies remained a constant source of strength and purpose for me. I'm sure that if I hadn't been confined to the house for two years, I never would have gotten to know them so well. I would get lonely up in my room and make my way down to the porch at least a few times every week to listen to their conversations. When I grew stronger, I began to take them on their errands again. My car had been totaled in the creek accident, but a friend who worked at a gas station found me another one, a '65 Mustang with the floorboard all rusting out. I felt like Fred Flintstone driving that car.

Spending all that time with the old ladies, I couldn't help but get drawn into their dramas. The most obvious one was the feud between Ma Hayworth and Mika. Great big Ma was always picking a fight with pint-sized Mika. "What are you doing on the porch, Mika?" she'd blare at her. "Why do you have to sit on the porch when I want to sit on the porch? Move aside!" Or, "Mika, you've been crocheting since you were fifteen years old. You'd think you'd have finished one of those damn things by now."

"How does Ma know that Mika's been crocheting since she was fifteen?" I asked Carrie one day when it was just the two of us.

"Don't you know?" she cackled. "They've known each other since they were girls. Only they never thought they'd end up together here."

"What happened?"

She inhaled deeply and lowered her voice, which didn't help me much. I hunkered closer to her.

"When Hayworth and Mika were growing up, they both fell in love with the same boy. They each wanted to marry him, but he chose Hayworth."

"So why is Hayworth so mad at Mika? She won."

"I guess he wasn't such a prize after all," Carrie laughed.

"But that was seventy years ago! Has she been angry all this time?"

"Who knows? Mika moved away from town right after high school. She and Hayworth never spoke to each other again, until they both ended up here in this house a few years ago. Neither of them knew the other one lived here! It was a fluke. They saw each other and picked up the fight right where they had left it off in 1900."

Although Mika seemed mostly unperturbed by Ma's constant haranguing, the contest would erupt anew each Friday night, when the two ladies would try to outdo each other with their baking skills. Mika made coconut cream pie and Ma made banana cream pie. We all had to taste the pies and tell them which was better. The rest of us had an unspoken pact that it would always be a tie. I used to wonder why they always made cream pies, until I realized that none of them had her own teeth.

I'd moved in with the old ladies and had the Jeep accident in 1974. Toward the end of my stay, in 1976, Ma got sick, really sick. She had cancer. Her family wanted to put her in a hospital, but she didn't want to go. She said if she was going to die, she wanted to be in the house. I offered to take care of her, but I was too young to understand what I was getting into.

We all pitched in and started caring for Ma, and it was hard. She barely ate, and then she started losing control of her bowels, so I was always cleaning up after her. We rented a hospital bed and did everything possible to make her comfortable, but we had nothing to help alleviate her pain. Finally her family came and put her in a convalescent home. Our hearts were broken, but we had no say in the matter.

Two weeks after Ma left, I took the ladies to the home to visit her. Much to my surprise, Mika wanted to come also. I figured that after all the abuse she had endured from Ma, she wouldn't be interested. It was an hour-and-a-half drive—not easy with four female bladders in one car. You'd think at their age someone would have been packing a catheter. But despite the sad reason for our journey, we had a good time, talking and laughing and admiring the scenery.

When we arrived at the convalescent home we stayed close together. The residents, most of them in wheelchairs, sat silently in the lobby or hallways. Some were wearing drool-covered bibs, others were slumped in their chairs, their hands limp in their laps. The home's walls were painted in juvenile pastel colors that made it even more depressing. It was a frightening place for the ladies, so I quickly hustled them to Ma's room.

I hardly recognized her. In two weeks' time she had become so small. She wasn't really big-boned. Her eyes were sunken and her voice was ever so soft. I thought to myself, *How could someone so powerful become so fragile?* I hugged Ma and told her I loved her, and then I whispered in her ear, "You know, Ma, your banana cream pie is the best." She smiled. I stood by and watched Betty and Carrie visit with her, while Mika waited at the back of the room.

We stayed for about an hour and then said our good-byes. As we were heading out the building's front door, I saw that Mika wasn't with us. I returned to Ma's room to find her sitting next to Ma on the bed. As little as she was, Mika had managed to slip her hand behind Ma's back and lift her to hug her. They just held on to each other for the longest time. I saw two teenage girls making peace in their nineties.

A few days later Hayworth passed away, and about two months after that Mika died in her apartment. A week later there was a knock at my door. It was Mika's daughter, whom I'd never met. Holding up a brown paper bag, she said, "My mother made a doily for you and wanted to be sure you got it." I was so touched that Mika had thought of me before she passed on and that I'd be receiving one of her exquisite doilies. Eagerly, I took the bag from her daughter and opened it.

Inside was the ugliest doily I had ever seen. Who makes a red and blue doily? The reds and blues were all blended together to create a putrid purple, and the colors managed to camouflage the delicate crochet work. I tried to hide my disappointment as I thanked her daughter, wondering if she had kept all the good ones for herself and dumped this one on me. I had never seen Mika crochet anything but a white doily, I thought to myself as I guiltily stashed the gift in a bottom drawer. Why did she have to start experimenting now? Then it struck me. At the age of 91, Mika was still taking chances—making peace with Ma, getting adventurous with the doilies. She was still trying new things, bless her heart. It was the last lesson I learned from my old ladies. I treasure my red and blue doily to this day, and yes, it is still in the drawer.

Soon after Mika's death I received a long-delayed payment from Social Security. For some reason, my being run over by a Jeep hadn't impressed them, and they had spent two years assessing my disability. I'd been on welfare in the meantime, but now the folks at Social Security had decided they owed me some money. Just before Christmas they sent me a check for $3,062.

With Ma and Mika gone and my legs finally beginning to work again, there didn't seem much reason to stay in Ohio. I couldn't bear the thought of seeing the rest of my old ladies pass away. And I wanted to escape the lawyers, the doctors, the hospitals, the pain, and the constant reminders of the Jeep accident. For the past two years my life had revolved around it and my "fame" had spread. Whenever I met someone new, it was, "I heard you were run over by a Jeep. How are you feeling? Did it hurt?" No, no, I think everybody should have a two-ton piece of metal run over them. My luck—I finally get laid and it's by a Jeep.

Besides my ladies, the only thing holding me in Ohio was my grandparents. To Grandma and Grandpa, I had remained an equal partner, a Musketeer, despite all the misfortune and craziness. When I was little I had made Grandma promise never to leave me, and the poor thing had waited until I was 19 to break the bad news: "Kathy, I have something important to tell you. Don't be made at me. Honey girl, you're old enough to know that I can't keep my promise to you. I won't always be here. The time will come when I'll have to go." I had started sobbing when she said it. Luckily I pulled myself together before she could feel too guilty about her eventual death! "I understand. It's part of reality," I had admitted. "But don't you even think of going anytime soon. When I get married you have to be my maid of honor!"

Now, as I stood knocking on the door of the mobile home where she and Grandpa lived, I thought about that day. I did not have the heart to simply inform Grandma and Grandpa that I was leaving.

They were sitting in their small living room, near the color TV I had bought them years earlier with my first check from JCPenney. Grandma was crippled with arthritis by now and her leg was stiff from a knee operation that had been badly botched. I sat on the floor beside her, as I had since I was a child, and she stroked my hair with her little fingers. Finally I asked them if I could leave Ohio. Grandma didn't hesitate. "Honey girl, I would miss you terribly, but there is really nothing for you to do here and I wouldn't want to hold you back. I know you love us, but I think it's time for you to go." Grandpa just sat there quietly.

I almost hated her for saying it, but at the same time I was relieved. I don't think I would have left if they hadn't let me go. But they did, so I cashed the Social Security check, bought a used AMC Matador, and started driving.

12

A California Scramble

My grandma named the AMC Matador "Pedro." Pedro was long and white with an orange vinyl roof, and I thought it was beyond cool. I used to feel like James Bond behind the wheel of that car. I guess the Jeep accident had done more damage to my head than I realized.

I had Pedro and my grandparents' blessings about leaving Ohio, but I had nowhere to go. My mom's brother lived in California and I had visited him once and liked it, so that's where I chose. Los Angeles seemed like a nice place, and more important, it wasn't Ohio. Good enough for me. I left Willoughby with eight hundred dollars in my pocket, feeling like a Rockefeller. As I drove west I visualized Ohio growing smaller and smaller in the rearview mirror. California, here I come, to start my new life. I thought I could leave everything behind. The only problem was, I was taking me with me.

It took about a week to drive to the Pacific Ocean, and by that time a lot of my money had been dribbled away on gas and food. I lived in my car for a while, sleeping in the backseat covered with a blanket so no one would know I was there. I took sponge baths at gas stations or used the outside showers at the beach, where I spent most of my time. At first I thought it was cute the way they colored the curbs in Los Angeles—we didn't have that in Ohio. Each night I would pick a new color to park on. I got a lot of parking tickets, all of them pink.

I had promised my old ladies that I'd let them know when I arrived in California. I wrote to them the first week I was there, although of course I didn't tell them I was living in my car. I continued to write to them often, and the only way I knew if someone had passed on was when I didn't get a letter in return. Betty is the only one left now. She's taking care of her 96-year-old mother and she still writes, telling me that she can't see very well anymore. It's obvious by the way her writing keeps running off the page. I'll make a bet she still has that push-button washer and a can of red paint sitting somewhere.

Finally I called Mom's brother, my Uncle Frank, and he invited me to stay with him. He told me I should get out, go to some dance clubs, meet a nice guy. The L.A. nightclub scene in 1976 was about as far from Willoughby as you could get without leaving the planet. It was the height of disco, and I had never seen so many people in so little clothing and so much jewelry. Gold and diamonds were hanging on every body part that could hold them. The first few times I went to a club I felt so out of place that I ended up spending most of my time in the ladies' room. I guess the girls in there were saving on cigarettes, because there was a group of them all puffing off the same one. In one of those rest rooms I met Ann, a college student and my first California friend. Ann's roommate was leaving and she was in need of another one, so I moved in with her. She was a cute little blonde, about 5'1". The two of us were like Mutt and Jeff sharing her North Hollywood apartment. I had every cupboard space that hit the ceiling and she had the ones that hit the floor. After about a year Ann decided to move closer to campus. I stayed in the apartment for eighteen years.

As soon as I moved in with Ann I made a big push to blend in with my new environment. Tanning seemed to be a priority here, so

I set about getting dark. I might as well have stuck a skewer up my butt and hopped on a rotisserie, I did so much tanning when I first got to California. I thought I had to get it all in at once, not really grasping that the sun shined here all year round. Then there was the jewelry to go with the tan. I bought myself a fake diamond ring and a gold necklace with a pretty star on it. Little did I know I had just become Jewish. And what good are diamond rings without porcelain nails? I didn't really have the patience for them—halfway through the manicure I was asking the lady, "Do you have to do all ten?" But by the end of the session I had perfect, clawlike fingernails to go with my star of David and my tan.

The first night I had my new nails, Ann and I went to a dinner party. I was in the kitchen when I felt a bit of food stuck between my teeth, so I tried to pick it out with my pinkie nail. Nothing unusual there, except this time the nail got stuck. The "porcelain" was too thick, and was wedged in between my molars. My hand was jammed in my mouth and I was starting to panic when Ann came in to see what had happened to me.

"If I have to go to the emergency room for this, I quit," I garbled from behind my hand. "Please, help me get my fingernail out of my teeth before anyone else sees me." She gave my hand a good yank and it flew out of my mouth. "Welcome to Hollywood," she said.

One of the first things I did when I arrived in L.A. was go to the Social Security office to continue my Social Security disability compensation. I needed to survive; I needed to feel secure. Physically I was doing pretty well, but emotionally I was not at all confident. The Social Security office had my file sent from Ohio, but they didn't show it to me and I had no idea what was in it. Whatever it was, I'd have to live up to it in order to continue my disability checks. I figured deaf and dumb must be in there somewhere, so I felt a need to play that up. I was so afraid of SSD declining me that I would act more disabled than I really was. It was like I was the puppet and they pulled the strings. I knew what to do from my days at the Dunbar School—if they wanted disabled, I could give them disabled. For extra credit, I'd also complain about my back and legs hurting from the accident, which was really the bulk of my concern. But that didn't seem enough for them. I hated having to behave in this manner, performing for the almighty dollar, but my fear of abandonment was overwhelming. My act for the SSD people stripped me of any self-respect I had left.

I qualified for SSD, but there was always a little voice down deep inside me saying, "You don't need this." There's nothing like receiving a check and feeling both grateful and guilty about it. I didn't need a wheelchair, I could talk, I could drive. It just didn't seem right. At the same time, a part of me felt that society owed me the money for putting me through so much misery and giving me all the labels I had believed were true—retarded, limited, can't speak, can't comprehend, too tall, dumb—to the point where I didn't know what my abilities or disabilities were. Yet the price I paid for receiving SSD was to be saddled with still another label. I was now officially *disabled*.

To the government I was disabled, but to my friends I seemed as able-bodied as anyone else. It was like having an on/off switch. The question was, when did it go on or off and who controlled the switch? On the surface the solution was to simply get a job. In order to stop receiving the checks and being "disabled," you had to prove that you could support yourself. But I'm sorry to report that when it came right down to it, I couldn't hold a job. I kept getting fired, and it was starting to remind me of high school. I took odd jobs as a warehouse manager and a waitress. I even worked at an auto shop for a while, but the problems were always the same. I couldn't do the work correctly because I couldn't comprehend people. My waitress position lasted one day.

"I'll take an order of pigs in a blanket, please."

"You want *what* in a blanket?" Sure sounded like "kids" to me.

I knew that couldn't be right, so I ended up writing a Chinese order in a coffee shop.

"Squid and snow peas."

"What? That's not on the menu."

"Well, that's what they said they wanted!" It was a whole new menu every time I went back to the cook. I didn't do much better at the auto shop. I did learn that *tire* rhymes with "fired."

Then, about two years after I arrived, I got a call from my lawyer back in Ohio. They had settled my Jeep case out of court. By the time the doctors and lawyers had taken their shares, my portion was the cash equivalent of "Oops! Sorry." Still, it was enough to buy a new car—my Toyota Corona—and to pay for my latest plan: enrolling in one of Southern California's best fashion-design schools. My grandma had always told me that I ought to be a fashion designer, and I was determined to make her proud of me. Besides, I was already making all my own clothes. At six feet tall, I didn't have much choice. There seemed to be a law that once you grew past 5'7" you were no longer entitled to clothes that fit.

At first, the school I chose didn't want to accept me because of my extremely low grade-point average from high school. (Nobody had told *me* we were collecting points!) Then I offered to pay the whole tuition up front. The check cleared and I was in. It was fun being creative, and although I still had trouble hearing the teachers, there wasn't so much reading and I had no problem producing the merchandise. I graduated from the fashion-design school and even won their award for best designer that year.

With my degree and award, I set out to find my place in the fashion industry. But I kept misinterpreting little things like prices, quantities, colors, and number lots. Once again, I was fired from job after job, still denying to myself that I had a hearing loss and assuming I was just slow in the head. I could hear enough so that with my lip-reading I was able to communicate, and I still thought I heard the same way everyone else did. If someone said, "How are you?" I heard, "Hi R wo?" I knew by syllables what was being said, but I was missing enough so that that I consistently messed up on the job.

My world had always been based on sight. I believed what I saw and didn't think to doubt what I heard. I saw the big red "Fails" on my report cards, the faces of disappointment because I wasn't achieving, the fingers pointing out the door. I saw the kids' faces as they laughed at me for not getting it. Those sights left a deep impression on me, and now that it looked like I wasn't making it in the fashion world either, they all came flooding back. I kept getting the disability checks and going to my appointments at the Social Security office, where I continued to play deaf and dumb. I was afraid that maybe the people at Social Security were right to label me disabled. Maybe they knew something about me that I couldn't accept.

Old habits die so hard. Without work or a place to fit, I started picking on myself again. My jaws began to hurt and I was convinced that it was some sort of after-effect of the Jeep accident. I ended up having surgery to fix my jaw (and an overbite people made fun of). During the three-month recovery period my mouth was wired shut and I could only drink liquids. Luckily, there was someone to take care of me—the amazing Rosemary Meyer, another surrogate mother. Born and raised in Switzerland, she was a tough cookie from the old school and was determined for me to have a life in spite of myself.

Rosemary was "Mom" Meyer not just to her married daughter, Sue, and her two grown sons, Rick and Randy, but also to the numerous strays she took in to feed, comfort, and care for. One of these strays led me to her in the first place. His name was David and he was a friend of Randy and Rick. I kind of had a crush on David. Who am I kidding? I did have a crush on him, I just didn't know what to do about it. We weren't dating, I was just hanging out with the guys, and then David got into a motorcycle accident that left him with third-degree burns on the top half of his body. I don't know where his own family was, but he ended up staying with Mom Meyer to recuperate.

I met Mom Meyer when I went over there to help take care of David, hoping to be his Florence Nightingale. With her heavy Swiss accent and my speech impediment I don't know how she and I communicated, but we hit it off right away. At first I sensed some competition about caring for the patient, but the contest ended when I realized David didn't want me around. By the time I got the hint, I had already become good friends with Mom Meyer.

Since I wasn't working, I would often spend afternoons at her house doing crafts with her. Together we tackled everything from knitting and crocheting to cooking and baking. On Sundays she'd cook a big dinner, and Rick, Randy, and I would battle one another for the last helping. Mom Meyer was an incredible cook and introduced me to foods I had never heard of. Some of them, like *leek* and *bok choy,* didn't even sound edible. When we were finished with dinner we'd clear the table and play Boggle, which wasn't my favorite. I didn't care for any game where I had to spell. But I liked the card games, such as hearts, gin rummy, and crazy eights. Those we played into the wee hours.

The round table in Mom Meyer's kitchen was the scene of all those dinners and card games, and it was also where she and I spent countless afternoons talking. As I got to know her, I realized she had a lot in common with my own mother. She lived for her children and was an extremely hard worker. The big difference between her and my mom was that she and I could talk about anything. There was another difference, too. Mom Meyer encouraged her children. She had dreams for them, whereas my mom had no dreams for us. While I was growing up, she had never once asked me what I wanted to be. Years later she admitted, "I just figured you'd get married and have kids."

As I got to know Mom Meyer better I opened up a little bit, telling her how much I needed to get off SSD. "I just want to be able to support myself," I'd grouse as we sat at her table making our crafts and knitting our afghans. I was good at it, just as I had been good at all the projects in Home Ec. Mom Meyer couldn't understand why I didn't turn my talent at crafts into a business. I would always surprise her with something special for her birthday or Christmas, and she was in awe at what I could do with stained glass and woodworking. Seeing the potential there, she became hell-bent on getting me off SSD.

"Kassy. This stained glass is beautiful. No one else does the glass this beautiful. Why don't you sell and make money?"

"I don't want to make my crafts for money. My heart goes into making these things for the people I love. It's my way of showing how much I care for them, and I get such joy watching them receive it. To make these things and sell them will take all that away."

"But Kassy, you need a job. You need income. You can sell these things!" *You can do this,* she kept telling me, and I think it was those words—*you can*—that started setting off my memories. I had to teach her that no, *I couldn't.*

"You don't understand," I would correct her. "There is no way I can start my own business. I never get instructions right. Look how many times I've been fired! Even I wouldn't want to hire me."

"Kassy, you have beautiful skin. I have a friend who is selling makeup from Switzerland. You could sell it, too. Let me give you her number."

"No, I could not sell makeup. You don't understand. I'm not pretty. I didn't get a date to the senior prom until the last second, and that was only because I paid for the tickets. Besides, I am not a good saleswoman. I'm not comfortable taking people's money. Giving money away, maybe, but not taking it."

"Kassy, this woodworking is wonderful. I never have seen woodworking like this. You can sell these woodworkings." It was getting to the point where I didn't want to make things for her anymore. Everything I made, she wanted me to sell.

You can do this, you can do that is all that came out of the woman's mouth. What was wrong with her? *I couldn't.* That was all I knew, that was what I had been taught, that was what I believed. What was it going to take to get her to understand? For every *can* she gave me, I had to fight it with a *can't,* as if I had been pro-grammed. In bits and pieces, mostly to try to explain to Mom Meyer why *I couldn't,* I told her the whole story of my life. I com-plained about my mother, my father, every school I'd been to, all the labels that had been put on me, every failure and humiliation, the Jeep accident, and other memories that I had never shared with anyone before. "You don't understand," was my refrain. "You weren't there when I was in the school for retardation. You weren't there when my mom made me wear hearing aids that hurt and I felt like an alien and all the kids laughed at me. You weren't there when I got kicked out of every class in high school. You didn't hear me cry at night. You weren't there when I graduated with a one-point grade average."

But she was there when I graduated from fashion-design school with a 3.5 grade point average and won the award for best designer. She was there when I did my woodworking and stained glass. Mom Meyer saw a beautiful young woman with loads of potential, but that young person couldn't see anything except the lies that had been programmed into her all her life. Mom Meyer saw all my tal-ents, she saw me for the loving heart that I had, for my sense of humor, and she kept reminding me of those things. But it was as if I had a force field that would repel any compliment. "Kassy, you look beautiful today." "Yeah, yeah, yeah. Shampoo and makeup." I'd brush it off instead of just saying thank you.

Through all my odd jobs, the fashion-design school, the jobs I tried and failed at after I graduated, and my stint in bed with my jaw wired shut, Mom Meyer was like a broken record that just kept repeating *You can.* She never let up. She had been telling me *you can* for eight years when the conversation finally blew up.

I was complaining, as usual. I don't even remember what we were talking about, but I was on some variation of my unfair past. This time instead of shaking her head in sympathy, she let me have it.

"What are you going to do about it?" she shouted in frustration. "Wallow in it the rest of your life? How many times are you going to relive this shit? Where are the good memories?"

"The aren't any!" I yelled back, stunned that she would attack me and that I would lash back at her. I couldn't believe that after all this time together, Mom Meyer would cut me like this. All my life I had felt as if there were a monster inside me trying to crawl out, and now the monster took over.

"You're supposed to be a mom to me," I accused her. "You're supposed to be my best friend. Why aren't you listening to me when I tell you *I can't?*" My stomach was burning. It felt as if there were a creature stomping around in there with a pitchfork. I walked out of her house and slammed the door, enraged. Who the fuck did she think she was? She was never going to understand my feelings. She was never going to feel my pain. Nobody was ever going to feel my pain.

I kept on fuming, but after a while I couldn't avoid asking myself why I was so angry. I thought about the look of shock and hurt on Mom Meyer's face as I had walked out on her. And then it dawned on me. She did feel my pain. I kept giving it to her because I *wanted* her to feel it, to really understand how it had been for me. I had never before been close enough with anyone to share it all. What a terrible thing to do to her. Her expression had been so full of love and sadness for me, as if she were asking how much more I could possibly put myself through. I was causing her pain and she was doing nothing more than believing in me. Instead of gratefully receiving her love and support, I had been rejecting it.

"What are you going to do, wallow in it the rest of your life?" she had asked me. *Yes,* I thought to myself. *Sounds good! That way I don't have to date, no one will see my ugly body, and I can be a victim my whole life.* As a child I had been a victim of circumstances and a lot of stupidity, so I would be a victim as an adult, too, because I was really good at it. But instead of allowing other people to victimize me, I would victimize myself. I would blame everyone else when things went wrong and I'd never take responsibility. I could be pissed off at the world because they deserved it after everything they had done to me. And I would have a life filled with loneliness, rejection, bitterness, and resentment of my own making.

In truth, I didn't confront myself with quite so much clarity at the time. It came to me more like a sick feeling, a realization that I couldn't do this to Mom Meyer anymore, she didn't deserve it. It hurt me to see her suffer. Mom Meyer had told me about when her husband left and how it had almost destroyed her. She couldn't talk to her kids about it because he was their father, so she had confided in me. I felt brokenhearted for her whenever she talked about it, and yet I had never considered that when I was in pain, it hurt her, too. I had to stop saying, "I can't," at least out loud.

I went back to Mom Meyer's house and apologized. "I'm so sorry," I told her. "I don't know how to let someone in. I can't imagine anyone really believing that I can do something. You kept fighting me where I found comfort. I understand now that it hurt you to watch me put myself down and limit myself, but that's all I know how to do. So from now on I'll try my best not to tell you about my past anymore, about my pain. And I'll try my best to believe you when you tell me *I can*." I didn't have much faith that I could do that last part, but at least I said the words. It was a beginning.

13

The Fourth Gift

IT WAS HARD for me to let anyone in completely, even Mom Meyer. And trusting a man, believing that someone could love me? That was a whole other story. Luckily, I was never one who thought my life wouldn't be complete unless there was a man in it. Granted, every once in a while I wished there was someone special, but most of the time dating felt like another minefield to me. I never actually dated, I just fell into relationships. I didn't even want to take a chance with a blind date. Sitting at Mom Meyer's kitchen table, I told her about the men I did connect with, holding back a lot of the racier details. My relationships tended to go in three-year spurts. I'd see somebody, have a three-year dry spell, then meet someone new.

By the time I got to California I wasn't totally naive about sex anymore. During my last year in Ohio I had dated a fireman named Barry who had taught me a few of the basics. I was crazy for this guy and lost all inhibitions when I was with him. Lots of women have fantasies about firemen, but after about six months of being with Barry my fantasy became about the day he'd return. He'd been shipped west for the fall fire season, and while he was away he sent me postcards or letters every week. I couldn't wait for him to come back. I knew he would be home for Christmas, so that whole autumn I devoted myself to making his return unforgettable. I had it all planned out. I knitted him a sweater, crocheted him an afghan, made enough Christmas tree ornaments to fill three trees, got him all kinds of gifts, baked cookies, set up his apartment with a tree, decorated the whole place, made all his favorite food, and had a surprise party with all his friends to welcome him home.

When Barry finally returned he was totally indifferent toward me. I wanted to believe he just needed time to adjust, but I could see in his face and body language that he was hiding something. He showed me pictures of his trip, and when he wasn't looking I went through the packet and found photos of him with a beautiful, auburn-haired girl. My heart sank, my stomach ached, and any confidence I had about being a woman went out the window. I felt ugly and rejected, and reverted right back to my old feelings of "What's wrong with me?" I didn't understand how Barry could brush me off after all I had done for him. At least, I thought I was doing it for him or for "us." In reality I was looking for approval, a pat on the back. "Wow, you did all this for me? Gosh, Kathy, you're the best. I love you."

Unfortunately, this was a pattern I tended to follow whenever I got involved with someone. I smothered him with kindness. Later on in life I thought of the perfect metaphor for what I was doing: I was on a tennis court, and on the other side of the net was someone I liked. His racket had no strings. I, on the other hand, was standing next to a ball machine. I started the machine on low. My partner swung at the balls but couldn't return them with his stringless racquet. When nothing came back I turned the machine up—now he was ducking the balls, and still nothing came over the net for me. I turned the machine on full blast. Now he didn't have a chance in hell, he was being bombarded with all these balls beating on him. He had no choice but to quit the game and I was left standing alone on the court.

I wasn't playing fair. I wasn't giving the guy a chance to participate. Now I've learned that when I play tennis, both parties need to have a tennis racket with strings, and you play with one ball. When I hit the ball over the net I wait patiently for it to return, and if it doesn't, then I'm off the court. But back then I was a long way from understanding how the game was played.

It wasn't just that I was needy. Part of my problem was that I never felt comfortable around men unless I was being their buddy. My Grandma Virginia, always popular with the gentlemen, used to tell me, "If you can't flirt, you're no granddaughter of mine." I must have been adopted, then, because I didn't understand flirting. It's not that I didn't want to be with guys, I just didn't know what to do with myself around them. I wasn't comfortable in my own body, let alone having to share it with someone. I grew up believing it was broken, and I didn't want anyone else to find out. It was better to keep men at a distance.

To add to my ambivalence, there were things that would trigger contempt, anxiety, or fear in me for no good reason. If a man looked at me in a particular way I'd recoil, barely conscious that I was doing it. The smell of beer on a guy's breath would fill me with disgust and I'd find myself thinking, *What a weak, pitiful person.* I hated the expression on men's faces when they were looking at a *Playboy* or ogling a girl on the street. I knew a lot of women felt the way I did, and I identified with the women's movement. But those women had boyfriends or husbands, many of whom even drank beer. Clearly I was the odd woman out. The upshot was that throughout my early and mid-twenties, I dated only a few men. I'd start lobbing the tennis balls fast and furiously, and while I was lobbing away the guy would quietly put the racquet down and leave the court. They always came back, though, wanting to be friends. Just what I needed.

Then, in my late twenties, I met Ryan. My first California roommate, Ann, was marrying his cousin and we met at the wedding. Ryan had a wonderful sense of humor, wavy brown hair, and brown eyes. He was a good-looking man, but at first I wasn't very attracted to him because he was shorter than me. At six feet tall I usually felt big and clumsy around men, but Ryan got my attention by just taking over. All my clumsiness vanished because he didn't give me time to think about it.

Without fanfare, as if it were the most natural thing in the world, Ryan moved into my apartment and made us a couple. He convinced me to get rid of my furniture and replaced it with his. I had very few preferences of my own, and if he felt so strongly about the way the apartment looked, that only seemed to be proof that he cared about us. Other women may have chafed at a man who was such a take-charge type, but it was just what I needed. Anything less, and I would have doubted that he loved me.

When I realized Ryan was safe, he started to look very good to me. I couldn't keep my hands off the guy. He made every holiday special and bought me my very first Valentine's Day gift, a heart-shaped mirror with gold roses around the frame. I still have it. I think Ryan even made up some holidays, because he was always bringing me surprises. He began to buy me clothes, too. No one had ever done that, and I was thrilled. It was a rare gift to have someone take care of me. Before I knew it, I was wearing shirts with little polo players stitched on them, yuppie stuff I would never normally choose. We joined a bowling league with his sister, whom I adored. In fact, his whole family was pretty great. And Ryan wanted to be part of my California family, too. He would come over to Mom Meyer's with me for Sunday dinner, and he fit right in.

Like a lot of people I was beginning to meet, Ryan had a job in the entertainment industry. He was a sound-effects editor for a television show. We would be sitting there watching TV and he'd say, "Listen! Hear that door slam? I did that!"

"Looks great, honey," I'd reply. The whole time we were together, we never discussed my hearing loss. I'm sure he realized I had one, but I didn't mention it and he didn't push. He just accepted me.

I was still getting Social Security, and Ryan helped me find a job I could excel at, working in the warehouse at a sporting goods store. I managed to get my five days' worth of work done in three because I was alone. There were no people to misinterpret, just me and the order forms, merchandise, and ticket machine. I was in heaven. I received a letter from Social Security Disability stating, "Your case shows that you are now able to do substantial gainful work. You are no longer entitled to benefits." At last I was not disabled.

Even though I was content, Ryan prodded me to aim higher and look for a more challenging job. I took it as an insult, thinking that he didn't like me as I was, but later I realized that he had seen potential in me and was hoping I would see it, too. He was teaching me to dream. I often wondered if he and Mom Meyer had teamed up.

Ryan and I spent hours making love, planning projects, laughing, sharing, completely losing track of time. It was wonderful, but I didn't quite trust it. I felt as if I were still not quite connecting with him.

Late one afternoon, when we had just returned from a camping trip, I received a phone call from my gynecologist. He told me to come see him in his office the next day. I had been in for a checkup a few weeks earlier, but when I didn't hear from him I assumed everything was all right. As I settled into the chair across from his desk, I wondered what could be going on. I had no idea what they tested for during those checkups.

Dr. Jamison folded his hands, and with a completely neutral expression said something that looked like, "Kathy, we've discovered some indication of invasive carcenomansitoo. Squamasels."

"I'm sorry, I don't understand what you're saying."

"It's another name for cervical cancer."

Cancer? I instantly remembered Ma Hayworth, how she had become so small and fragile and had died within a few months of getting cancer. Cancer was death. That was all I knew about it. There was nothing in between the two words.

"We'll need to go in and see how much it's spread," the doctor continued. "We'll do some cervical biopsies and then decide on a course of treatment." I searched his features for some bit of information that I could use, but there was nothing. No fear, no hint of, "It'll be okay." Dr. Jamison had probably developed this detached expression to keep his patients from panicking when they heard the word *cancer*. But I depended on faces to tell me what I couldn't hear, and his blank look made the conversation even more frightening.

When I left the doctor's office, my whole being shut down. I didn't exist; I was in complete shock. I didn't think, "I'm going to fight this and beat it," because I didn't realize that beating it was an option. Ma Hayworth had died, and now I would die too. I kept seeing that big woman all shriveled up in the nursing-home bed. I was never very big to begin with, so I would probably shrivel up to nothing.

That night the fear was overwhelming. I felt entirely alone, even though Ryan was lying right next to me. I couldn't tell him, I didn't know how. I didn't want him touching me anymore. I felt ugly, disconnected, empty. It started happening all over again, the terror at not knowing what was wrong with me. Worst of all, the cancer was in the one part of my body that I didn't want to think about. I was so scared that I started having a seizure, shaking and curling up in the bed. Ryan woke up and tried to calm me. "Kathy! What's the matter?" I didn't know what to do. I couldn't communicate my feelings. Whenever I suffered, I did it alone.

I couldn't bear to see the look on Ryan's face if I told him I had cancer. All I could see was me dying, and I didn't want to put him through that. I had to get rid of Ryan but I didn't know how, so I simply shunned him. Overnight, I stopped letting him touch me and refused to make any plans. I hated myself for it, but I wanted him away from me. Finally, we both agreed that he should leave.

The day Ryan moved out he looked like a trauma victim, confused and lost, just as I was. It killed me to watch him be hurt, but

I told myself this was how it had to be. I asked Ryan to take all his furniture with him; I didn't need any material things. I was left with a refrigerator, some silverware, a TV, and one chair, but I didn't care. I was going through something I didn't understand so I reacted the way I always had, by retreating into myself until the siege was over. At 27, I went through the cancer alone. I didn't even know how to share it with Mom Meyer.

It was one of the scariest times of my life. I couldn't see the cancer or feel it, and I didn't know what it was doing. Questions on top of questions confronted me, and there seemed to be no answers. The diagnosis of cervical cancer was especially disturbing, since anything pertaining to the female parts of my body had always been mysterious and frightening to me. Pain I could handle. The Jeep accident hadn't been all that long ago. But cancer elevated my fear about my body to a whole new level.

The biopsies were horrible, more painful than any surgery. They were done in Dr. Jamison's office with no anesthesia. The doctor would be positioned behind a sheet draped over my legs, which were up in stirrups like they are for a Pap smear. To make matters worse, I couldn't hear anything he said. He'd peek up from behind the sheet to tell me something and then go back down, making me crazy. Lip-reading someone who's between your legs is not an option unless you're a contortionist. Finally I just blurted out, "I can't hear you! I don't understand what you're saying!" I was so frustrated. The nurse, whose name was also Kathy, was my saving grace. She sat in a chair next to me and repeated everything the doctor said. I was seeing the words but I wasn't understanding them. I just had to trust that they were doing what was best for me.

Dr. Jamison used a long metal instrument with prongs at the end that would bite little chunks of flesh out of my cervix. He inserted it in my vagina and would yank pieces of skin from my insides, up to 13 times in one session. It was painful as hell and left me with cramps and heavy bleeding. I hated it. I had to wait for weeks to get the test results, only to find out that I had to go back and do it all over again. When he would hit the same spot he had sampled before, all hell would break loose. Kathy the nurse would have to hold me still. I don't think I could have done it without her—her look of concern and hope kept me going.

The cycle progressed: test, wait, heal; test, wait, heal. It was the waiting that was slowly killing me, the not knowing, or understanding, or having control. I didn't tell anyone how much fear and pain I was in, but I think Mom Meyer knew. It was during this waiting time that I started having more seizures like the one that had struck me that night with Ryan. They'd happen out of the blue, and suddenly I'd be beating myself and screaming. The old familiar feeling of being possessed, of something inside trying to climb out, was back. At one point my neighbor asked a priest to come to the apartment and bless me to get the evil out of me. Another friend took me to a hypnotist to get to the bottom of the seizures, but they had to pull me out of the trance because I was digging my nails into the palms of my hands and hurting myself. I didn't have the money to go back for a second session, and besides, I was afraid.

Everyone thought the seizures were from the Jeep accident, but I knew otherwise. To me the Jeep accident was physical, not emotional, and whatever this was, it had lived in me a long time. It had taken up residency in the space where my self-confidence, happiness, courage, and faith were supposed to be. Instead, there was a black cave where a demon lived. Having the cervical cancer had somehow given this creature more life, and I lacked the tools to fight it because I didn't know what it was.

Amid all this, Christmas came. I didn't go home to Ohio because I was emotionally drained, and my family was not a good support system. I didn't dare tell my grandparents about the cancer because I didn't want to worry them. No, the best thing to do was stay in California and wait for the test results.

For people like me, who grew up with white Christmases, December in California can be depressing. That year I wasn't in the mood for the harsh, slanty sunlight and dry weather of Christmas in L.A. But my family back home did not forget me. They all sent me presents, which was unusual. In fact, they all sent the same kind of present. They sent music boxes.

My dad sent me a musical jewelry box; my mom sent me a musical figurine; my own grandma sent me a musical clown doll; and my brothers sent me a clown music box. I'm 98 percent sure it wasn't some plot to drive me completely insane. I opened the presents one by one, in shock. I knew in my heart I would not be able to hear these. Why would they send them?

I wanted so badly to hear the musical gifts. I closed all the windows and curtains in my apartment and lined them up on the kitchen counter, thinking, *I can hear them, I can hear them* as I wound them up. I could tell they were working because I could see the cranks moving and feel the vibrations when I put my hand on the counter, but I couldn't hear a note. I lay my head on the counter. Nothing.

In a rage, I took my arm and swept all the music boxes off the counter, wanting them to shatter, yelling out loud, "Who am I? What is wrong with me?" Obviously I was supposed to be able to hear these things, because my own family had sent them. If they didn't know who I was, how could I know myself? They didn't mean any harm by it, they were just giving me Christmas presents. But all in one year, on the same occasion? Only my Grandma wrote, "Honey girl, I know you probably won't hear this, but I thought the clown was so beautiful." Thank God for Grandma.

I called my mother and asked why she sent the musical figurine, hoping I could tell her how I felt about it.

"I sent it because of the song, Kathy."

"Mom, I can't hear the song."

"Yes you can! That's why I got it, the song is special. I got myself one, too. It's 'The Way We Were.' " She was trying. But "The Way We Were"? The way we were was messed up, Mom! Why the hell would I want to remember that? I ended up lying and telling her that I could hear the figurine so I wouldn't hurt her feelings. That's the way "we" were.

Finally, after a year of biopsies, I had surgery to remove the cancer. Yes! I was on my way to recovery, I shall live once again! Six months later I went in for a follow-up. The doctor told me he didn't get it all, that he would have to perform another surgery.

To hear this for a second time was too much. I went home so scared, angry, and frustrated that I could barely see to drive. This could not be happening. I paced my apartment, trying to understand what I should do. Dr. Jamison had told me that it was my choice. "But we strongly recommend the second surgery to make sure all the cancerous cells have been removed. If you elect not to have the surgery, Kathy, we can't guarantee how long you will have to live. Six months, six years—there's no telling."

Should I go in for the surgery? Should I refuse? I was walking back and forth, my thoughts flying around inside my head, when I ran out of steam in front of a wall mirror. Suddenly it was as if a hand came out of the mirror around to the back of my head, pressed my face up to the glass, and said, *"What's your name?"*

"Kathy."

"What's your favorite color?"

"Pink. Well, it's pink if Mary likes pink. But it's blue if Joe likes blue."

"What's your favorite food?"

"I don't know. I'll eat whatever anybody else is eating."

I was looking in the glass, I could see my reflection, but I didn't have a clue who I was. I was looking into a flashback of all the "Kathys" I had been up until that moment. I was born a perfect child of God, and then society had yanked me by the back of the neck and said:

"You are retarded."

"I can do this work, I can do these blocks, why doesn't anyone expect anything of me?"

"Now you're not going to be retarded anymore. You're going be deaf and you're going to learn how to talk."

"Wow, what a wonderful teacher. I love Miss Joan Dailey. I'm learning how to talk. I'm going to be just like her. I am going—"

"No, now you have your hearing aids and you're fixed and you're going back to public school."

"But I don't understand the work! The teacher has her back turned toward me, I can't lip-read her. Why are the kids making fun of me? Mom? Mom? If you could just listen to me I could tell you what that man is doing to me. You could get him to stop touching me."

"Now you're going to be run over by a Jeep and you'll never walk normally again."

"God, please don't forsake me. Don't leave me like this."

"Now we're going to give you cancer. And you have to have surgery if you want to live."

At that moment, I learned how to say, "FUCK YOU!"

How dare you say I can't talk? How dare you say I can't walk? How dare you say I can't have a life? *How dare me for listening to you.*

I had spent my whole life wearing society's stupid labels. You can't read; you can't talk; you can't write; you're retarded; you're too tall, too ugly, too flat; you can't, you won't, you will never be able to. Sticks and stones may break my bones but names will never hurt me—bull! Words can have the power to last a lifetime, it all depends on how much life you give them. I had given those words almost thirty years, but as I stood looking into that mirror, I remembered. I saw it as clear as day, the fourth gift I had received at the Jeep accident, when I had the life-after-death experience. It was the gift of choice. I remembered saying, "No. I'm not ready yet." Someone had loved me so much that He had let me decide whether to go or stay. I ended up staying, and I had better start making the most of it.

I took a chance. I never went back for the second operation. I decided to take that incredible gift called choice and start taking charge of my own life. I changed my diet, I changed my attitude. My Uncle Frank had once told me, "Fear knocked upon my door, faith opened it. No one was there." I lived by that. And I flew home to confront the man who had made me so afraid of my body.

14

~

The Missing Piece

I WAS GOING to do it. I had made up my mind. But every time I started to call the airline to book a ticket home, I chickened out. In the end I decided that what I needed was professional help, so I got the name of a therapist who held group sessions in her home for women who had been molested as children.

My molestation was my deepest, darkest secret. For years, not only didn't my family know about it, but even I had managed to block it out. It was manifested in my uneasiness around men and the weird reactions I'd have to them. Those feelings had been a mystery to me, but getting cervical cancer had cracked the wall of denial. In the year that I had the biopsies, the scattered pieces of my memory slowly came together to form a complete picture. Once I could see what had happened, I began to understand why I felt and acted the way I did around men. Suddenly my life made sense to me, but the memories were sickening. I didn't want to face them, but the time had come—they were all oozing out. I'm sure that's why I kept having the seizures.

Even though I knew it hadn't been my fault, I was so ashamed of the molestation that the only person I dared talk to about it was

Mom Meyer. I sat at her round table and told the story again and again, feeling more enraged and helpless and confused every time I repeated it. Yet even though I could now remember the events in detail, there was still a part of me that wondered if I hadn't made it all up. Before I actually confronted the man, I needed feedback from other women who had gone through the same thing.

There were about ten ladies at the therapy group the first night I went. Each one talked about her experiences, including me. Their stories were all so horrible that I felt like mine was a picnic in comparison. I almost wanted to thank the man who molested me for not doing anything worse than he did. But regardless of the different degrees of molestation, we had all experienced the same pain and betrayal, and we were all left feeling totally inadequate. Talking about it in front of the others was a huge relief. For once I didn't feel all alone with it. I left there on a real high and couldn't wait for the next week, when we would learn how to deal with the memories and let go of the pain. I felt I was finally taking my past into my own hands and was on my way to healing. Maybe I wouldn't have to confront him after all.

Next Wednesday night came. I took my chair alongside the same women. The meeting began and, one by one, they started telling their stories all over again, just like they had the week before. I was baffled. When it came my turn, I went into a little more detail about my experience, but that was it for me. As each lady spoke, I watched her body language, trying to get a sense of her fears and doubts and what was in her heart. I saw a lot of emptiness and blank faces. My heart went out to them, taking my mind off my own pain.

Week three rolled around, and I wondered whether I should return to the group sessions. I decided to give it one more try. We started the meeting and again everybody went into the same stories, for the third week in a row! I really liked some of these women, but something seemed off-kilter here. So at snack break (which I think was the real the reason some of them kept showing up), I asked each one, "How long have you been coming to these meetings?"

"Six months."

"One year."

"Three years."

"Seven years."

"You've been repeating your story here every week for seven years? The snacks aren't that great!"

I was afraid to ask the woman giving the meeting how long she had been holding them. None of the ladies seemed successful. None had a decent job, self-confidence, or was in a good relationship. They were reliving their molestation over and over again, holding on to the past and not willing to let go, as an excuse not to try and make a happier future. As far as I could see, they were being molested every week they were there. I didn't want to be sitting there in seven years. Hell, I didn't want to be there another minute, so I walked out and never returned. I guess I needed to see for myself the damage I was doing by holding on to the bad part of my past and forgetting any of the good. I knew that if I was going to have any kind of a future, I had to get on that plane to Ohio.

It started when I was eleven. He was someone close to the family (not my grandpa), someone who had always been there for me. I was taught to trust him. He had known me since I was born and was like a surrogate father to me.

Every Saturday my mother went to work early in the morning. I could never hear her leave. He was there baby-sitting us. My brothers were downstairs watching Saturday morning cartoons, and I was upstairs.

My body was starting to make some changes and I was already uncomfortable with it. No one had explained that these changes were going to happen to me. He would either wake me up or follow me into the bathroom. He would have me take my pajamas off and then he would play doctor. He would touch every part of my body and comment on it.

He touches my eyes, looking into my face as I lip-read him: "What is wrong with your eyes? One is smaller than the other."

"I, I, I don't know." I'm scared. *What is wrong with my eyes?*

"What is wrong with your nostrils? One is larger than the other."

"I don't know." *What is wrong with me?*

I am lip-reading him, taking every word for the truth, believing he is concerned for me. I trust him. There is something terribly wrong with me.

With his hands on my shoulders: "What is wrong with your shoulders, why are they slanted?"

As he works his way down my body, I watch his face. It no longer looks familiar to me. What is happening to him? I don't like this.

His hands are on my nipples: "There is no milk. Where is the milk?"

What milk? I don't understand what he is talking about, I just know I hate this. I am screaming inside, standing there naked, frozen in my feet, not understanding any of this and wanting it to be over with. *Please,* I scream in my head. *Stop! Stop touching me! Stop with all that talking! Stop looking at me with that expression, it is horrifying! I need my friend. You go away! What is wrong with you? What is wrong with me? I don't want to be broken anymore. Oh, God, please stop. This feels awful.*

It was never sex, it was him playing doctor, sneaking up on me, touching me, telling me everything was wrong with my body and never giving me a remedy to fix it. When it was over I would go on with my day as if nothing had happened. By the time my mother came home from work, it would be totally blocked out of my head. I never thought to tell my mother. We didn't communicate.

My mom would have us kiss him good-bye if he was over at the house. He reeked of beer. I hated the smell of it and to this day if I see a man drinking beer I automatically think he is a weak person. Now I know it's nothing more than my reaction to my past—beer represents molestation and molestation represents weak, hollow, evil, sick, lonely, scared, and out of control.

The molestation changed the core of me. It left me in fear of my own body, unable to trust anyone. It made me believe that I could never be loved, that I was ugly and broken. I can still recall, as if it happened only hours ago, how the face I loved and trusted turned into a stranger's face as he was touching me. It was the same expression I saw on men when they looked at *Playboy* or whistled at a woman on the street. I hated that expression so much that I would do anything to avoid having it directed at me, so I made myself look unattractive by not using makeup and wearing baggy clothes to hide my body. Only with Ryan had I begun to feel safe enough to love. But in the end, I had failed. I hadn't trusted him enough to tell him I was sick.

Would I ever be able to trust a man who said he loved me? Would I know what it felt like to be a woman confident in her own body? I wanted to feel worthy of all the lovely things in life; to receive compliments and believe them without making a joke. I wanted to look at myself naked in a mirror without being afraid or ashamed and say, "I like you, you are okay." Would I ever love myself enough to let someone in? So many questions, and only one place I could go to begin to answer them.

I flew to Ohio intending to control how and when I confronted him, but when I went with my brothers to visit my dad, the man was there, too. He sat down on the couch next to me and started telling me how proud he was of me, considering all I had been through. He meant the Jeep accident. "You've really gotten your life together, Kathy," he said.

"Yeah," I agreed. "I do feel like I'm putting the pieces of my life together. It's like a puzzle. Except there's this one big piece right smack in the middle of the puzzle that's missing."

"What's that, Kath?"

"You. Every Saturday morning upstairs in the bathroom or bedroom with me. Remember?"

"No, I don't remember anything like that."

I felt like cold water had been injected through my veins. *Had I made it up after all?* Without any noise or heaving or shaking I started to cry, the tears pouring out of my eyes while the rest of me sat still as a statue. It was the strangest sensation. Before anyone could see what was happening I ran upstairs to a guest room. I sat on a couch, thoughts and feelings tearing around inside my body. A few minutes later he came in and kneeled in front of me.

"My God, what have I done to you?" he said, and as I looked down at him it seemed as if his face was aging before me. "I did do those things. Don't hate all men, just hate me." He was crying.

I felt so bad for him that I started to comfort him.

"I don't hate you," I said. "I just don't understand."

"What I'd give to have one-tenth of your heart, your courage, your compassion," he told me, and then he pulled himself to his feet and left.

I was numb and it was over. The conversation hadn't lasted five minutes. He had admitted it, and I knew it wasn't a dream or my imagination. Maybe that was all that needed to happen.

But the next day I woke up feeling like something wasn't right. He had gotten away with it again. A simple "I'm sorry" was not enough to erase everything he had done. I needed more, so I called him at his home. He didn't sound surprised to hear from me.

"We have to talk," I said coldly.

"We can talk, Kath. How about if we meet in a restaurant?"

I hated the way he said *Kath,* so familiar, old friends.

"No, I don't want to meet in a restaurant. I can't say what I want to say in public, and this is going to take more than five minutes. We can do it at your house, but I want someone else to be there, too."

We talked in his home office while his wife waited downstairs.

She had no idea what was going on. For at least an hour we went over it, but the conversation just kept going around in circles.

"I need to understand why. Why did you do this? How could you do it? What were you thinking when you were touching me?"

He had no answers. He just kept saying, "I don't know why I did it. What can I do to help you now?"

"I don't know. Just make the pain stop."

"How can I do that?"

I just looked at him. I had no answers either.

I left that day feeling worse than I had when I arrived. Driving back to my mother's house, I cried in the car—the pain was still there. Then, all of a sudden, it was as if a spirit were sitting in the seat next to me, demanding that I face the facts. *How many times did he ask you, "What can I do to help you?"* Finally, I understood that what had happened was done and over with. He had already done what he could do. He had admitted it and was sorry for it. Nothing could change what had happened, but I was the one who had carried on the tradition of replaying the scene in my mind. Now it was up to me to break that tradition. I couldn't be like the women in the therapy group, using the memories as my excuse for not being successful at anything, whether it was a job or a relationship. I made a promise to myself to let it go, and chose to get on with my life.

15

My Audio Angel

WHEN I CAME back from Ohio I felt lighter. I had returned to that man what was rightfully his, not mine. I wasn't angry with him, or at least I told myself that, but I was hurt and confused. I just could not reconcile how someone I was taught to love could do such harm to me. The negative feelings he had instilled in me had changed the course of my life. I would never know who I might have been if he hadn't cornered me those Saturday mornings, and it was hard not to dwell on it. There was nothing to be gained by doing that, however, and too much to lose. I had to trust my gift of choice. By being aware when those old feelings of self-hatred and fear started to well up, I could choose how I wanted to handle them. Either I could give them life, or I could banish them from my mind. It was time for me to rewrite the script, and for now that meant putting the confrontation behind me and concentrating on my biggest enemy, cancer.

I had turned my life over to the cancer out of fear, and now I wanted it back. There was no way I was going in for the second operation; the first round had taken too much out of me. I needed all my strength to focus on understanding the cancer and taking charge of it. Dr. Jamison was great about it, although he continued to encourage me to have surgery.

"I want one year of no doctors," I told him. "No tests, no invasions of my body, nothing pulling at my heart or mind. I just want to see what I need to be myself. But after that first year, I promise to come in for a checkup every six months." As long as I agreed to the checkups, he went along with my plan.

Mom Meyer's son Randy had opened an aerobics center called Sweat with Us and he asked me to manage it. Since I was intent on getting well again, this seemed like a good idea. I could surround myself with beautiful, healthy bodies, and maybe some of it would rub off on me. I was surprised to see that most of the people who bought a membership in the club were already in great shape. Some came in two or three times a day. The aerobics instructors were stunning young men and women who wore the tightest of workout gear to show off their amazing bodies. I was in awe of how hard they pushed themselves.

One day an aerobics instructor didn't show up. The people were waiting, they wanted their workout. I called several instructors to cover for the one who was supposed to be there, but no luck. It was up to me to teach the class of 25. I figured, "I can do this, I've watched enough classes," but I was scared to death. First, because the only thing I wore under my sweats were leotards—no protective T-shirt or shorts to shield me. Second, I would have to stand up front where everyone could see me. Third, there were mirrors everywhere and *I* would see me. But I had no choice, the customers must be served. What the heck, how hard could it be?

I had noticed that the instructors always turned on music before they started the warm-up, so I turned the music on. I started going through the routine, and everyone followed along. Looking down, I saw that one of the women in front was moving her lips. I lip-read her: "I can't wait to get you alone tonight, babe, just you and me." *Oh really? I don't think so!* Then I realized everyone was mouthing the same thing. Man, I must be good! They all want me. Soon I was teaching three classes a day. I looked spectacular.

After six months of this I almost resembled one of the girls I used to gawk at when I first started managing the club, minus the silicone. Looking good, feeling healthy, getting on with my life—almost. There was still the question of men. I thought that after my confrontation in Ohio everything would be different, but it wasn't. I was still picking the wrong guys. Brandon was a good example. Taller than me, he was the type of man other women drooled over. I could actually wear high heels with him. And he liked me, too, with just a few ifs: "You know, Kathy, if you'd get a nose job and a boob job and dye your hair red, you'd be perfect." I wasn't totally nuts. I put some auburn highlights in my hair and let it go at that.

While I was dating Brandon, Ryan came back into my life. He started dropping by my apartment leaving gifts and flowers, which infuriated Brandon. Now two men wanted me, and I had no idea how to handle it. For one thing, Ryan's reentry into my life came as a complete shock. We hadn't spoken since he had moved out nearly two years earlier. During that time I had been consumed with fighting cancer and thought of little else. Occasionally Ryan would cross my mind, and I always felt a twinge of regret when I remembered how much fun we had together. But I believed I had done the right thing by releasing him when I did. He was never one to sit around and mope, and I assumed he was happy and getting on with his life.

It turned out that Ryan had proceeded full steam ahead to save money so that he could buy a house and win me back. I wished he had told me of this plan. But he wanted to surprise me, and it caught me off balance.

I flew home to Ohio for Christmas that year, and Ryan sent a cassette tape that was waiting for me when I got to my mother's house. It was a song by the Survivors with lyrics that went something like, "The search is over. I knew you were always there. I was caught up in a dream, but you were right before my eyes all the time." I couldn't hear the words, so my mother had to recite them to me. That took away from the romance a little bit, but the message was clear. Ryan wanted to share his life with me.

When I got back to Los Angeles Ryan was still pursuing me, leaving gifts at the apartment where Brandon was sure to see them. Finally Brandon blew up and said, "It's me or him. Go stop this, now!" I was torn and, I have to admit, a little afraid of Brandon. My misplaced sense of justice told me I had to dance with the date who brought me. I was with Brandon now, so I had to choose him. I didn't have enough self-esteem to pick the man I truly cared for.

Dreading my mission, I went to see Ryan. I fumbled around trying to explain myself, but he cut me off. "Just tell me you don't love me anymore, Kathy," he challenged me.

"I don't love you," I lied.

For a long time we cried and held on to each other, but at last I left. I'd made a choice and I had to stick with it. I wept all the way home and was angry at Brandon that night, but the die was cast. Like they say in comedy, timing is everything. I had never realized Ryan loved me so much, and at that time in my life I didn't know how to accept it. I cared for him, but the feeling was buried under guilt about Brandon and my desire to be loyal. God provides several paths; I chose one, and I'll never know where the other would have taken me. Maybe instead of being a comedian I would have been a wife and mother with a large collection of Polo shirts. I have to trust that I took the right path, but I will always regret the biggest lie I ever told.

Brandon ended up dumping me for his next-door neighbor, who then dumped him.

I had kept my promise to Dr. Jamison and gone in for checkups every six months after a year without doctors. At my very first checkup, after taking charge of my life, I was found to be completely cancer free. To my great joy I still am to this day. There is and always will be an underlying fear whenever something goes wrong with my body that the cancer might be back. But when that happens, I let faith answer the door. I refuse to give the fear any life. So far, it has worked.

I worked at Sweat with Us for two years, and then they went out of business. With my experience in aerobics, I was able to get a job as an exercise therapist at Vita-Fit, a medical and chiropractic clinic. One of my childhood dreams had been to become a nurse, but by now I knew I would have trouble getting accepted to nursing school. They would probably worry that the patients would ask for "bedpan" and I'd give them Percodan. (True, but I'd be a very popular nurse.) Vita-Fit employed massage therapists who seemed to have a lot in common with nurses. Their work was very hands-on and therapeutic, and they got to wear a white uniform. Massage therapists also made twice as much money as exercise therapists. It seemed like a good career move for me, but the hitch was that I would have to go to massage therapy school, and that would cost money. I didn't have enough for tuition, so I went back to the only family I knew—the government.

At the California Department of Vocational Rehabilitation, I was introduced to my career counselor, Colleen Hasson. I knew how to play the system now, and I figured I could pull some of her strings. I just needed enough money to get through massage school, that's all I wanted. *Just help me out this one last time.* But I had met my match in Colleen, who happened to have a hearing loss herself and was not about to play the game with me. She picked up on my speech impediment right away.

"I will agree to process your application."

"Yes!"

"After you have a complete physical exam, including a hearing test."

"What? A hearing test? I didn't think that would be part of the deal. I don't need hearing aids."

"I think you do."

"I'll take the physical, but please, no hearing test."

"Kathy, the government is not going to pay for your schooling if you can't hear in the classroom. You go have the hearing test, and if you need hearing aids we'll provide them for you."

"I had hearing aids when I was a kid and they were no help whatsoever. If anything, they caused me a great deal of pain and confusion. I don't need them! I haven't worn hearing aids since sixth grade."

"It's totally up to you. You want the money for tuition, you have to have the complete physical with the hearing test."

In any other situation I would have ignored the requirement, but I had my heart set on being a certified masseuse with a white uniform. The next week I kept my appointment with Michael Shannon, an audio technician at AAA Hearing Service. He was in his thirties, a nice guy and very good looking. We met in the lobby. "Ready for the exam?" he asked pleasantly, as if it were no big deal, just like getting your shoe size measured. As he led the way to the soundproof room I started sweating, overcome with anxiety.

The room wasn't as big as I remembered from my first hearing exam. In fact, I felt like I was too big for the room. The walls weren't padded with old gray mattresses, they were just plain walls. Michael sat me down in the chair and left the room. It all came flooding back—the schools, sitting out in the cold, bad report cards, rejections, corduroy pants, hospitals, and being fired from all those jobs. I kept telling myself, *It's just a hearing test. All I have to do is raise my hand if I hear something.* Tears were streaming down my face as I sat with the headset on. Michael appeared in the window and mouthed, "Are you okay?"

"Please, just get it over with."

I raised my sweaty hand with each sound I could hear. I knew the drill. When the test was over I got up from my seat and made a beeline for the front door. Michael stopped me. He took me back to his office, laid a piece of paper on the desk, and said, "This is your audiogram." Then, for the first time in my life, at thirty-two years old, somebody—*anybody*—explained to me about my hearing loss.

"This is where it would be hard for you to understand on the telephone."

"You mean I'm not retarded?"

"No. This is where it would be difficult for you to understand music."

"I am not slow?"

"No, you just don't hear normally. See this flat line? This is where it's difficult for you to understand in a group of people."

"Michael, look at me. Are you sure there is nothing wrong with my brain?"

"Kathy, you just don't hear normally. In fact, you're very intelligent. You've managed to maintain in the hearing world solely by lip-reading. You're a great lip-reader."

"Can you say that again?"

"You just don't hear normally."

"No, no, no. I got that part. The other part."

"Intelligent?"

"*Yeah!* Intelligent!" No one had ever said that to me. "I just don't *hear* normally?"

"That's right, Kathy," he said, giving me a puzzled look. "You have a hearing impairment. But you knew that, right?"

"I guess so," I mumbled, staring down at the audiogram. There had been so much denial of my hearing loss, first by my family and then by me, that I couldn't honestly say what I had known or understood.

He gave me my audiogram to take home. That piece of paper didn't just show me my range of hearing, it answered questions I had agonized over for as long as I could remember. *I am not retarded,* I repeated to myself on the way home, finally believing it. *It's just that I can't hear normally, so I don't understand everything that people are saying. And this piece of paper explains exactly what I can and cannot hear.* The audiogram was proof of my true identity. Intelligent. Not retarded. Hearing impaired.

Even though I was on cloud nine with a whole new perspective, I still had no intention of wearing the hearing aids. For now, knowing my identity was enough. When I returned a week later to pick up the aids, I informed Michael that I wouldn't be wearing them. "Hearing aids didn't help me in the past," I told him. "They just made everything loud and painful."

"Technology has changed a lot in twenty years, Kathy. These hearing aids won't give you perfect hearing, but they'll block out a lot of the background noise that makes everything sound dull and fuzzy, and they'll amplify other noises that you can't normally hear."

"I'm only here because I have to be. My counselor said that if I didn't get the hearing test she wouldn't give me the tuition for massage school. Well, I took the test, but that's all I have to do."

"Look, just promise me that you'll wear them for a week."

I didn't want to. I was content living my abbreviated life, hearing only vowels, not consonants; deciphering only low-pitched sounds; and pretending not to notice when others were hearing noises I couldn't hear. In the end, Michael told me that if I didn't wear them for one week he wouldn't turn in the paperwork for Vocational Rehab, so I had no choice.

I put the hearing aids on in his office.

"SSSSo, Kathy, what'SSSS it SSSound like?"

I sat straight up and stared at him. What was all that "*sssss*"? I had never heard an *S* sound and Michael had to explain it to me. A little excited, I left the office building wondering what would happen next. The first thing I heard when I walked out to the street was traffic. It was annoying. I got into my Toyota Corona. As I started the engine, I noticed an odd beeping noise. These damn hearing aids . . . I went back into Michael's office, convinced they had gone haywire like my old ones. He checked them out and declared them fit to use.

I returned to my car. *Beep, beep, beep.* "This guy is on crack," I muttered. Storming back into his office, I announced, "Michael, there is something wrong with these things. Maybe the Toyota is too small for the hearing aids, but they keep beeping every time I get into the car." Michael checked the aids again and decided to walk me to the car himself. I opened the door and sat down in the driver's seat. *Beep, beep, beep.*

"Kathy, that beeping noise is just your car telling you to fasten your seat belt."

"Oh . . . Like I'm supposed to understand Japanese now? Is there anything else you'd like to translate for the car before I leave?"

Suddenly the neighborhood I had lived in for a decade was both familiar and foreign. For the first time I heard my keys jingle as I unlocked the door to my apartment. The door squeaked as it opened. I heard the clock ticking, the refrigerator humming. Heaven only knows how long the toilet had been running! More thrills were in store when I heard myself pee for the first time. Scared me to death! I thought my liver had fallen out. I sat there holding it, releasing it, holding it, releasing it—Old-Mc-Don-ald had a farm, ee-i-ee-i-o—into the toilet bowl. As I left the bathroom, it occurred to me that I should have done that when I was two.

The pee sound worried me. I couldn't tell how loud it really was. How far did the noise travel? At work, I wondered if everyone in the building could hear me peeing. I asked one of the therapists, who assured me that she couldn't, but I wasn't convinced. I was so self-conscious about it that I trained myself to pee against the bowl so it wouldn't make noise. My curiosity was killing me, so much so that I'd hang out at the bathroom door to see if I could hear other people peeing. After about three days of this I realized I had to get a life.

One of the things I was most curious about was sleeping. Now that I had better hearing aids, would I be able to hear my dreams? I wore them one night, but every time I rolled over the hearing aids would let out a piercing *"crealll!"*—feedback—that startled me awake. My eyes were still my ears, so I tried to keep one eye open at a time to see if I was hearing anything. I didn't sleep much that night.

It was as if all my life I had been squinting through a tiny, blurry peephole, seeing just enough to keep from walking into walls, and now the view had opened up to include the whole, huge world. My hearing was still far from perfect, as I would find out a few years later when I got better, computerized hearing aids. But I was hearing much more than I ever had before. It was the equivalent of giving a blind person a pair of thick, somewhat distorted glasses. A big improvement over blindness, but not exactly 20/20 vision. By contrast, when I got computerized hearing aids, it was like replacing the Coke-bottle glasses with ultra-sharp binoculars. The sound was so crisp, clear, and *big*. These allowed me to hear laughter for the first time in the comedy club.

That first set of hearing aids from Michael Shannon was the best toy I ever had. Every sound was new to me—the wind as it rushed past my ears, leaves crunching as I walked, birds, crickets, and the rain. When I first heard rain, I ran downstairs to the pool and sat on the edge, watching the drops hit the water and trying to hear the sound each one made. I looked up at the sky and thought, *Do you have to bring it all down at once? This is hard!* Then it occurred to me that I was in the rain, I was plugged in, and I could get electrocuted. I ran back and stood under the metal awning, listening to the rumble of the amplified drops. Rain is still one of my favorite sounds.

The ocean was one of the sounds I went looking for. Water, first Lake Erie and then the Pacific, had always been my greatest source of comfort. I felt closest to God when I was by the water, and I even used the sand as a kind of spiritual message pad. There's an old saying, "Give your burdens to God." Whenever I felt my burdens to be heavy, I would take a stick and write all the problems I needed to leave behind in the damp sand. Then I would stand back and watch the waves take them away. It made me feel as if God had taken care of them for good. To make sure He received my love as well as my problems, I would also write Him little notes thanking Him for the good things in my life.

I had often wondered what people meant when they talked

about listening to the waves. They used words like *soothing* and *hypnotic* to describe them, and I couldn't wait to hear it for myself. I set aside a whole day and drove to a private beach for the occasion. With my hearing aids in my pocket, I wiggled my butt into the sand right by the water's edge and watched the waves quietly for a few minutes. Then I placed the hearing aids in my ears and turned them on.

It sounded like a freeway. Talk about disappointed! Forcing myself to really listen for a while, I finally understood. My heart was totally content.

I kept the hearing aids, completed my course at the massage school, and got my license. I'll never forget the day I put on my white uniform for the first time. I was in my glory! I felt so significant. Now I was qualified to do what I loved most, which was to care for people. It was as close as I was ever going to get to being a nurse. And there was one big advantage to having a hearing loss in this line of work. I found out that when people get naked on a massage table, they don't shut up. Whenever that happened, I just slipped my hearing aids back into my pocket. I believe it's called selective hearing.

The one request I made as a massage therapist was that I wouldn't have to work on men. I wasn't comfortable with the idea of being with a naked man behind closed doors. The management was fine with my request, but apparently the other masseuses were not. After I had been massaging for a while they managed to slip in a regular, Bill, who was sixty-something. When I entered the massage room Bill was lying on the table naked, with a sheet pulled over his body. I worked him like I did my female clients, starting on his back. After giving him a nice, long back rub I asked him to turn over, tucking the sheet around his body and thinking, *I am totally okay with this.* I pulled the sheet off his left leg and proceeded to work on it. The leg was stiff as a baseball bat, which made it very difficult to massage. "You can relax," I said gently, but it remained rigid. Eventually I looked up to ask him again, only to find him asleep, with a little soldier standing straight up under the sheet. Apparently this was something Bill was known for, because when I left the room five of the other masseuses were hovering outside my door. "So, how did it go?" they asked, big grins on their faces.

"Very well. I got a standing ovation."

Ever since high school I had used laughter and wisecracking to win people over. They would tell me, "You should be a comedian," but I never took them seriously. The only thing I dreamed about when I was a kid was becoming a nurse, because I wanted to help people as Miss Joan Dailey had helped me. But while I was working as a masseuse at Vita-Fit, I had an experience that changed my way of thinking.

My client was a woman who had been in a bad car accident the day before I saw her. She could barely make it into the office and it took two people to get her up on the massage table. My instincts kicked in. There was no way I was going to touch this lady. She reminded me of myself after the Jeep accident. The look on her face made it obvious that she was full of fear, which would make her body too tense to massage. Working on her could do more harm than good, so instead of massaging her, I asked her to tell me about the accident.

"You always have two people carrying you around?" I asked her.

"No," she said, starting to laugh a little. "I was in a car accident yesterday."

"And you figured that since your body didn't get enough of a beating, you could come in here today for more? Well, I'm sorry to disappoint you, but I will not be massaging you today. How about if you just lie there and tell me all about what happened, and let's see if I can help you eliminate some of the fear that is causing your shoulders to sit in your ears."

As she told me her story I joked about it, all the while stroking her head and arm, comforting her. I listened, and then I had fun with it.

"I was so mad at that guy for driving right out in front of me," she said.

"Oh, be honest with me. You're pissed 'cause you missed your hair appointment."

We laughed in there for more than two hours. When we were done she got up off the table herself. She was far from being physically healed, but her fears were lifted and that was more than half her battle. That day, I saw the power of laughter.

16

~

Crashing the Comedy Party

MY SUCCESS AT the massage school gave me the confidence I needed to pursue another dream, one that had started percolating long ago but that I had never let myself take seriously. I wanted to be an actress.

I got the acting bug from Anne, my first roommate. She was a film major and had asked me to act in some of her student films. Since I've been a chameleon all my life, acting came easily to me. I loved slipping out of my skin and into someone else's. By the time I was ready to make some moves—go out on auditions, take acting classes—I was already friends with a couple of successful actors. I didn't know much about their work because it was usually aired on television, which I had no use for. Close-captioning wasn't available then. But the warmth and friendship I got from these two people made the whole profession shine even brighter in my eyes.

I met Anne Baxter not long after I moved to Los Angeles. My cousin Kitty had a friend, Katrina, and Anne was her mother. One night I went to a party at Katrina's house. She had a mike hooked up to her sound system and was singing a song, and I had my back up against the speakers to feel the vibration of the music as I lip-read her words. When Anne came into the room and saw me, she waited until Katrina was finished and then cornered her: "Good heavens, what is that young lady doing so close to the speaker?" Katrina told her that I read lips and had a hearing loss, which I guess was more obvious to other people than I imagined.

Anne fixed me with a big smile and swept across the room, her arms outstretched. "HELLO! I AM ANNE, KATRINA'S MOTHER!" she bellowed, overemphasizing her lips so that she practically looked like Mr. Ed. Throughout the night she introduced me to everyone who came in, exaggerating her words and telling them that I lip-read. After a few of these introductions I said, "You don't need to overemphasize your lips so much. It's all right to speak normally. If you don't, your face is gonna need crutches in the morning."

I managed to get hold of Anne the next day. "So, how's your face?" I asked.

"Sore!"

"You should feel my eyes," I told her. We had a laugh and became good friends.

Anne had an assistant, Dottie Edwards, a petite Londoner who was in her early seventies. Dottie was Anne's dresser, secretary, traveling companion, and probably her best friend. She had been with Anne long enough to have seen all her daughters grow up. I was fascinated with Dottie's English accent, which was different than anything I had lip-read before. One night, when Anne and Dottie had downed a few glasses of wine, I told them I wanted to learn how to speak like her. For several hours I sat with my hands on Dottie's throat feeling the vibrations of her voice and mimicking her accent while they howled at my efforts. From what I can remember, Dottie's elocution lesson went something like, "Buckley, I want you to talk like a lady and I don't want you swearing. Do you hear me, you little bitch?" A seventy-year-old lady calling me a bitch! I don't think any of us had ever laughed as hard as we did that night.

Anne, who died several years ago, was an incredible, fun lady with a real passion for life. She dearly loved her daughters—Katrina and her two teenage sisters—but seemed to have a hard time convincing them of it. Being an actress was very demanding, and she worried she didn't give them enough time. We would often talk about her girls and how concerned she was for them. Once, when Anne was traveling in India, I got a phone call from her at about 2:00 A.M.

"Whatever you do, Buckley, do not give your money to Indian charities," she warned me as I struggled awake. "These people are not getting it. It's a shame to think that someone is pocketing all that money! Oh, Buckley, I just love you. You are an angel."

"Anne, is there wine in India?"

"Why, yes, Buckley."

"Did you have some?"

"Drinking it right now, Buckley." Anne was by no means a drunk. All it took was one glass and she was tipsy. That night she was hurting for her daughters, and as we talked I felt so sorry for her. I wanted to reach through the phone and tuck her in for the night. Little did Anne know she was my angel, too, because she planted a seed in me during all those conversations about her daughters. Listening to her made me realize that my mother may also be hurting, that she might be a person in her own right and not just the distant, uncaring woman I had perceived her to be.

At the same party where I met Anne I met another lifelong friend: Max Showalter, an amazing man and one of the most generous spirits I have ever known. Max was an old-time Broadway character actor who had made a successful transition to movies and TV. He was tall and handsome, with white hair and big, buggy blue eyes that reminded me of a fish. Max was Anne's good friend, and over the years he ended up becoming a surrogate father to me. In fact, one day I sat him down and told him, "You're the daddy I never had. You're so easy to talk to."

"Well then, call me Daddy," he offered, and I did.

Max was in his sixties when I met him, and we connected instantly. Our bond was so strong that it almost felt as if we were two spirits who had been together in some other lifetime and had met again here on earth. We both shared a love of gardening, and when we were working in the yard together I became aware of his greatest talent, which was to see beauty in just about anything. He'd pluck the ugliest dying flower and say to me, "Look, Kathy, isn't this the most exquisite blossom you've ever seen?"

"No, it's dead. What's the matter with you?"

"I want you to look for the beauty in that," he'd command in his gravelly smoker's voice.

"Get me another flower, something that's blooming, opening up! I'll see the beauty in that one." It got to be a running joke between us, but eventually I did learn to see the beauty in a flower that was returning to the earth, because at least it got here in the first place.

A few years after we met, Max decided to move to Connecticut. I helped him pack his house up, which was not an easy feat. He was friends with many Hollywood legends, including Katharine Hepburn, Marilyn Monroe, Mary Martin, and Lucille Ball, and he had saved every memento anyone had ever given him. I kept wanting to throw things away to lighten the load, but Max resisted.

"See this, Daddy? This is a garbage can. It's empty. We can put things in here instead of a box." I held up a candy wrapper that I had noticed lying on his coffee table and went to toss it in the can. Max snatched the wrapper out of my hand and tucked it into his pocket. Months later, when I visited him at his new house in Connecticut, I saw the same wrapper lying on the coffee table.

"What *is* this?" I asked. "Why is it still here?"

"Oh, back in 1970 when I was shooting that TV series, Matthew gave me that wrapper when he had a piece of candy."

"He probably gave it to you to throw away," I said, beginning to wonder about Daddy's mental health. I would have asked who Matthew was, but I didn't want to know. He had a long story to go with every little item, and I was sure the candy wrapper was no exception.

Daddy Showalter gave me another priceless gift, the gift of trust. By knowing him, I understood that not all men would mistreat me. It was possible to love and trust a man and to have your love returned without being harmed. In Daddy I saw not just a kind and beautiful soul, I saw a little boy. It made me realize this might be true for a lot of men.

Daddy supported me in anything I wanted to do, and when I confessed that I was going to try to be an actress, he was all for it. "My darling daughter, you can do and be anything you want. Just have faith." Max had never let go of his acting. He was also a musician and composed a lot of songs with his friend Peter. At one point he and Peter were putting on a fundraising show in their little Connecticut town, and Daddy wanted me to sing one of his songs in it. I tried explaining to him that deaf people don't sing—it's not pretty—but he believed anybody could do anything so he went ahead and taught me the song. The night of the show, just when I thought I was going solo, he had Peter come out and sing the song with me. I believe it was to drown me out.

Anne wasn't quite so supportive of my potential new career. In fact, she discouraged me, saying, "It's not a nice business, Kathy." But once I had come out and told people about my plan, there was no turning back. I took classes and started going out on auditions. Unfortunately, the industry people didn't know what to do with me. "She's not deaf, but she doesn't quite hear everything and she talks funny." They weren't comfortable with me, and I wasn't comfortable with myself. I still didn't know where I fit.

When I started explaining my situation to people, I began to hear about a comedienne named Geri Jewell. Geri had cerebral palsy and had a recurring role on the TV series "The Facts of Life," which was a big hit. She was the first person with CP ever to become a TV star. "You should meet her," my friends would say. The opportunity came when I was invited to go to the Media Access

Awards, which honor people for their efforts to hire and promote actors with disabilities. Geri was one of the stars receiving an award that night.

Shyness was never my problem, so when I spotted her I walked up and introduced myself. "Hi, Geri. My name is Kathy Buckley and everyone is telling me I should meet you." As she was about to speak to me she got called to the stage, so she handed me her card and told me to phone her.

Later that week I called Geri and invited her over to my apartment for lunch. She agreed right away. When she got to my place, I realized why she had been so friendly—she thought I was someone else. We laughed about it and she stayed for lunch anyway.

Cerebral palsy was a mystery to me. I had never known anyone with the condition and I didn't understand it. When I asked Geri if she would be more comfortable eating at the table or the couch, she said the table, because of her involuntary movements. She was afraid she would spill food on the couch. We had only been eating for a few minutes when her arm suddenly jerked and the food on her spoon flew across the room, landing on the couch. Without saying a word I got up, made another plate of food, put it by the couch, and said, "Look, you eat wherever you want to." She cracked up, and after that, she was totally at ease.

Geri told me a lot about herself and her career that afternoon, things you only tell your closest friend. I told her about myself, too. I didn't think much about it, but apparently it scared Geri because after that day she didn't return my calls. When I finally got hold of her I asked if everything was all right.

"Well, to be honest with you, I got a little nervous," she admitted. "I realized how much I told you, and for all I know you could be from the *Star* or the *Enquirer*."

I had to reassure her that I was from neither. "I was just someone who wanted to meet you because several people thought it would be a good idea. I was hoping maybe you could give me some advice about being an actress. They said I should get to know you, and now that I know it all, you have to be my friend because I can blackmail you." We've been friends ever since.

At that time, the only goal I had was to convince casting directors I could play a part. People were still telling me I should be a comedian, but it sounded terrifying. I didn't want to stand in front of a room full of people trying to make them laugh. Comedians were fully exposed and vulnerable, and I wanted none of that. With acting you could hide behind a character, which was old hat for me. I had been acting all my life.

A friend of mine had clipped out an article about a comedy contest called "Stand-up Comics Take a Stand," which was being held to raise money for children with CP. I showed the article to Geri and she explained to me about what children with CP had to endure. Cerebral palsy is not a disease, it's a condition, and it ranges widely in its severity. Some children's muscles are so spastic that they need shots every day just to help them relax; others use wheelchairs or crutches; some just have CP in one hand. The movements are involuntary and unpredictable. People often think that children with CP are retarded, which makes their lives even more disheartening. The more she talked, the more I wanted to help. Within minutes, she was daring me to enter the contest.

The only problem was that each contestant had to write a letter to the organizing committee explaining why he or she wanted to compete. Back then I still was not comfortable with writing, and the last thing I wanted to do was write a letter that would be read by a bunch of strangers. But I loved children and it was for them— and Geri had dared me. So the letter was a must.

The response was supposed to arrive by April 13 or not at all. For two weeks I was a nervous wreck, but at last April 13 came and went. No letter. Hooray! I'm off the hook, the dare is off, I'm free.

On April 15 the letter arrived. I panicked. Now I had two weeks to come up with material. I knew nothing about comedy, so I went to comedy clubs to see how the professionals did it. A lot of the humor was lost on me. I remember one comic talking about Indians with dots on their foreheads. "What's that for, target practice?" he snickered.

That's not funny! I thought. *That's their culture, they need that dot.* It seemed cruel to me. I also had a hard time understanding the comedians because they always had the microphone right in front of their mouths, making it difficult to lip-read them. Even though I now wore hearing aids, many sounds were still hard to discern. I depended on lip-reading, as I always had.

My next maneuver was to rent comedy videos and study those. Unfortunately, they were not close-captioned. Robin Williams had the fastest lips I'd ever seen, and Whoopi Goldberg barely moved hers. I rewound and rewound the tapes, finally giving up in frustration. I must have sat there for an hour crying. Why was I trying to do something that was totally impossible for me? When I was too tired to cry anymore, I resigned myself to my fate. Even if I messed up, it was for the kids. It wouldn't be the first time I made a fool out of myself, and I could pretty much guarantee it wouldn't be the last. All I needed was three minutes of material. Yeah, three minutes of the unknown.

My efforts to learn from the comedy masters had failed, so my only guide had to be myself. I would focus on what I knew best— me. I started coming up with material about being six feet tall, flat-chested, having a hearing loss, and going without a date for two years. Gee, talk about plenty to work with. I called all my friends, invited them over, lined them up on the couch, and did my jokes for them. Mom Meyer was my best audience and at the same time my worst. If I had used half of the stuff she laughed at, I would have been thrown offstage. Most of my friends were great cheer-leaders, but a few were afraid for me. My Aunt Angie, who was staying with me at the time, kept asking, "Are you sure you want to do this, Kathy? There are thousands of people out there who want to be comedians. What makes you think you can make it?"

"I won't know unless I try."

While I was going through all of this I enrolled in Stanley Marion Handleman's comedy class. The class was helpful in that I got to watch other people get up, bomb, and still live. It gave me hope. I learned to edit my stories to get to the punchlines, and how to feel comfortable with the microphone. Basically, all you did in class was get up in front of the room, tell your joke, and allow the others to critique you. If they didn't laugh, that said it all.

Geri helped me, too. She was the one who gave me the big plastic hand to place by my ear and dreamed up my opening joke: "You'd think with today's technology they could come up with hearing aids that are just a little less obvious than this."

The big night arrived. I wore a peach-colored shirt with jeans and Keds—I wanted my feet to be as close to the floor as possible so that I could feel the vibrations of the audience's response, if there was any. I arrived at the LA Cabaret early and began pacing in front of the club. You could see the skid marks I was making with my Keds on that sidewalk. The club was packed. There were nine other contestants; some were inside watching the performers, others were waiting out front with me. To calm myself, I struck up conversations with my fellow comedians.

"So, is this your first time doing comedy?" I asked a young man in his twenties.

"I've been doing this for three years."

"Three years?" Oh my gosh, I have a professional here.

Next I asked a woman who looked to be about my age. "So, is this your first time doing comedy, too?"

"No, this will be my seventh year."

"Seven years? That's nice." My heart sank. I went back to pacing, feeling very confused now. A guy pulled up in a truck and I ran over to him, tapping on the window.

"Are you here for the contest?"

"Yes."

"How long have you been doing comedy?"

"Ten years."

"Ten years?"

I had thought this was an amateur comedy contest. What the hell was I doing here? I made a mental note to kill Geri. *It's for the kids, it's for the kids,* I repeated over and over in my head. I kept looking to the sky, to the moon and stars, for some kind of comfort. I drove one of the producers crazy pestering him, "Did they call me yet? Did they call me?" My biggest fear was not hearing the emcee call my name, but at last he did.

It was show time. It's difficult to describe the feeling that came over me as I walked down the aisle through the audience. I could see my friends from Vita-Fit, Mom Meyer, Randy, my good friend Gail, and Aunt Angie, who looked more scared than I was. Hang-gliders must feel this sensation just before they leap off a cliff. As I continued to walk toward the stage through the audience, it was like a spirit entered me. All my fears were lifted.

I got onstage and the lights were so bright they just about blinded me. Can't hear, can't see—Helen Keller is in the house. I stood in front of 250 people and started sharing my jokes. The room was so big that my hearing aids were of little use. I could hardly hear the laughter, but they *were* laughing! I could feel the vibration through the floor. I couldn't wait to get to my last joke: "I have not had a date in two and a half years. Now, I don't know if it's 'cause I haven't heard the phone ring, or what! Thank you!" I bowed, walked off the stage—flew off—and went right out the door. Looking at the sky, I said, "Thank you. Can I breathe now?"

The manager of the club found me out there. "You brought the house down," he said.

"I didn't touch anything," I responded.

People were coming up to me, clapping me on the shoulder and shouting, "You killed!"

"Who?"

I won the contest. It was such an incredible rush! And knowing that it was over with was almost as good as winning. What I didn't know was that if you won this contest, you went to the semi-finals. Which meant five minutes of material. More jokes, *nooo!*

I made it to the finals, which were held at the Wilshire Ebell Theater and broadcast on PBS. Steve Allen, Carroll O'Connor, and other celebrities were there that night as judges. I couldn't tell how many people were in the audience, but it was big and beautiful. I spoke slowly and clearly to make sure everyone could understand me, and I ended up placing fourth out of eighty comics who had been in the business from three to ten years.

After the contest, Steve Allen wrote me a lovely letter congratulating me and sent me a copy of his book, *How to Be Funny*. On the inside he wrote, "To Katherine, who already knows."

About a year and a half later, I found out I wasn't supposed to be in the contest at all. First, because I had no experience; and second, because of the way I wrote the letter—it had been rejected. But Geri knew the producer and had asked that he let me enter the contest as a favor to her.

So you see, I shouldn't even be here. I wanted to help raise money for the children, and in return I ended up with a career making people laugh and a place for my puzzle piece to fit. There's an old saying, "You want to make God laugh, tell him your plans."

17

America's First Hearing-Impaired Comedienne

AFTER I WON the comedy contest I decided I'd try to make a career out of stand-up. What better job could a woman have than to talk about herself? And for me there was a special bonus, because I didn't have to worry about getting the information wrong. On this topic there was only one expert—me. Hello, comedy.

To break in, I took the tried-and-true route of going to open mike night at different clubs around L.A. On those nights you sign up to go onstage for a few minutes and audition for the club managers. If they like you, they'll give you a try on one of the other nights. I got into the Improv, the Laugh Factory, and some other popular clubs. My favorite was the Ice House in Pasadena, which was acoustically set up so that somehow all the laughter from the room ended up onstage with me. It was a total high. The owner, Bob Fisher, was a big help and gave me some tips about doing stand-up.

"Don't look away from the audience," he advised. "Keep eye contact with them."

"Then turn up the house lights so I can see them."

"Don't jump offstage when you're through, Kathy. Stand there, take a bow, and receive your audience's applause." It was strange at first just to stand there and receive the applause, but I learned to love it. It was a sign of acceptance.

Many of my fellow comedians warned me about hecklers. They said they would always be in the back of the room, where I couldn't see to lip-read them. I took to carrying a flashlight on stage with me just in case I had to see what a heckler was saying. Sure enough, I was playing the Ice House one night when I began to notice people's heads swiveling toward the rear of the room. I stopped and asked someone in the front row what was happening.

"You're being heckled by a guy in the back."

I grabbed my flashlight and said to the heckler, "Will you please put your lips in my light so I can see what you're saying?" The man in the front row started chuckling and told me, "He said he can't. He's blind."

"Leave it to a blind man to heckle a deaf woman."

It was while I was working at the Ice House that I first heard what is still my favorite sound, an infant's laughter. I had no idea babies could laugh. That night, when I went into the greenroom, another comic and his wife were sitting in there with their six-month-old. As I chatted with the comic, I felt a warm sensation come over me and asked him, "What is that noise?"

"It's the baby."

"The baby?"

"Yes, the baby's laughing."

I turned around and saw the mother dipping the baby to make her laugh. "Dip her. Dip her some more!" I urged her. The sound of that baby laughing was so wonderful to me that it brought tears to my eyes. I was crying, the baby was laughing, and I kept shouting, "Dip her! Dip her!" It was a wonder the baby didn't turn blue. I was so caught up in my new sound that I didn't hear them call me to the stage. When they finally got me up there, I was still crying. Let's just say that crying is not a good opening line in a comedy club.

Maybe because of the comedy contest or the fact that I stood out among the crowd of comics, my career started to take off without me. Before long I became known as America's First Hearing-Impaired Comedienne, and soon I had to come up with five, then ten, then fifteen minutes' worth of material. Elaine Cardone, the Ice House's booking agent, was nice enough to give me stage time as emcee at the club so I could work out material there. Trying out new stuff was scary. I hated the thought of bombing, but I told myself I wouldn't hear it if I did. So I forged ahead and mined material from my past, my perceptions of other people, and eventually from my experiences on the road.

Elaine took me under her wing and really promoted me. She believed in me and let me know it. She was also the booking agent for road work and got me my first out-of-town gig, in El Paso, Texas. I was looking forward to it except for the flying, which made me very nervous. When I boarded the airplane I made sure to ask the flight attendant if there were any connecting flights. She said no, I swear she did. Just one brief stop in Phoenix, and then the plane would continue on to El Paso. The plane landed and some of the passengers departed. I sat there, knitting away, until I looked up again and realized that everyone had left and the cleaning crew was on board. Did it ever occur to anyone that if there is one passenger left on the plane maybe, just maybe, that passenger did not hear the announcement of a plane change? I missed my flight, but luckily there are lots of flights from Phoenix to El Paso.

When I finally arrived, I took a cab to the address Elaine had given me. It was a condo. "Cool," I thought, "I have this huge place to myself." Not quite. I had to share it with two other comics, both male and both smokers. Before I left L.A. I had asked Elaine if there was anything I should take with me. I thought it was odd when she suggested sheets and towels, but one look at the bed cleared up that mystery. The first thing I did was turn over the mattress, only to find a nest of used condoms underneath. Yuck! *Okay, Kathy,* I thought, *look at the bright side. This means you could be getting laid in this business. You're living with two guys under the same roof for two weeks.* I walked out to the smoked-filled living room to find them both unshaven, sitting in their boxers watching the football game. It was like living with a husband and an ex at the same time.

I learned in my first week on the road that you can spend most of the money you earn just on eating out. So I told the guys that if they'd pitch in for groceries I'd make dinner before leaving for the club. "There's just one condition. You have to put your pants on." I ended up spending three weeks in El Paso, and I can report that Texans have the slowest lips I have ever seen. They can actually get five syllables out of a four-letter word. I thought I'd go into a coma lip-reading in that town.

After I got the hang of air travel I began to love the road. I toured the country on the comedy club circuit, and during the first few years of my career spent maybe a month at home. No matter how many times I got up on a stage, it always amazed me to see an audience sitting there just to hear me tell jokes. There was something powerful about making a room full of people laugh, taking their troubles away for the few moments they spent with me. Soon I was doing thirty minutes, which took me from being an opening act to the middle position. Then I got up to 45 minutes, then an hour, which made me a headliner. My favorite spot was the middle. When you open, the waiters are taking orders and it can be distracting. When you're headlining, the bill comes and everyone is half-drunk and fighting over who owes what, which is even more distracting. In the middle spot they're just sitting back and enjoying the show, although I must admit the pay is better as a headliner.

My greatest moment as a headliner came when I played Las Vegas. Seeing my name on the marquee was surreal. My first thought was, *Who the heck knows who I am?* I was working at Bally's Catch a Rising Star and the room was unlike any of the clubs I'd performed in. This was a theater, and it seemed immense. The show went smoothly, but when I got offstage I was disappointed.

The other comic asked me what was wrong and I told him, "They barely laughed."

"What are you talking about? You killed."

"No, I didn't. I didn't hear them laughing." By this time I had my new, computerized hearing aids and was used to getting the full roar of the audience's laughter. That night they had sounded as weak as infants.

"Kathy, the whole room is carpeted all the way up the walls. The laughter gets absorbed by the carpet."

The next night I made little earrings with dangling pieces of carpet. I related the story to the audience and said, "If the laughter is going into the walls, well, I am going to get some of it."

By this time I no longer used the plastic hand "hearing aid" in my act. My friend Mark Lonow from the Improv had told me to give it up, that I shouldn't need a prop. I thought I would feel naked onstage without it, but it turned out that my computerized hearing aids came with a pen-shaped control that I could show the audience. I felt as if I had to prove to them I had a hearing loss. I had spent my whole life in denial about my impairment and now I wanted the audience to know about it so that they wouldn't think I was making fun of deaf people. Even so, someone would occasionally come up to me after a show and ask if I really had a hearing loss. I'd always tell them, "No, I'm blind with a limp."

Sometime during the first or second year of my comedy career, I was asked to do a spot on a TV show called "Funny People," produced by George Schlatter of "Laugh-In" fame. I fell in love with this big, jolly fellow who looked like the Santa Claus of comedy. Marianne, his assistant, encouraged me to continue with stand-up. It meant a lot, coming from people who had worked with the best comedians in the country. As cable television started to grow, so did the number of comedy shows, filling cable's need for programming. The big comedy clubs taped their live shows and sold them to the cable companies. I did TV shows like "The Improv," "Comic Strip Live," and Rosie O'Donnell's VH-1 show, "Stand-Up Spotlight," which I appeared on a couple of times. That's when I bought 500-dollar jumpsuits and realized that everyone else was wearing jeans, a T-shirt, and a blazer. Oh well.

At the time I met Rosie she was beginning to branch out of stand-up comedy and into acting. I was performing at a club in Seattle when she was there to film *Sleepless in Seattle,* and we spent a day together in the city. That afternoon we went to the movies, and I was amazed by the way Rosie absorbed the film. She experienced it the way a child would, totally free and unrestrained, singing the songs, saying the lines she knew. The thought occurred to me, *If I had been born a normal child, would I be able to absorb all this, too?* For the first time in my life I felt that I had missed out by not being able to hear. I wasn't so much envious of Rosie as I was in awe of her. She astonished me with her knowledge of music, movies, Broadway musicals, and all the other things I had never had access to.

I worked like a demon the first few years of my career. But my biggest thrill as a fledgling comic had to be when I was invited on "The Tonight Show with Jay Leno." To get on "Leno" you have to perform a showcase for the producers, five minutes of your best material. If they don't like one joke, just one, they tell you to replace it and you have to reschedule the showcase and do it all over again. I was lucky—they liked my material but insisted that I clean it up a little. I couldn't say *tits,* for example. I had to say *breasts* instead, which isn't as funny and sounds so much more . . . bosomy. And I had one line about "strapping an alarm clock between my legs" that they made me change to "up my thigh." The last time I checked, "up my thigh" was between my legs, but I didn't mind changing it. Whatever was best for the show. I was in!

The first order of the day was to get a custom-made outfit for the occasion. I wanted bright colors, so I hired a designer to make me a coral pantsuit with a royal blue blouse. It turned out way too bright, but I figured that I had paid so much money for it, I had to wear it. Besides, I didn't want to hurt the designer's feelings. After all, I was the one who picked out the fabric.

On the day of the shooting I brought some friends to the studio. I would have been a lot more nervous if Jay Leno hadn't taken me on the set to adjust my hearing aids before the audience arrived. That meant a lot to me, because the only thing I was really worried about was whether my hearing aids would be affected by the electronic equipment. Once I adjusted them and knew where I was going to be standing, I had no fear. Except about the outift.

I went out and did my five minutes. It was awesome. Unlike the clubs and theaters where I usually worked, the studio was all lit up so I could see the whole audience. They were all laughing, and it went off without a hitch. Afterward the owners of the Improv, Bud Friedman and Mark Lonow, threw me a party there. With that, I really felt like a member of the gang. Doing "The Tonight Show" made me a legitimate comedian.

A short while after I did "The Tonight Show" my agent called to relay the message that Howard Stern was looking for me. He had heard about the "deaf comic," and apparently he was trying to locate me through the radio. I cannot hear the radio. I can feel the vibration of music, but if people are talking I can't understand what they're saying. I knew nothing about Howard Stern, not what he looked like, not how he acted, not the kinds of things he talked about on his show. Eventually his producer got hold of my agent, who asked me if I'd be willing to go to New York and do an interview with Howard.

"Is he a nice guy?"

"I think you can handle yourself," he said.

I went to Howard's studio in New York. The first thing that came out of my mouth was, "Whoa! Who didn't do your hair?" I looked over and saw Robin Quivers in a glass booth by herself. "What is she, a *bad* black person? Why is she in a box?" I asked. In about a minute I grasped what was happening on the show: this man talked dirty. All he talked about was sex, sex, sex. I didn't know they could do this on the radio. God, I wish I could hear radio.

Howard kept asking me personal questions. "Who are you getting it on with? Who are you dating? Are you married?"

"No, Howard. I'm deaf, not dumb."

"Would you date a man with a disability?"

"Yeah, I'd consider going out with you."

I had a ball, and it was a good thing I didn't know about the show. Had I known prior to the interview what Howard does, it probably would have intimidated me.

Since I had never been on radio, I didn't get it when Howard began to do promos for his sponsors. He flipped through this big notebook, stopped at a page, and asked me, "So, Kathy, do you like wearing jewelry?"

"No, I never wear the stuff." I had no idea he was asking for my help. Next he started talking about Seaman's Furniture Store, pronounced "semens." Not being from New York, I had never heard of it.

"What is that, a couch with a wet spot?" I asked. He shot me a panicked look—these were his sponsors. No one had told me! Give me a little warning, I'll catch on eventually.

I had a great time. During the breaks we talked about his kids and wife. When I left I said, "I promise I won't tell anyone what a nice guy you really are." Oops!

The first five years of my career were intense. I did more television, was asked to be on "The Tonight Show" twice again, and kept up a hectic schedule of road work. But by the mid 1990s the comedy scene had started to change. Cable TV became glutted with comedy programming, and that had a direct impact on the clubs, which started to fold. Fortunately, I had already begun to branch off into an area that in some ways was even more fulfilling to me than stand-up comedy—motivational speaking.

18

Me, Motivate?

GOING ON THE road had brought me enough income to be able to quit my day job at Vita-Fit during the first year, and after a while traveling became a way of life. I was gone for weeks at a time, popping back to my apartment in North Hollywood every month or so. During one of these rare visits home, I got a call from Geri Jewell. She wanted to tell me about a firm she was doing some work for, Milt Wright & Associates. They had a program called Windmills that educated employers about disability issues, with the goal of removing the attitude barriers that made it so difficult for people with disabilities to get hired. Milt Wright paid Geri to be a trainer and present Windmills to corporate groups, and she thought I might like to do the same thing. I was all for it. Here was a chance not only to entertain but also to educate people.

I'd been in comedy for a year or so at this point, and in my act I sometimes swore. Okay, more than sometimes. Most comics are pretty foul-mouthed, but I didn't do it to be part of the gang. I found myself doing it because I was nervous. When people have been asking, "What did she say?" all your life, and suddenly you're standing on a stage with a microphone performing in front of hearing people, it can be very nerve-racking. I'd always wonder, *Do they understand me or are they just being nice?* I doubted myself, so I'd get anxious and swear. It was safe, too. People always understood the curse words. They were the only words I could enunciate clearly.

Well, the same thing started happening when I gave the Windmills speech, although I was very careful never to use the F word. The Windmills program was written down in a huge book full of guidelines about hiring people with disabilities, changing your attitudes, equal employment laws, and so on. I'm not a book learner, but to give the presentation I was supposed to read this and teach from it. I basically didn't know what I was talking about—the best I could do was call out a page number—and I'd end up cussing here and there because I was uncomfortable. I felt like telling the room full of earnest, polite business types, "He's a crip. So what? Get over it." Instead I'd try to stick with the program and end up swearing without even realizing it. Milt Wright & Associates would get reports back: "She swore!" No shit. They let me know that if I kept it up, they'd stop booking me.

Determined not to curse in class, I started veering away from the Windmills program and into my own background, where I felt more comfortable. I shared stories about my life, the prejudice I had experienced, and how it had affected me. A lot of it came from my comedy routine, but in front of the corporate groups I could slow down and really explain how it felt to be excluded just because other people didn't understand your differences. Instead of teaching Windmills, I drew the audiences into my world. I would open my heart, cry, and get emotional not only because of my past pain but on behalf of all the people who were having a hard time gaining acceptance due to the wall of ignorance. I was determined to break that wall down. Before I knew it, I was having my therapy session in front of 500 people and getting paid good money for it. Who needed a shrink?

The business groups liked me because I was funny and they related more to the human stories than to Windmills. Windmills may be a great training program, but no book can teach more than the person who lived it. Besides, I'm no good with pie charts. My approach was to appeal to people's common sense, using stories like the one a Milt Wright trainer had told me.

We sent over a little person to do a filing job. The company called back and said, "There's a midget in the room."

"Yes, that's the person you hired to do your filing."

"But she's a midget."

"That's okay. She's only going to file from M to Z. Would you like to hire someone else for A to L, or just get a footstool?"

People who have disabilities know how to deal with them. A person who is unable to walk knows how to use a wheelchair, a deaf person knows how to communicate with the hearing world because he lives in it, and a blind person can get around without sight. They have acquired survival mechanisms. Instead of assuming what their limitations might be because you can't fathom being in their situation, why not let them take the challenge and find a solution? After all, you're hiring the person, not the disability. All you have to do is open the door. Today, the only real disabilities are people's attitudes.

You know, any one of you could become disabled at any time. So look at the person first and the disability last, if at all.

The more personal I made my presentations, the more the audiences listened. But despite my success, I still couldn't grasp the Windmill training for Milt Wright & Associates. Eventually I cut my ties with the company, but I kept giving motivational workshops. The more I did it, the more I loved it. With each new audience, my self-confidence grew and my swearing decreased. I began to branch out, getting more involved in organizations for people with disabilities and other nonprofit groups. My biggest passion was children's rights, especially when it came to education. I wanted to erase every destructive label children were saddled with, especially *learning disabled,* the one that had hurt me personally. I don't believe in learning disabled, I believe in teaching disabled. Every child can be taught if we have enough patience and dedication to reach them. In my workshops I wanted to speak to parents everywhere, instilling hope and optimism to replace their fear and doubts.

Whether I was working with parents, children, college students, people with disabilities, or just average citizens, motivational speaking filled some sort of void in me. It allowed me to preach my gospel, the gospel of choice. I wanted everyone to know that they could choose to live, not just exist. No matter how hard their life had been or how they had been treated, they were worthy of all the good things the world had to offer. But it had to be their choice to focus on the good things and let go of the bad. They could go for it, or they could just sit and dream.

Young or old, it seemed to me that people needed to know about choices. I loved doing colleges, sharing my story with young people ages 17 to 25, who I came to think of as the lost generation. So many of them felt they were ready to be on their own, yet to me they seemed terribly unprepared. They were too old to go to Mom and Dad, and too young to find their way. Or in some cases, just too scared.

One fall I was at the University of Washington and asked the audience of students, "How many of you are afraid of your future?" Nearly every hand went up.

"You know why you're afraid? Because you grew up with your mom and dad telling you to clean up your room, stop fighting with your brother or sister, brush your teeth, do your homework and so on. Then, after eighteen years, you graduated from high school and went to college. Now that you're on your own, you can't even figure out if the fabric softener goes in the washer or dryer." That always got a big laugh.

"How many of you believe that the career choice you make today is what you'll do the rest of your life?" Again, almost every hand went up.

"Well, let's stop and think. People are living to be eighty or ninety years old these days. Let's say you're all about twenty. Are you telling me that you're making a decision that will influence the next sixty to seventy years of your life, when you can't figure out if the fabric softener goes in the washer or the dryer? Hey, I'd be afraid, too."

They laughed again, a little bit nervously.

"How many of you are making your career choice purely at the suggestion of someone else?" At least half the students raised their hands.

"Now you have every reason to be afraid, because you have yet to decide what your interests are. See, the great thing about choices is that they're unlimited. You can make a bad choice and it will still be valuable because of what you learn from it. Then the next choice you make might be better. But none of that can happen unless you're making the choices yourself."

Every time I went onstage to do stand-up or motivational speaking, I was aware of something changing inside me. The monster that I used to feel crawling around in my stomach was withering away. It had begun sometime after my big blow-out with Mom Meyer. "When are you going to let go of this shit?" she had demanded. When I screamed back, "Why won't you believe me when I tell you *I can't*," I could feel the monster fighting for its life. That's when I first made the connection: the evil thing inside me lived and fed on *can't*. When Mom Meyer kept telling me *you can,* she had threatened this creature that had been a part of me for as long as I could remember.

I'm a visual person, so in order to control it I began to imagine an actual monster living in the pit of my stomach, growing with every negative word or thought that I allowed myself to consume. I had come into the world a perfect, innocent child, and then I had started getting the messages *you can't, you won't, you're ugly, you're broken, you're stupid.* Each time I swallowed one of those messages the monster developed a little bit more, growing two arms, two legs, ten toes, and ten fingers, so that by the time I was an adult it had taken on a life of its own. It was this monster that had sent me to Holloway Mental Hospital, roared out of my mouth at Mom Meyer, and driven me to seizures. I had created it myself by accepting the negative things people said about me, and it grew fat on the negative thoughts I created by replaying in my mind all the bad things that had happened. My thoughts and words had become my enemy, my limitation, my disability.

When I remembered my fourth gift, the gift of choice, I realized that I could take the monster apart just as I had created it. The creature hated it when I faced fear—it scared him. I began to visualize him shrinking away, piece by piece. When I went onstage for the comedy contest, that took off a whole arm. When I ignored someone's mean-spirited or narrow-minded words and mentally replaced them with positive ones, a toe or finger would fall off. Max Showalter had taught me about finding beauty even in a dead flower, and I took it to heart. Each crumb of beauty took away a little piece of the monster. With every speech I made, as I shared my life and comedy with people, the monster got smaller, sometimes so small that the only thing left was a toenail. I knew he'd never disappear entirely, but I could keep him down to hangnail size if I chose to, by making positive words and thoughts my best friends. That was why I preached so hard about the gift of choice in my motivational workshops. The day of the Jeep accident I had been given the choice to live, and with the gift of choice I was going to live my life to the fullest.

I got my biggest break at motivational speaking through my comedy act. I was working at a club in Oceanside, California, just north of San Diego. On this particular night, show time came and went and they still didn't call me up onstage. "What are we waiting for?" I kept asking the club owner. Finally he said, "Tony Robbins is on his way over here with a group of people to celebrate his birthday. We're waiting for them."

"Did anyone bother to tell them what time the show starts? It's twenty minutes late and it's not fair to the people who are here."

Just then Tony's party walked in. At first I didn't know who he was because I'm terrible with names, but when I looked more closely I realized he was the motivational speaker I had seen on TV. Fair game! When I got onstage I started ragging on him about being a motivational speaker and being late, and we all had fun with it.

After the show I ran into Tony and his gang in the parking lot. I told him I admired how he helped people and thanked him for the lift I got whenever I saw him on TV. To my surprise, he asked me if I would do my act at his Life Mastery Program, and if he could ask me some questions about my life afterward. I was flattered and agreed right away.

As promised, I did my stand-up routine for Tony's group. When I was done I called out to him from the stage, "Do you want me to continue, or would you like to ask some questions now?"

From the back of the room Tony yelled something inaudible.

"I can't lip-read that far," I reminded him, "so I'm just gonna keep talking." I continued with my stories, and when I was done Tony was speechless. I, Kathy Buckley, made Tony Robbins speechless. And that was the beginning of our beautiful relationship.

After that night, Tony asked if I'd like to join the faculty of his Life Mastery Program along with General Norman Schwarzkopf; Deepak Chopra, M.D.; John Gray, author of *Men Are from Mars, Women Are from Venus;* and several other world-class speakers. I was the only woman on the program at the time. It was a tremendous compliment and a real milestone for me to be invited into this group, and of course I jumped at the chance. But the real treat for me was the audiences. These people had a sincere desire to change their lives, and I really wanted to be there for them. Tony made it a safe place for me to open my heart and let it all pour out.

One of the great things about the Life Mastery Program was that it took me to some terrific vacation spots. Every year they have an event in Hawaii that's very popular. At the first one I did, Robbins Research treated me to something I'd always fantasized about—swimming with dolphins.

When you're swimming with dolphins you have to follow the trainer's rules. Everyone wants to touch and pet the dolphins, but you're not supposed to approach them. The morning of my swim, we all waded out into the lagoon and waited for the dolphins to come to us. I didn't have to wait long. One dolphin zoomed right over to me and would not leave me alone. Everywhere I went, he followed me. The other people were getting a little annoyed—they wanted their turn—and I was getting embarrassed. "Go away! You're getting me in trouble," I told the dolphin, but he kept rubbing up next to me, almost climbing up my back. It went on for about ten minutes, and then the trainer waved me over.

"Open your vest," he ordered. We all had wet suit vests on.

"Why?"

"I want to see if you have fish in there."

"I do not have fish in my vest!" I protested, flashing back to those cans of tuna I got busted for so long ago. This time I was clean. But I was getting really uncomfortable. Did I smell fishy? Maybe I was sick—dolphins were always trying to save dying people. *Get away from me,* I thought, aiming all my energy at the dolphin. *Go to that old man, he's about to croak anyway!* The trainer was calling to me, "Let the dolphin go!" I put my hands up in the air, shouting, "I'm not even touching him."

That was it. I was outta there. I waded out of the lagoon and walked toward the beach. The damn dolphin followed me! Now the trainer was yelling at me, but I couldn't hear him because I was walking in the opposite direction. People on the beach were shouting, "Turn around! Turn around!" I turned to see the trainer screaming, "Bring that dolphin back!" Meanwhile the dolphin had his belly on the sand, coming up out of the water after me. I took off my sun hat, put it on the dolphin, and tiptoed out of the water, saying, "Come on, let's get out of here. They'll never know it's you."

The Life Mastery Programs were always full of odd surprises. One year I had just returned from another Hawaii program when my agent, Amy, called to relate a very strange message she had received from a Dr. Peter Anderson.

"He's a Beverly Hills plastic surgeon who does lots of celebrities," she explained. "He said he was in your audience in Hawaii and was so moved by your speech that he wanted to offer you a gift."

"What, a boob job?"

"Yes."

"Are you kidding?"

"Nope. He wants to offer you breast augmentations and asked me to have you call him at the hotel in Hawaii."

I was stunned. I had always contemplated getting implants, thinking they might make me feel more attractive, but I had never had the money or nerve to actually investigate it. I left a message for Dr. Peter Anderson and he called me back at home.

"You know, Peter, when most people make a crank phone call they just breathe heavy, they don't offer you a couple of tits," I told him.

"No, I'm for real, Kathy. I've done lots of people you've heard of."

"Didn't you watch my show? I don't hear." He ran off some names and he was right. I did know who they were.

"I really would like to offer you this gift."

I kept declining, but he was very persistent. Finally I said, "I'll tell you what. Can I take a rain check?"

"A rain check?"

"Yes. When I travel around the country doing my workshops, I sometimes come across kids who have been disfigured in an accident or were born that way. Would you be willing to do the plastic surgery on a child in lieu of a boob job?"

"I'll do two of your children and still give you the breast augmentation," he offered graciously.

"You just want to see me naked."

I was touched but mystified by Dr. Anderson's offer. Later I found out that after I had given my speech in Hawaii and left the building, my tits were the topic of the day at Life Mastery. Dr. Anderson had suggested the free implants and it had caused an uproar. Some people were offended, others thought I should take him up on it. The debate had lasted more than an hour. I couldn't believe it—my little tits had made a bigger impression than I had.

The following year I went back to Hawaii to do the Life Mastery Program with Tony. I usually give him a big hug as soon as I see him, but this time I avoided him. I didn't want him to see me until he called me up onstage.

After checking into the hotel, I went looking for a girl with gargantuan boobs who worked on Tony's staff. I asked to borrow one of her bras. It was so big that if I had put it on my butt I couldn't have filled it. I got two huge water balloons and arranged them in the bra, put on my T-shirt and dress, and made my way over to the convention hall.

Tony had no idea whether or not I had taken Dr. Anderson up on his offer. He always gives me a bear hug and lifts me up in the air when he introduces me to the audience, but this time as I walked up to greet him I whispered in his ear, "Be gentle, they're still tender." He sprang back as if he'd been burned, gave me the briefest of hugs, and retreated offstage. Staring at my chest, he took a seat in the first row directly in front of me.

I launched into my act as if everything were normal, but I couldn't keep it up for long because I kept getting distracted by Tony. He looked stricken, and I could lip-read him grilling his wife,

Becky: "Did she really do it? They're too big. Do you really think she did it? They're too low. *They're too low.*" He looked so concerned about my bad boob job that I finally took pity on him.

"That's it," I suddenly announced into the microphone. "Here, Tony—you like tits? Take 'em!" I pulled the water balloons out of the bra and tossed them at him, while the audience cheered. He was so relieved those boobs were fake.

The offer of a free boob job led me to do some serious thinking about my body. I couldn't imagine what it would be like to have big breasts after all these years. They would be like puppies—I'd have to give them names and decide how to dress them. Leather or lace? I knew I'd always be hyper-aware of the silicone balloons attached to my chest. And if I weren't flat anymore, there went half my material!

I had been making fun of my body ever since I was a teenager. My brother Mark had given me a head start with all his cruel jokes about it in high school. Underneath the humor, of course, was a great deal of unhappiness. At twenty, I had hated my body for being so tall, skinny, and flat. At thirty I had missed the body I had when I was twenty. Now, at forty, I missed my thirty-year-old body. And God knows when I was fifty I would miss my forty-year-old, still reasonably firm bod. If I were smart, I would start loving it now.

Getting a boob job would have been one more attempt to gain entrance to a society that had rejected me. How many times was I going to knock on that door? When I turned down the offer, I decided the door could stay closed forever. I would never completely fit in with the "normal" world anyway. I was not deaf, and I was not hearing. I was six feet tall and flat-chested, and that was the way I was going to remain.

Just for the record, I'd like to say that I appreciated Dr. Anderson's generous proposal. He's a plastic surgeon and boobs were what he had to offer. I only wish he were a banker.

19

Dear Kathy

MOTIVATIONAL SPEAKING CAME naturally to me, and before I knew it, my schedule was full. I'd end each seminar with a question-and-answer session, which brought me a little closer to the people in the audience. Afterward, a few would usually linger to talk to me personally. Some wanted to hug me, as if they needed to physically reinforce the bond they felt between us when I was speaking. Every so often someone would confess, "When you were up there I really felt like you were talking only to me." For once, maybe my speech impediment was actually a good thing. They had to concentrate so hard to follow what I was saying that they ended up hanging on to every word. Or maybe it was that my story was similar to theirs—so much has happened to me that almost anyone with a problem can find something to identify with.

But there was one aspect of the work that I wasn't prepared for—the emotions of the people who came to hear me. Those who approached me after the show didn't just want to thank me, they wanted to tell me *their* stories, too. And many of those stories were horrifying. I needed to figure out a way to deal with the tragedies these strangers were pouring out to me every week. The best way to help, I decided, would be to shake them up a little. I developed my own brand of therapy, where I would try to get them to shift gears.

Hal was a good example. A short, round man who appeared to be in his fifties, Hal came up to me after a workshop saying, "I want to thank you so much for sharing your life story." He looked extremely depressed and withdrawn, and I assumed something awful had happened to him recently. I gave him a hug and asked, "What's wrong?"

"I lost my son," he said softly.

"That's terrible. When did this happen?"

"Ten years ago."

"Ten years ago, and you still look like this?" I was too shocked to be tactful.

Hal's shoulders slumped and his voice started to get shaky. He wore round, wire-rimmed glasses, and behind them I could see his eyes tearing up. "I just can't get over it," he said. "Sean died in a car crash. He was only sixteen. I haven't worked since. I used to be a fireman. The other driver was drunk, and he walked away from the accident—"

From his tone, I knew that Hal had repeated these sad facts to himself and other people hundreds of times since the boy's death. So I cut him off.

"There's only room enough for one person in the coffin," I said.

"What?" He stared at me, hurt and surprised that I had broken into his lament.

"Tell me something. If you were to reverse the roles, and you passed away and were looking down from heaven at your coffin and saw that your son had been lying in it with you for the past ten years, how would you feel?"

He stood still, waiting for me to continue.

"You have a life. I'm sure your son is up there in pain, wanting you to live your life. How can you do this to him? How can he enjoy his afterlife knowing that you're lying in his coffin?"

Hal looked as if he'd been punched, but he let me hug him again before he walked away.

I rarely know if my words make a difference, but sometimes I'm lucky and get to find out. About two years later, I was performing in Los Angeles. After the show, a man knocked on my dressing room door.

"You probably don't remember me," he said.

"Honey, I see so many people that even white folks are starting to look alike," I told him. "You're right. I don't remember you."

"I'm the man who lost his son. Twelve years ago."

"Oh, my God. You look great!"

The change in Hal was phenomenal. The only thing I recognized about him was his glasses. He was thirty pounds lighter now, and his face was animated instead of slack and hopeless.

"I thought about what you said," he told me. "And I realized that if I were in heaven looking down and watching my son lying in my coffin, it would break my heart. I'm back on a regular schedule at the fire department, and I'm going to the gym."

"I can tell," I said.

"It's funny," he continued. "It was like I had been sleeping. You woke me up. I miss my son, and I love my son, but I hadn't realized that I had given up my life when he died."

It's almost as if people like Hal have been painting a picture using only the darkest colors. When I interrupt their stories and give them a different perspective, I'm splashing new colors on the canvas—bright yellows, oranges, pinks. Then I hand them the brush and say, "Paint!" No one else—not even their therapist— tells them to get over it and get on with life. They've gotten used to thinking of themselves as tragic cases. I know how it feels, and they know that I know. But at some point you have to force yourself to stop grieving and choose brighter colors.

Kimberly was 18 years old when I met her at a conference for children with disabilities. She was gorgeous, the typical coed with long blond hair. Physically she looked fine, but Kimberly had been in a car accident and suffered brain damage. She talked to me several times during the weekend, always listing the things that she couldn't do anymore: "I used to be able to swim and play tennis, but now my arms don't work right, so I can't play. And I can't think the way I used to—everything's so hard. My brain just doesn't work as well. I can't make the same connections. Homework takes twice as long. Everything takes twice as long."

I genuinely felt sorry for her, but after a while I had to put the brakes on. "Tell me, what grade were you in last year?"

"I was a senior in high school."

"And now?"

"I'm a freshman in college."

"Well, sweetheart, college is harder than high school! But even so, I'll bet the only reason you're working twice as hard is that you're subconsciously thinking that it's not as easy as it used to be. You know, life is going to get twice as challenging as you get older, with or without the brain damage. But you're a beautiful girl, and no one could tell by looking at you that there's anything wrong unless you start complaining about it. The disability you're going to have won't be brain damage, it'll be *complaining* about brain damage. It's going to be annoying as hell for people to see a beautiful young girl complaining about something she could do yesterday that she can't do today. I can give you a whole list of stuff that I had yesterday that I don't have today. If you keep hanging on to what you had yesterday, you're never going to have tomorrow."

Kimberly made the dean's list that year. Later, she wrote to give me an update about her life:

You said, "You're trying to be who you were. Why don't you try being who you are now?" So I decided the week before Spring Break I wasn't happy trying to be what I wasn't. I was just gonna be myself, that's all, and if people had a problem with that it's not *my* problem. It's *their* problem.

Here's how it's been for me . . . after my accident all my

close friends and my fiancé deserted me. I don't know why, maybe they were scared. I went to a picnic recently, and a lot of Jason's friends were there, and they told me they thought it was too bad Jason didn't stand by me when I was going through rehab and whatnot. All this time I've blamed myself for the break-up and I thought everyone else blamed me too. But they didn't, and don't!

. . . I'm sorry I never got in touch with your friend who has a brain injury. I did try, but got no response. But like I told you, he's probably not ready . . . I can understand that, I remember that . . . Don't get me wrong, I'm still struggling every day. But the struggles are different somehow.

No matter how bad something is, it has a limit. It all depends on how long you're going to drag it out. No matter how good something is, that has a limit too, so you'd better get in the moment and enjoy it. I believe in that message so strongly that I'm willing to tell anyone about it, regardless of what they've been through.

One evening after I'd given a seminar for a women's group, a lady approached me. She was overweight and had short, strawberry blond hair and crooked little teeth. But what I really noticed about her was her eyes, the loveliest blue eyes I'd ever seen.

She walked toward me hesitantly, but when I smiled she gained confidence. "You've changed my life," she said. "I see life in a whole new perspective now, and I can't thank you enough."

"Whoa," I responded. I get a little nervous when I'm being praised. "So, tell me about yourself."

She wasted no time. "My father molested me most of my childhood. I gave birth to his son. I was gang-raped by thirteen men. I developed agoraphobia for five years, and that's when I gained a hundred pounds. I haven't owned a mirror in fourteen years."

I looked her straight in the eyes and said, "Have you always had big boobs?"

"Yes."

"Well then, don't come complaining to me."

She laughed so hard she had to grip my arm for balance.

We all have something someone else is envious of. Unfortunately, we get caught up in what we don't have instead of appreciating what we do. I told her that the first thing I had noticed about her was her eyes. "You mean to tell me that all these years you've denied yourself the gift of looking in the mirror at those beautiful eyes and seeing what God has created, instead of what men have messed with? You would give men that much power? Let's go in the bathroom and look in the mirror."

"No!" she said, pulling back from me. She was terrified. I would never force somebody to do what she wasn't ready to do, so I let it go. Three days later I got an e-mail from her. It said, "I bought a compact mirror. I thought I would start out small."

20

Marathon Evan

"I'VE HAD ENOUGH! I don't care about that donkey's butt!"

The blind kid sounded like he meant it, so I finally stopped spinning him around. He giggled wildly and felt his way back to the circle of children waiting to play Pin the Tail on the Donkey—kids in wheelchairs, deaf kids, blind kids—all laughing, jostling one another, and shouting, "My turn! Spin me!" I looked around for my next victim as they shrieked and hooted. What else is camp for?

When I was a kid, there were no such things as camps for children with disabilities. By the time I'd started giving motivational workshops, there were plenty of places where these kids and their parents could go for two or three days of fun and relaxation. Boys and girls who'd spent years cloistered at home got to live it up a little in the countryside. Parents got a break, too, and a chance to talk with other moms and dads who understood what it was like to raise a child with a disability. The worst part, most would agree, was the isolation. In fact, the real goal of these camps was to provide support and coping techniques for the parents.

I had been doing motivational speaking for about a year when the director of a camp in Iowa called to ask if I'd do a workshop.

She and I laid out a vague plan. I would meet with the parents in the morning, have a workshop with the children in the afternoon, and at night I'd do my comedy act. The curriculum was up to me.

After the morning session with the parents and a hot-dog lunch, I went outside to get to know the children before our afternoon powwow. First the counselors and I played with them, and I do mean we played with every single child. If they were in wheelchairs we'd tie ropes to the chairs and pull them around, banging them into one another like bumper cars. We played Pin the Tail on the Donkey, and while the kids were waiting for their turn, I'd choose one child, then another, to joke around with.

"You don't even know what color the cane is, do you?" I asked a blind girl. "They could have given you a blue one for all you know."

"It's white!" she hollered. "Hey, why does my cane have to be white, anyway?"

"Because society associates a white cane with blind people," I answered. "They see the cane and know you're blind."

"I'm going to paint it orange and let them guess!"

A little boy teased me about my height and I shook my fist at him. "You keep that up and I'm going to flatten that tire in your chair."

"There's no air in it—it's all rubber!" he shouted.

I wanted them to come back at me, and they always did. Just as my Grandpa Oliver had egged me on and made me defend myself, I wanted these children to correct me, stand up for themselves, show me that they knew how to handle me. Instead of shying away from their disabilities, I engaged them, and they loved it.

Finally I led the children to a small conference room that featured a two-way mirror. This is where I'd lead my workshop, which was really just a free-for-all conversation between me and the kids. The parents would sit on the other side of the mirror, eavesdropping. I pretty much knew where the conversation would go, but I doubt many of the parents did.

It didn't take long to draw the children out. As I expected, every one of them had the same anxiety: "I don't want Mommy to be worried." Their disabilities didn't bother them nearly as much as the feeling that they had disappointed their parents. They were ashamed when they saw the frustration in their fathers' eyes, and when their parents fought, they blamed themselves even more than healthy kids do. They told me of the gifts they made their mothers to cheer them up—paintings, clay mugs, cards, and potholders.

Talking about it out loud and listening to other kids who felt the same way was a tremendous relief for them. After they'd had a chance to vent their worries, I steered the discussion to happier themes. "If you could do anything you wanted in the world, with or without your disability, what would it be?"

An eight-year-old named Evan, who had spina bifida, immediately piped up: "I want to run a marathon."

"A marathon! What for?"

"My friends are running in a marathon to help raise money for the school band."

"Do you think you could do it if you didn't have a wheelchair?" I asked.

"I think I can do it *in* my wheelchair!" he declared. "I know I can do it. It's not that long of a run."

"Well then, why don't you do it?"

"My mom doesn't want me to. And my dad's just left and I don't want to upset her."

"Why does it have to be a marathon? There are other ways to raise money," I suggested.

"I want to be with the other kids," Evan replied.

"They'll probably run ahead of you."

"Yeah, but at least I'll start out with them."

It was time to toe the party line. I knew nothing about Evan or the marathon, but I remembered the single mom from my workshop that morning, and I could feel her watching us from the other side of the mirror. "Do you think that maybe Mommy loves you so much that she's protecting you from something? Maybe you could get hurt," I told him.

"How could I get hurt? I'm already in a chair!" he protested.

"Maybe you could fall out of your chair and skin your forehead."

Evan rolled his eyes and grinned at me as if to say, *We both know that's ridiculous.*

"Sometimes it's really hard for your parents because they have to make the decision for you," I said, as much for the other children as for Evan. "A lot of times when they make a decision, they're not a hundred percent sure it's the right one. They only know they're responsible for you. You have to respect that."

The kids looked dubious and Evan was plainly unconvinced. "If she's so confused, why can't *I* decide?" he demanded.

I took another tack. "You know what your job is?" I asked the group. "It's to introduce yourself to Mommy and Daddy so they can find out who you are. You need to tell Mommy and Daddy what you believe you can do. Evan told his mom, 'I want to be in this marathon.' If she says no, then he'll have to deal with that, but at least he's put the idea in her head. His mom might think, *If I were in a wheelchair I could never run a marathon*, but she might not realize that Evan can do it because he's so focused on the goal. Even if she won't change her mind, though, Evan has made her think about the possibility. And that's what you all have to do—be strong and teach your parents about yourself."

I felt I had done a tidy job of turning the debate into a lesson, but later that night I found out that Evan wasn't quite finished with the topic. We had just eaten dinner and the parents and children were relaxing in the cafeteria. From across the room I saw him waving me over to where he sat with his mother.

I'm not much good with names, and for the life of me I cannot remember the name of Evan's mom. She was a tall, freckle-faced woman with short-cropped auburn hair. I had noticed her fear and nervousness that morning in the workshop, before I knew she was

Evan's mother. In fact, the anxiety coming off her blocked out every other impression, including her name. Her husband had left them just a month earlier, she had told the group.

Before I had a chance to say hello to her, Evan blurted out, "Mom, can I do a marathon to raise money for the school band?"

"I told you, no," his mother replied.

"Why not?" I asked. Then I looked down, and that little stinker had a smile on his face from ear to ear. The kid had used me!

"I can't be responsible," Evan's mom was explaining. "My husband's not here anymore, it's just me and Evan. If something happened to him I'd never forgive myself."

"What could happen? It's not that big a deal," I said.

"Yeah, Mom," Evan chimed in. "What could happen?"

"You don't understand. I have to make sure he's going to be okay."

"Look at that face, look at that enthusiasm," I teased her. "Don't you wish you had something in your life to go for like that? Why would you take that away from him?"

"But you don't understand," she repeated.

"Listen. If you need support, I'll go to the marathon with you. I'll come back here to Iowa."

Evan was delighted. "You'd come back?"

"Sure," I said breezily.

His mother looked stunned, and then she seized on the offer. "I hold you totally responsible for this. You want to do it, fine."

Damn. I didn't think she'd take me up on it.

Before the evening was over, she approached me again, with Evan at her side. Handing me a piece of paper, she said, "I want you to sign this. It says that you promise to come back here for the marathon and that if Evan gets hurt you'll be totally responsible." She was only half joking.

I signed with a flourish. The next day I flew back to California and forgot all about the conversation.

Two months later I was sitting at my desk catching up on some

mail when the phone rang. I answered and a little boy's voice said,
"Kathy?"

"Yes."

"The marathon is next Saturday."

"What?"

"You're still coming, right?"

He had caught me completely off guard. I could picture Evan
sitting there, gripping the agreement triumphantly. The kid would
never need assertiveness training. I could also see his mother, standing behind him with arms folded across her chest, ready to console
him when I backed out of our deal. If I didn't go, I knew my name
would become household slang for "insincere stranger." She'd send
him off to school each morning with, "Just you be careful—there
are a lot of Kathy Buckleys out there."

"I've been practicing the whole time," Evan was telling me.
"Practicing so hard my hands are sore. So, are you coming?"

Plus, I had a job that Saturday night.

"Of course I'll come," I told him. "We have a deal."

I canceled the job and flew back to Iowa. All the way there I
asked myself, *Why do I do these things? How can I get my brain and
my mouth to work together? What about stopping to think before I
talk?* I stared glumly out the window, calculating the bills I could
have paid with the money I could have earned.

My mood lifted a bit when I got off the plane and saw Evan and
his mother waiting for me. She couldn't have been nicer—I'm sure
she never thought she'd see me again. Evan, meanwhile, was nearly
out of his mind with excitement. I had brought along a child-sized
pair of leather gloves with thick rubber palms on the inside, where
his hands would grip the wheels of his chair.

"Normally I'd buy somebody running shoes for a race. You'll
have to make do with these," I said, handing him the gloves.

He pulled them on and stretched out his hands, admiring them
like a concert pianist.

The next morning we drove to the site of the marathon, a little patch of parkland near the school. The trail looped through the woods for about a mile, and the runners would be out of sight from the first minutes of the race until they rounded a curve back to the finish line.

"What about a helmet?" I asked as Evan angled into position alongside his classmates.

"What for?"

"In case you fall and skin your forehead."

"Will you get off my forehead already?" he said, laughing. We put a baseball cap on him and kissed him good-bye, then moved to the sidelines. A few moments later the starting shot rang out and Evan wheeled down the path, bumping along in the pack of racers.

His mother had cheered him off along with the other parents, but the minute he was gone her cheering stopped. She turned and gave me a look of pure despair, as if she had just watched her son roll off the deck of the *Titanic*. I could see the tears welling up and stepped over to hug her.

"He'll be fine," I told her. "You don't realize this, but while you're sending him off to do this marathon so that he can be like the other kids, he's also giving you the opportunity to be free to live your own life. He wants you to be happy. If this is what he has to do to show you he's strong enough to start taking care of himself, this is what he'll do. He loves you that much."

She looked at me and shook her head, tears leaking down her cheeks.

"You're not letting him go, you're letting him grow," I said urgently. I felt like I was in a race too—I had half an hour to plead Evan's case. "Let him spread his wings! While you're holding him back from living his life, you're missing your life. He wants you to have a life. Don't let him be your mother."

She nodded. Then she said, "I still hold you responsible for this."

At last the racers started coming in, and the parents began to whistle and cheer again. Evan's mom joined them, a little dazed but thrilled at the realization that her son had actually pulled this off. She was rooting, and the kids were coming in, and she was yelling, "He's going to be here any minute!"

And he didn't come.

"Any minute!"

And no Evan. Then she started giving me The Look.

"I didn't sign anything too detrimental, did I?" I joked.

She smiled, but I could see she was starting to get tense. Almost all the kids had arrived by now, and Evan still wasn't back. Before the race began he had made me promise him, in front of his mother, that I wouldn't go look for him until ten minutes after all the other runners had returned. It had only been five minutes.

"Kathy, go get him," Evan's mother ordered.

"I made that promise."

"You can't keep it! He's just a boy."

"If I break that promise, I'm telling him I don't respect him. I need to let him know that he's worthy of my respect. I have to give him that much."

At eight minutes I thought, *I better start heading out there.* She was staring at the trail, literally wringing her hands.

"Okay, I'll go get him," I said, and started to walk—very, very slowly—toward the trail. Just as I neared the finish line, out he came. He saw me and yelled, "I've still got a minute and a half!"

I cracked up. "I wasn't coming!"

"Yeah, yeah, yeah," he said. Then, "I did it, Kath! I did it!"

"What the heck took you so long? You could have been here a lot sooner, and I know that."

"My bag broke," he said in a stage whisper.

"What bag?"

"You know, the bag I pee in."

"So what did you do?"

"I didn't want to come in with a trail of pee, so I had to wait in the woods until it all drained out, and then I could keep going. Next time I'll keep it inside the seat, away from the wheel." He was unfazed, already planning for next time. "Kath, you should have seen! I'm going, the kids are passing me by, I don't care! There was this lizard, this butterfly—"

A few people were still waiting for Evan, and they hollered his name as we came down the trail. His mother was weeping openly now, out of relief but also to see her little boy so excited. He was only eight, and he had been in and out of hospitals for so long, he hadn't had many reasons to be excited about life yet.

Evan made four hundred dollars for his school from that race. He was ecstatic. The next time I sign an agreement with him, it'll be as his agent.

21

You'd Be Surprised

AFTER ELEVEN YEARS on the road, I had it down to a science. Before I got onto a plane I'd check to see if it was full, and if it wasn't I'd try to get three seats in a row. Not that there's enough leg room even with three seats, but this way I figured I got three times as much air, and some of it had to be fresh. The only place on an airplane with enough leg room for me is the exit row, but I'm not allowed to sit there. It's a law—people with disabilities, children, and senior citizens cannot sit in the exit row. Well, I didn't plan on being six feet tall and having a hearing loss, but I do plan on trying for that exit row every chance I get. After all, deafness is the *invisible* disability. They'll never know.

One time I had just settled into my favorite spot—exit row, aisle seat—and was reading a magazine when a flight attendant came up behind me. I didn't hear her but suddenly I realized that she was standing over me, talking. Startled, I looked up and said, "I'm sorry, I'm hard of hearing. What did you say?" Oops. I guess my big mouth is the real disability.

She quickly invoked the law. "If you're hard of hearing, you can't sit here."

"Why not?"

"This is the exit row. If an emergency should occur you wouldn't understand what the captain is saying."

"No one understands what the captain is saying."

"Well, if something should happen you wouldn't know when to open that door."

"Yes, I would. If I'm sitting here reading my magazine and I look up and all two hundred fifty passengers are charging at me, I'll pretty much know to open that door. Besides, I can smell smoke."

She didn't go for it and insisted that I move. The funny thing was, about twenty minutes later the same flight attendant asked me if I wanted a headset for the movie.

I just said, "No, thank you. I'm hard of hearing, and I don't think I'll be able to hear out of those."

She paused for a moment, then said, "Oh, well . . . would you like two sets?"

"And where do you suggest I put the other pair?"

Being a relentless advocate of common sense, I proposed to her that the airlines should close-caption the movies on all flights. She looked at me as if I were crazy and replied that if they did that, no one would pay four dollars for the headset. Exactly. Free movies for everyone, thanks to the deafies.

I am always aware of the other passengers, especially those who happen to have disabilities. I was flying from Las Vegas to Burbank a few years back and noticed such a lady sitting next to the window across the aisle from me. She had no legs from the upper thigh down and no arms from just above the elbow. She seemed uneasy, so I went over and asked if she was okay.

"I hate being on a plane," she admitted. "Flying makes me really nervous."

"Would you like me to sit next to you?"

"Please. That would be great."

I got my things and moved next to the woman, who told me her name was Nancy. She wasn't terribly attractive—her skin was on the rough side and she had a little body odor. I couldn't help but imagine how hard it would be to care for yourself without arms or legs. How could she wash her hair if her arms didn't reach her head? But then again, who was I to assume anything. She probably had a routine.

We struck up a conversation and I found Nancy to be a total delight. At this time I was doing the Windmills presentations and had access to job training programs. I thought maybe I could be of some help to her with a few employment leads, since she must be on Social Security Disability. Buckley to the rescue!

"Do you mind if I ask what do you do for a living?" I said.

"If you promise not to laugh," she replied.

"If I have the opportunity to laugh, I won't pass it up," I assured her.

Nancy giggled and said, "I am your fantasy caller."

"My what?"

"Your 976 number. You know, the number people call for sex."

"Oh, my gosh. Do they know who they're calling? 'Cause if they do, there would be no such thing as a boner out there."

She started laughing and I realized what I had just said. "I am so sorry," I stuttered, but she had no problem with it.

"It's so refreshing to have someone say it out loud instead of seeing it in their eyes," she confided.

"So, how do you like your job?" I asked her. "I could never work for a 976 number. I wouldn't be able to hear if someone was breathing on the other end. I'd be asking, 'Are you done yet?' I can just hear the complaints: 'I can't get off with this chick going, What? Huh?' They'd probably end up charging me for the call."

"A lot of these guys are my regulars," Nancy told me. "I develop a relationship with them over the phone. One of them really wants to meet me and I can't do it, though there's a part of me that wishes I could.

"The best thing about the job is that I get to be whoever I want with every phone call. I can be tall or short, I can be a redhead or a brunette or a blue-eyed blonde. Black, white, Asian, whatever. I get to call the shots."

Wow. What a perfect job for her. She had her independence and got to be part of a nonjudgmental world she had created for herself.

You'd think that after meeting Nancy and hundreds of others like her in all my stand-up and speaking engagements, I would have stopped making assumptions about people. But I still fall into that trap sometimes, and no more so than the night I was invited to Washington, D.C., to perform at the Kennedy Center for the National Council on Communication Disorders Awards. When I arrived, the stage manager took me to the greenroom and warned me, "You have to be quiet in here because the noise from this room can travel to the stage." There were several people in the room, and as I looked around I saw that everyone was mingling except for one lady in a wheelchair who was pushed up against the wall. She was a quadriplegic, sitting motionless with her eyes shut. My first thought as I looked at her was, *My God, what kind of life is this? She can't walk, she can't talk, she has nothing to contribute to society.* In five seconds I had her pegged for death.

I hated the fact that she was sitting there all alone in a room full of people, so I walked over and said, "Hi, how are you?" She started to open her eyes, a little bit at first, then wider and wider. I was taken aback. By the time they got really wide, her assistant had materialized behind me. "When Ruth opens her eyes it means yes, when she closes them it means no."

"Great. I spend my whole life learning how to read lips, now I've got to learn how to read eyelids?"

Ruth started to laugh. It was a horrendous noise, a gravelly "HEH HEH HEH" that sounded like a stalling engine. But to me, it was the most beautiful sound I ever heard. I realized right then and there, I could communicate with this woman. Who better to tell my jokes to than someone who couldn't heckle me? So there we were, Ruth and I, in the middle of the greenroom and all you could hear was this "HEH, HEH, HEH."

"Come on, Ruth, let's get some dancing shoes on and get outta here."

"HEH HEH HEH."

The stage manager was standing in the wings, in a total panic: "Get the deaf broad away from the quad!"

That night Ruth received an award. She'd written a top-selling book with the blink of an eye, using a computerized word board that recognized her eye movements via a wire attached to her eyelids. She could look at a letter, blink, and the computer would record it. After the show, Ruth had the word board print out a message for me. "Thank you so much for making me laugh. But more than anything, thank you for treating me like you would have treated anyone else."

I took the printout and scribbled something on the back of it. "There. That's my bill."

"Heh heh heh."

Just then a gentleman in a wheelchair rolled into the room. He had cerebral palsy and no front teeth. Me being who I am, I had to ask: "Where the heck are your teeth?" The man started to laugh, "HEH, HEH, HEH." It was her husband! Ruth was married. I couldn't believe it.

I looked at her and said, "You know what, Ruth? I came in here tonight, and when I saw you I thought to myself, *My gosh, what kind of a life is this?* I didn't think I could live it if I were in your situation. Here you wrote a book, and I can barely read one. You're married, I can't even get a date. I hope you get pinkeye!"

"Heh heh heh!"

That night I realized once again that I should never pass judgments upon anyone that I wouldn't want passed upon myself. Because believe me, I have seen that there are no limits to what people can do with their lives.

I suppose Ruth and I are good examples of how varied people

with disabilities can be. In 1990, the Americans with Disabilities Act was signed into law. The pressure to pass the act came from 43 million persons with disabilities in the United States, the single largest minority group in the country. The passage of the ADA meant that everyone was now entitled to equal access to education, transportation, recreation, and employment. Overall I've seen a big improvement in access, but sometimes the results go a little haywire. Traveling as much as I do, I have seen the way lots of people and places interpret the idea of equal access.

In the drive-through lane of a fast-food restaurant in Iowa, I pulled up to the speaker and noticed that in addition to being posted on a big sign, the menu was also displayed in Braille on a little metal plaque near the car window, for all the blind drivers out there. Pretty much explains the little bumps on the freeway. I rolled down the window and shouted into the speaker: "I am deaf. I can't hear and I cannot read Braille, so when I drive through just throw the food into the car, okay?" You should have seen the look on the face of the kid at the window.

In Chicago I asked for a room that had a television with close-captioning. That's all I wanted, close-captioned TV. I ended up in a room that was wheelchair accessible. The bathroom had bars going in every direction—I didn't know whether to pee or start doing pliés. The mirror was slanted downward so that people in wheelchairs could see their reflections. It gave me a great view of my belly button. The odd thing was, they had the whole room fitted out to be wheelchair accessible but the hair dryer was mounted so high on the wall that I could barely reach it standing up. Fun room, no close-captioning. I've always wondered why the people who build these hotels don't just hire someone in a wheelchair to design the wheelchair-accessible rooms. They know what they need better than a designer who's read a book about ADA requirements. Let the people who live the life do the job.

But the hotels are trying. In Indiana I stayed at a place that had a sign on the counter of the front desk: "Handicapped Rooms

Available." What the heck is a handicapped room? Is all the furniture missing a leg? Lamps with no shades? Black-and-white TV? No room service? Am I going to walk out of there with a limp in the morning? *Handicapped* is a word of the past. It sounds so broken to me, and knowing its origins makes it even worse. The word comes from "cap in hand," as in standing on the corner, cap in hand, begging for money. *Disabled* is almost as bad. I wish none of these words were necessary to describe human beings. What is *abled,* anyway? I don't know anyone who is able to do everything. As Mr. Hintz told me back in high school, "Use what you do have instead of worrying about what you don't."

Then again, there are those people who are just a little too confident about their abilities. One September I arrived in Chattanooga, Tennessee, to do a fund-raiser for the Chattanooga-Hamilton County Speech and Hearing Center. I had booked a reservation at the Choo-Choo, a motel where they had old train cars set up as rooms. It sounded fun but turned out to be too claustrophobic—the room was long and narrow and done up in red velvet with gold trim, like a brothel from the twenties. I returned to the lobby to ask for a regular room, and when the clerk finished checking me in she rang for the bellhop to get my bags. Inching toward the desk came a skinny little black man who looked to be in his seventies, with pants hiked up to his chest and a zipper about twenty-two inches long. He couldn't have been more than 5'2", and he moved like a snail.

"Hello, ma'am. My name is John, and my job is to get your bags to your room."

"John, honey, my bags are bigger than you. It's okay, I can get my own bags."

"No, ma'am, my job is to get your bags to your room."

"John, by the time you get my bags to my room my plane will be taking off again."

"No, ma'am, I'll get them there by Thursday."

"Um . . . I leave on Wednesday."

I didn't want to let this frail old gentleman carry my bags, but this was his job and probably the only thing that kept him going. Still, I didn't feel right about it.

"Hey, John, I have an idea. I have wheels on my bags, so I can take them myself."

"No, ma'am, it's—"

"I know, it's your job to get my bags to my room."

The desk clerk finally solved the problem by calling for a golf cart. Slowly, slowly, John wheeled my bags outside and painfully hoisted them onto the cart while I towered at his side. We got into the cart and I asked John for the key so I could drive.

"Oh, ma'am, I don't know."

"Come on, John, it'll be fun."

Now, this golf cart didn't go more than ten miles per hour, and apparently John had never taken it over five. Because John panicked: "Oh, ma'am, you got to slow down! There's a big old speed bump coming up. Easy, ma'am. Oh, Lord!"

When we got to the room I managed to grab the bags before John. He opened the door—to a room full of people.

"Ma'am, are you expecting company?"

"Not before I get into the room."

"Well, it looks like we got us the wrong room."

"We?"

"I guess I better get on back down to the lobby and get us another room."

"Us?" Are we roommates now?

I knew that if John went down there by himself I wouldn't see my room till sunrise, so I suggested that I go and get the room while he stayed with the bags.

"No, ma'am, it is my job to get your bags to your room."

John left. By the time he returned with the new key, I'd pretty much rearranged all the pool furniture, emptied the ashtrays, and gotten to know a good half of the people staying at the hotel—who, by the way, already had their rooms.

"Ma'am, come with me," John instructed. I picked up my bags and followed him to my third room. When we got to the door, I saw that he had one of those card keys and was having a difficult time with it.

"Doggone card. Don't know why they don't use them metal keys no more."

"John, let me have a try. I travel all over the—"

"No, ma'am, it is my job to get those doggone bags into your room."

Finally I reached over, pushed on the card, swung open the door, grabbed my bags, and threw them on the bed. John was still out by the door.

"Doggone cards! Once you get them in you can't get them out."

He came into the room to give me the card key. "Why looky there, ma'am. Your bags are already in the room."

I gave him a twenty-dollar tip and offered him tickets to come and see my show.

"Oh no, ma'am, I don't think my wife would appreciate it."

"You're welcome to bring your wife with you."

"No, ma'am, I don't bring her on my dates with me."

Just before John left he said, "You need anything at all, you just call on me and I'll have it to you in no time."

No time sounded about right.

I was there for three days. I fell in love with John; he was this beautiful old soul, and whenever I went down into the lobby I'd look for him.

"Hey, John," I'd call out. "How's it going?" I'd grab him, give him a hug, and kiss his wrinkled face. He'd look at me like, *Get this white woman off me!*

On the third day John peeled my arms away and said, "Ma'am, do you know I'm black?"

"Okay, John. When did this happen? Does it hurt?"

He looked at me and said, "Sometimes. What about you, ma'am?"

"What do you mean, me?"

"Being deaf and all, does it hurt?"

"Yeah, John. Sometimes."

"Ma'am, you can't be kissing on me like that down here. People are gonna be talking at you."

"That's all right, John," I said. "I'm deaf, and I'm not gonna hear a damn thing they say."

22

Forgive and Live

IT WAS APRIL of 1991. I was sitting on my living room floor close to the TV, watching myself on "Live with Regis and Kathie Lee." There I was, strolling up to them . . . I had high heels on . . . my God, I towered over Regis and Kathie Lee. I must have been six foot four with the heels. Regis said with a laugh, "She *is* a tall one." I didn't care. The makeup woman had done a great job and I looked *hot*. What a kick to see myself up there goofing around with Regis. Good thing I was taping this so I could rerun it a hundred times. Suddenly my phone rang, interrupting my thoughts.

"Hi, Kath." I knew the voice instantly. It was him, the one who had molested me. I was so surprised to hear from him that the first thing I thought was, *He must be calling to tell me he saw me on "Regis."* It had been five years since I had confronted him. I had seen him from time to time since then, but I always kept a civilized distance. As far as I was concerned, I had put the whole thing behind me.

"Kathy, I'm calling from the hospital, a mental hospital here in Mentor. I want you to know that I had myself committed because I've been suicidal. I need to ask you a favor. The therapist I'm working with told me I have to come clean with my past. I need your forgiveness for what I did to you."

"*No!*" I hollered into the receiver. "I will not forgive you. Why the hell should I?" I was enraged and simultanouesly stunned by my own reaction. All this time I had thought I had forgiven him and moved on, but I was wrong.

"Kathy, please."

"No!" I started to cry uncontrollably and hung up the phone. How dare he ask me for this! I had no idea there was still so much fury inside. I sat sobbing silently, the phone in my lap. There was no way I could just say "I forgive you" over the telephone. Maybe I *should* go back, I realized. If there was a chance that talking about it with him and the therapist would inch me closer toward putting it to rest, it was worth a try. The pain I was feeling at that moment could not have been sharper if the whole thing had happened the day before.

I picked up the phone again. There was no dial tone—he had stayed on the line. "Look, I'm going to be in Chicago next week and I'll fly over to talk with you and your therapist. When you see me, do not hug me. Do not touch me." That was the first time I had said those words out loud. It felt good.

"Thank you, Kathy. I mean that," he said. I hung up.

The following week I was back in Ohio, meeting him in the hospital lobby. He didn't try to hug me, and I was grateful for that. Without speaking or looking at each other, we walked to the therapist's office.

The doctor sat behind a desk, and we sat on chairs in front of it. For the first time, I ripped into him with anger: "What the hell were you thinking, fooling around with me? You took care of me when I was little, you gained my trust, you were supposed to protect me, then you betrayed me. Why?"

"I don't know."

"Why did you say the things you said while you were touching me?"

"Probably to justify my actions." He couldn't even remember what he had said. The words that had broken me had just been a fluke, something to fill the air while he touched me.

"I trusted you!" was all I could say, repeating it and then screaming it so loudly that the doctor got alarmed and warned me, "If you continue with this we'll have to stop the session, Kathy. He's here for suicidal reasons."

"Don't worry! I'll kill him myself and save him the trouble!"

"Leave her alone," he cut in. "Let her say what she needs to say. I can handle it. She needs to get it out." It was him, the one who would always look out for me when I was little, defending me now. *Where have you been?*

"Tell me," I said, composing myself. "You have got to tell me why you did it. I need to understand it."

He sighed. "I didn't plan it. It started little by little. I remember it being in the bedroom, not the bathroom. If I had known that what I was doing to you back then would affect you this way, believe me, I never would have done it. I just wasn't thinking."

"Well, your not thinking cost me a lifetime of self-rejection."

He just looked down into his lap.

"How long did it go on?" I asked.

"No more than a few months." To me it had felt like years, but I could remember what I was wearing on those mornings—always the same pair of pajamas—so it made sense that it had lasted only a few months.

"What made you stop?"

"I got scared about what I was doing, and I knew it had to stop. One time I was looking for you, and you weren't there, and it was as if I woke up and I saw what I had been doing. I made myself stop."

But I remembered differently. There was a reason I had not been there when he was looking. It was the sex education talk from Lisa's mom: "Don't let nobody be touching on you. Just say no." Up until then, I hadn't known I could say no. This man was an adult, and the idea of saying no to him had never crossed my mind. The five-minute talk with Lisa's mother changed me profoundly.

On Friday nights I started wearing my clothes under my pajamas. I'd wake up when it was still dark and wait for my mom to get ready for work. I had to watch for the light to go on in the bathroom because I couldn't hear her. When I saw it, I'd make my bed, throw my pajamas off, grab some bread from the kitchen, and run down to a wooded area near my house. For hours I would sit on a log feeding the squirrels until I felt it was safe to go home. I had blocked out the reason I was doing it, but I kept going to the woods every Saturday morning for many weeks. Finally my mom told me that he was no longer baby-sitting us, and I stopped.

There was something about the therapist being in the room with us that day that helped me tremendously. Having a third person there brought it out into the open; it was no longer a secret between him and me. When the session was over I hugged him and looked him in the face. Out in the hospital hall, we shook hands.

"This is the last time we will talk about this, Kathy," he told me. I knew he said it because he didn't want me to suffer over it anymore.

"Yes," I agreed. "I don't want to do this again." I didn't want to have to pick up the phone and hear him beg for my forgiveness. I didn't want to come back and relive it.

Of all the things that have happened to me, those Saturday mornings were the worst. My childhood ended in that bathroom, where I was taught to hate and fear my own body. For the rest of my life I continued to look over my shoulder, always afraid that someone was coming after me. I do it to this day. The truth is, you don't live your life, you reenact it. If you are molested as a child, those awful feelings about touch and sex stay with you. The terror, helplessness, and sense of betrayal are impossible to describe to someone who hasn't experienced it. But from that point on, whenever someone touches you those feelings come flooding back. They're with you even when you have grown up and the touch is from someone you love. When adults molest children they don't think of the consequences. They are in their own moment, not realizing or caring that the innocence is being stripped from these children for the rest of their lives.

People ask me if I have forgiven him. Yes, but I have not forgotten. Lord knows I'd like to, but it's like a scar on my face—some days I see it and some days I don't, but the scar will be there for life. I just have to choose how to deal with it on the days I do see it. I have to believe I can rewrite the script that was given me and teach myself to trust.

I was speaking at a high school a few years ago and a young girl angrily asked me, "How could you possibly forgive him? If it were me, I would tell him to go to hell."

"I didn't do it for him, I did it for me," I replied. "I forgave him so I wouldn't have to carry the anger you are carrying right now. Forgiveness is about self-respect and self-love. Why would I want to continue to live like a prisoner dragging around a ball and chain, when I can choose to set myself free?"

I have made a decision to look at the events in my life from the most positive angle I can. From this devastating situation in my childhood, some good did emerge. In some ways I even feel blessed, because I was able to confront him. He didn't have to admit it. He could have lied, but he had a conscience and that was my saving grace. In confronting him, I was finally able to love and respect myself. Each time I faced him I became stronger, and knowing my own strength was an amazing and powerful gift.

Oddly, feeling broken as a child made me tireless in my quest to improve myself. Not that I would recommend molestation as a path to self-discovery, but for me, that was a positive outcome. I was always searching for ways to fix myself, and even though I am now in damn good working condition, those habits are still with me. I'm not one to pat myself on the back for too long, because I know there is always more I could do to better myself or improve things for other people.

But the most valuable lesson I learned from this miserable experience was that people really can change. I was not the same person I had been at age eleven, and he was not the same man who had cornered me in the bathroom. He had suffered, grown, and done the honorable thing by admitting his guilt. He had even defended me to the therapist, insisting that I say anything I needed to say.

Before I left the hospital that day, I asked him, "How would you feel about it if I were to use this story in my work? What if I'm on television and talk about this?"

"Kathy, if you believe that by sharing this story you can stop a single person from hurting a child, then by all means use it."

What he had done to me as a child was monstrous, but he was not a monster. He was a man who made a bad choice.

Whenever I thought about the molestation, my mind ran down another path that was almost as disturbing. I always ended up thinking, *Why didn't my mom save me?* My dad was never around, except for when I was in the emergency room. He was always working. Even if he had been there, I never would have been able to tell my father about the touching; it was far too personal and humiliating. Mom was working on those Saturday mornings and never knew I spent so much time in the woods. She didn't have a clue what was going on. But she was my mother, and if she and I had been close perhaps I would have had the courage to share this awful experience with her. Since we couldn't even talk about the most obvious things, such as my hearing aids hurting or why I had to wear them, there was no way I was going to tell her about this close family friend "examining" me. It all came down to communication, and she and I didn't have any.

Had it not been for my friendship with Anne Baxter, I might never have tried to understand my mother and see things from her perspective. Listening to Anne talk about her daughters had forced me to realize that my mother might have her own side of our story. After the trip to Ohio for that therapy session, I decided to try and get to know my mom better. Like the molestation, the reason for our bad relationship was a missing piece of my history. That part of my life would always feel hollow and wrong until I understood why she had acted the way she did.

My mother and I hadn't talked very often in the years since I had left her house. Her music box gift was a pretty good indication of how large the communication gap between us was. Mom hadn't been supportive of my comedy career in the beginning; I don't think she understood what I was getting into. Neither did I, for that matter.

The first time I played a club in Cleveland, Mom came and saw me perform. In the audience that night were also about 80 people from my high school class. Talk about nervous! Here I was, standing in front of the kids who had teased me, locked me in the girl's bathroom, and made me feel like I was dumb. I got onstage, and who was sitting right in the middle of the front row? Joey, the guy I had a crush on in sixth grade. I could practically feel my hearing aids starting to squeal again. But I went through my routine, and as I did, I realized that I was looking at a typical audience full of smiling men and women. They weren't high school kids anymore, they were adults. My classmates had not come to snicker at me, as I had feared, but to have a good time and root for me.

I would have been on quite a roll that evening except for one little hitch: Mom kept shouting out responses to my jokes. I was being heckled by my own mother! Finally I had to shout back, "Hey, Mom, save it for later. We're not at the kitchen table, you know!" When we *were* at the kitchen table, she gave me advice that made me wonder how much she really understood what I was doing. "Why don't you dress like Phyllis Diller, Kathy? She's very successful, you know."

"Should I wear a clown nose, too, Mom?"

As long as we kept the visits short, we could get along. She still did things that infuriated me, such as talking to me from the next room and, when I didn't respond, asking, "Why don't you answer me?"

"I'll give you three guesses and the first two don't count." A few days with her was about all I could handle.

But now I wanted to improve my relationship with my mother. Maybe she would never be a mom who doted over her daughter and took her to tea, but if I could get her to talk about what had happened when I was young, perhaps we could make up for lost time.

I knew enough not to drag her into a therapist's office and demand that we work it out there. Going at the past with klieg lights and a box of dynamite was only going to scare her away. Instead I went at it like an archeologist, picking around the edges of the site until I could get a sense of what was buried there. I began to ask her about her own childhood, but she didn't have much to say except, "I was the black sheep." It was clear that she didn't feel close to her family, the noisy, face-biting, toe-nibbling Italians I got such a kick out of when I was little. The aunts and grandparents had been wonderful with me. What had happened with her?

It was those very aunts who filled me in, before my mother and I got close enough to discuss it. Apparently Mom had been a short, average-looking brunette with two stunning, red-haired younger sisters who were the apple of everyone's eyes. The second child in a poor family of seven, Mom was the girl they would have sent to the nunnery in the old days. She loved school but was forced to leave in the eighth grade to help support her siblings. When she brought money home her mother would give her a hot dog, and that was about all the affection she received. She never had love and support from her family; they didn't hug and kiss her, they didn't compliment her or sit down and ask how her day was. My mother associated food and material gifts with love, so she gave us nice birthday parties and Hallmark Christmases and Easters. She had received a hot dog, so she gave her children a feast.

Mom and I never bonded in part because I didn't have the language skills until much later in life. But she was never one for heart-to-heart talks with any of her children. Her motto was, "You're living under my roof and you will do as I say." If only I could have heard what she said, I would have been okay. I couldn't, so it was like living with Dr. Jekyll and Mr. Hyde. I never knew when I would disappoint her. I was always afraid of getting into trouble, and my brother Mark made sure I was frequently in her line of fire.

I couldn't get around the feeling that my mother just didn't like me very much. Now that I look back on it, I think that she saw too much of herself in me. I was needy; I longed for hugs, kisses, and physical contact more than a hearing child would. Mom had needed love as a child, too, and she had been ignored. She must have seen her childhood pain in me, and it made her want to avoid me.

From a young age I wanted desperately to please my mother. I would make her things to show my love, but she rarely responded. When I was eleven I made her an apron in sewing class. She looked at it and simply said, "Thank you." Nothing more. A few days later I visited a neighbor who told me, "I heard about the beautiful apron you made your mom."

"How did you know I made my mom an apron?"

"She showed it to me and told me how much she loved it."

"My mother loved it? She said it was beautiful?"

I was ecstatic. From then on I continued to make her things, then go out into the neighborhood to see if she liked them.

A few years ago, when my mother and I were vacationing in Las Vegas, I couldn't resist hugging and kissing her as we were walking down the street. She stopped, looked up at me, and asked, "Why do you keep doing that?"

"What?"

"Hugging and kissing me."

"Because you're my mother and I love you. But if it bothers you, I can stop."

"Nah, that's okay."

That's when I realized that she didn't know how to receive my love, or anyone else's for that matter.

Each tidbit of insight made me want to keep poking around for more answers, but my mother was reluctant to look backward. "Why talk about the past? It's over and done with," she'd say.

"Mom, the past is like a closet where you store all your memories, good and bad," I tried explaining to her once. "Most of the good stuff is stored all the way in the back where we can barely get to it, while the bad stuff is right up front. We keep wearing the bad stuff because it's easy to get to and it's what we feel comfortable in, even though it doesn't look good on us.

"You store stuff in there forever, to the point where you can't squeeze in anything new. My closet was jammed with a lot of negativity, so I went in and threw out everything that didn't benefit my life. When I was done, the closet was nearly empty, and I had room for a whole new wardrobe of positive things that would look good on me."

After I had cleared my closet of all the bad memories, I was surprised at how empty it was. Where was my past? I forced myself to come up with some good memories and ended up being amazed. There was so much to put in the closet, all of which I had brushed aside before.

I recalled baking cookies with my mom and arranging them on a tray so she could bring them to my class the next day. I used to be so proud when the other kids gobbled those cookies up. I remembered how my mother had sat on my bed looking helpless and heartbroken when Jimmy hadn't asked me to the prom, and how she had known to call Lisa. I thought of how incredibly hard she had worked while we were growing up, standing behind the ironing board for a day and a half to iron the dozens of fancy dress shirts some jerk had crammed in the bushel basket. Five dollars a bushel, just so she could give us a wonderful Christmas.

And I remembered the birthday parties she threw, which must have taken weeks to plan. For years, whenever I thought of those parties I'd instantly tell myself, "Yeah, she gave good parties but she never hugged me." Now I dared to look at some old black-and-white photographs of my fifth birthday party. I saw an extravaganza with balloons, gifts everywhere, an enormous cake, and a crowd of laughing children gathered around me. In one photo my mom hovered beside me as I stared at the cake, my eyes huge. This was how she showed she loved me. I started putting those memories into the closet, because they were the past I wanted to keep.

I was determined to open up the lines of communication with my mother. If she didn't want to discuss the past, we could talk about the present. I started calling her regularly, and eventually it worked. We began chatting two or three times a week for an hour or more, and soon I was getting a much bigger dose of my mother than was good for me.

At that time, she was going through a difficult breakup with a man who had stripped her of her confidence. "He doesn't love me," she'd say. "If he loved me, how could he treat me like this? Nobody ever invites me over, nobody wants me around. I don't have any family. I'm all alone, I don't have any friends." It was agonizing to hear her put herself down and make herself a victim. After an hour of this I would get off the phone feeling drained and depressed. I didn't realize how much of her pain I was absorbing. I wanted to make her happy but I didn't know how. My friends advised me, "Don't call her anymore if this is how it's going to affect you." But I couldn't stop calling her—she needed me, and that is exactly what I had always wanted.

I began to see a lot of my mother in myself. I realized that from a very young age I had absorbed her vocabulary and way of thinking. Mom seemed always to be setting herself up to get hurt. She had a lot of rules and expectations that kept leading to disappointment. When I was little, I never felt as if I were good enough to deserve her love. As an adult, whenever I got close to loving someone I would freeze and back off, because to me love meant obligation. I would be obliged to repay the love, and I would come up short, as I always had with my mother. But now I could see that it wasn't only me coming up short, it was everyone. Nobody met her expectations.

It frightened me to realize how much her pain, negativity, and feelings of rejection had worked their way into my own personality. It was like I had a small version of my mother living inside me. I wanted her out, but I didn't know how to achieve that, especially now that we were finally talking. I was afraid that being honest with her might jinx everything.

Tony Robbins held a seminar called Date with Destiny, and as I had been working with him for several years by this time, I decided to take it. My goal was to get rid of all the negativity I was absorbing from my mother. The seminar itself was painful. I was too nervous and unhappy to sit still for the exercises and it was nearly impossible to read Tony's mile-a-minute lips, not to mention those of the twelve other people in our group. When he got to the part about "Close your eyes and imagine . . ." I nearly threw my chair at him. How was I supposed to close my eyes and read his lips at the same time, let alone imagine anything? Tony saw how frustrated I was getting and told Joseph, a seminar counselor and friend, to take me into a separate room for some intensive guidance.

"What is it you want out of this seminar, Kathy?" Joseph asked.

"I want to get my mom out of me. I want to help her but I can't, she won't listen to me. I want the negativity and pain to go away."

"What have you been doing recently?"

"Working, as always. I usually do three or four performances a week."

"Kathy, I've known you for a long time now, and I've seen you onstage. Whenever you're in front of an audience you give it your all. I see you up there, reliving the pain, the rejections, the retardation, all of it. When you talk with your mother, it puts you back in that place again. I think you're spending too much time in the past. Why don't you make a list of who you are today?" I did as I was told, eager to try anything that might work.

I am a comedian
I love and have a passion for people
I am forgiving
I am outgoing
I am a good listener
I am a leader
I am pretty (that was a hard one for me)
I am smart (Joseph put next to it, "Intelligent!!!" God love him.)

The list went on, and it was all positive. As I wrote it, I saw how easy it had been for me to forget the present and fall back into the past when I spoke with my mom. It crushed me to see her victimize herself, rejecting everything good that came her way. It was like looking into a mirror.

I had to take charge of my relationship with my mother. I could no longer feel responsible for her happiness, hoping that if she was happy I would be, too. I needed to look within to find my own happiness. If I could do that, maybe I could be an example for her. Our roles were reversed now—I had become the mother and she was the daughter. It is not easy raising your parents.

As gently as I could, I told my mom that I couldn't listen to her negativity anymore. "I love you, but I am not responsible for making you happy," I said. "You're going to have to want it. No more hour-long phone calls, Mom. I'll give you ten minutes, and if you start getting negative, I'll tell you I have to hang up. I only want to hear good things, and if you have nothing good to say, you can listen to me breathe."

To my amazement, she agreed. Even more surprising, she admitted that every day she listened to her sister dump on *her* for an hour. It dawned on me that I had been part of a vicious circle. When I broke it, my mother did, too. She called her sister and told her, "Ten minutes, and no more negativity." I had learned the power of words: The life you give them is the life you live.

Once, when my mom and I had gotten close enough to be honest with each other, she called me on the phone, crying. She had been thinking of the Jeep accident and blaming herself for not taking care of me afterward.

"Where was I, Kathy? I was your mother, I should have been there for you."

"You were living your life."

"But I was your mother!"

"Yes, but you were also a person. You had just gotten a divorce and for the first time you were finding yourself. You and I weren't connecting at that time, anyway." I didn't mention that I hadn't wanted her with me while I was recovering. She wasn't a source of comfort to me at that time, and it didn't occur to me to miss her. Now, all these years later, I didn't want her to feel bad about the past.

"You can't be there one hundred percent for any child," I told her. "Mom, had you been there, our relationship would be different than what we have today. And I wouldn't trade what we have now for anything in the world. We went on the paths we had to so that we could both grow."

I wasn't just being generous in my attitude for my mother's sake; I was doing it for me. I had made myself miserable because of her, convincing myself that she didn't love me. I had made her out to be a villain. She often asked, "Why didn't you ever come to me when you were little, Kathy?" I was a child and hadn't known I was supposed to go to her. The question was, why hadn't she come to me? At the age of forty-two, I made peace with the answer: Because she hadn't known she was supposed to, either.

It had been easy to blame my parents when things weren't going right in my life. As I got older I learned to see that they were just people with their own stories. Today my mother and I get along wonderfully. I appreciate the good qualities I inherited from her, such as her work ethic and sense of humor, both of which played a big part in my success. I didn't get her 44D chest, and she *should* feel guilty about that. But otherwise, I'm grateful for what she has given me. I have found the friend in my mother and put to rest the enemy I created.

Until the time I healed the rift with my mom, I was always collecting "parents." I would get attached to people and out of respect it seemed natural to call them Mom or Dad. I called Mr. and Mrs. Hintz Mom and Dad; I called Mrs. Reynolds, my teen board counselor at JCPenney, Mom; and then there was Ma Hayward, Mom Meyer, Daddy Showalter, and I called Anne Baxter Mom, too. Looking back, I can see that I was creating my own family with these people. Sometimes it's not the family you were born into but the one you create that has the most impact as time goes on. These moms and dads were the very ones who taught me to see my parents as individuals, and who showed me that my problems with my mother hadn't been entirely her fault.

With all my "moms" I was looking for love, warmth, and acceptance, but although they gave me plenty, I was not really able to receive it. It took a sister, my friend Jane, to teach me how to do that.

Jane and I met at a New Year's Eve party. I was sitting on the couch next to the front door watching people arrive, and in walked a pair of pants that nearly blinded me—tight, black-and-white-cowhide-printed jeans stuck into cowboy boots. I looked up and saw a tight black sweater belonging to a beautiful woman with naturally curly blond hair. The first thing that burst out of my mouth was, "You're going into the New Year with those freaking pants on?" I don't remember her response, but we've been best friends ever since.

Jane is from England. It figured that my new best friend was someone I was going to have to stand on my head to lip-read. She was a struggling single mom with a beautiful ten-year-old daughter named Katie who intimidated me. The little girl was scarily smart and always reading books. I had just started out in comedy and Katie, with her British sense of humor, just wasn't getting my jokes. Uh oh.

The following December I was home from the road and spent Christmas Eve with Jane and Katie. That night I became very ill with the flu. I didn't want them to catch it, so despite a high fever and the shakes I started making moves to drive home.

"You're not leaving," Jane said, gripping me by the shoulders and pointing me toward the bedroom. "You're going to bed and I'm going to take care of you." Bossy little Englishwoman Jane insisted that I stay. All weekend she played nurse, making me soup and force-feeding me Earl Grey tea. I think she believed that Earl Grey cured any illness. I had so much of that tea that I finally faked a recovery. After that, our friendship started to blossom, but I still kept Jane at arm's length as I did everybody—and I have very long arms. Like Groucho Marx said, if they wanted me in their club, I didn't want to be in it.

The following year, Jane and Katie had to move back to England. I couldn't bear it, so I booked myself out on the road as much as possible. I wasn't there when Jane sold all her belongings or sent Katie ahead while she tied up loose ends in California. Two weeks before she had to leave, Jane fell in love with a man named Jay. She brought him to the Ice House one night when I was performing there, so I could meet him. I saw immediately that this was a special relationship. When Jane left for England, I knew in my heart she would be back.

Jay, my knight in shining armor, went to England that Christmas, asked Jane to marry him, and brought her and Katie home. The following Christmas, Jane gave me the most exquisite gift anyone could have offered. She invited me to watch the birth of their new daughter, my beautiful godchild Julia. Jay, Katie (reading a book about childbirth, of course), and I were in the room with Jane when Julia arrived. Meeting her for the first time, it was as if my heart came out of my chest dancing—I could hear the angels playing their trumpets. When the nurse took the baby and started rubbing her briskly, I almost smacked her.

"What are you doing?" I yelled at her.

Poor Jane, still lying there on the table, had to grab my wrist and calm me down. "It's all right, Kathy, she's just rubbing the baby to help with her circulation."

"Katie, is that in the book?"

We all became a family that day. Katie was fifteen at the time, and finally beginning to get my sense of humor. Hallelujah.

In her first few years of life, Julia taught me many new things. She introduced me to Barney, which I did not appreciate. It's really difficult to lip-read a big purple puppet. At four years old, Julia attended her first day of preschool. I called from the road to see how she liked it, and while she was talking to me she suddenly started to whisper.

"Kathy?"

"Julia?"

"Kathy?"

"Julia, why are you whispering?"

"I'm just checking to see if you're still deaf."

Julia got my sense of humor from day one.

I learned a lot watching Jane raise her two girls. I wanted to be a better person and a healthy role model for them. Julia was as close to me as a child could be to someone who wasn't her own mother, and that did something to my heart. It would have been a sin if I didn't receive her love. I still had a difficult time letting other people in, even Jane. It was all right as long as I was doing the giving; that way I could stay in control. I was back on the tennis court with Jane, and it frustrated her to no end. It took something really big to get me to stop shooting those balls over the net and finally let her send some back my way. Luckily, Jane is a very determined person.

In April of 1995, after living in my North Hollywood apartment for 18 years, I finally rented a house. It took me almost three months to actually move into this house, possibly because I did it all by myself in my little Toyota Corona. I must have been home a total of two weeks in that three months, packing, unpacking, and hauling mini-loads of belongings to the new place. What with having to buy furniture and appliances in between road jobs, I was a wreck. Typically, I didn't think to ask anyone for help.

The whole thing climaxed with a job that took me to nine different states in ten days. I literally lived on the airplane, and we're not talking about a private jet here. There were times when I would change clothes on the plane, land, and go directly to the next gig. I don't think I slept in those ten days. I only packed one stage outfit for the whole trip—I figured I was going to be in a different place every day, and no one would know. By the end of the trip I was exhausted and so was the outfit. No one ever saw it again.

I was dreading coming home and having to get things settled in the house. In three days I would have to get up and leave again. There weren't even curtains in the bedroom, and it was hard to sleep late with the sun shining in. No furniture, just boxes piled everywhere and a feeling of total chaos that was torture for a control freak like me.

When I opened the front door I was hit with a peculiar smell. Pine-Sol. Did I spill a bottle before I left? It was dark, so I had to be careful not to fall over any boxes as I went for the light switch. I turned on the light, and there were no boxes. Everything was put away. I stood in the middle of the living room in shock, tears starting to trickle down my face. The house was spick-and-span. My bedroom was all put together. There was a bed in it, the bed was made, and there were curtains on the windows—blackout curtains, mind you. There were roses from the garden on the table next to my bed, with a note from Julia telling me that she loved me. I couldn't believe it. The kid was writing at a year old.

I went from room to room, bawling as I felt the love get stronger with each door I opened. There was nothing I could do but absorb it. I had never felt so full. My heart was like a sponge taking it all in. Jane had caught on to me. I needed to be out of town when she gave to me, so I couldn't block it by saying, "No, thank you. That's okay, I can do it myself." This way I had no choice but to receive, and I must say I loved every second of it.

I called Jane and asked her, "How could you find the time to do all this? You have your own family to care for."

"You are my family."

The most courageous thing I ever did was to receive Jane's love unconditionally, without feeling obligated to give it back right away. And that's what a family is all about: unconditional love, no expectations, and appreciation for all that is there. Well, Jane, you can give all you want—I have my heart set on a pool for the backyard.

I've always looked at myself as a package, and for most of my life I have felt half-full. I was so busy trying to get rid of what was wrong with me that I never bothered to look for what was right. I was afraid to be in a relationship because I felt I had very little to offer anyone. Although nobody except me could fill my package up, Jane and Jay's family showed me how to do it by supporting me and loving me unconditionally, as I did them.

I realize now that my package was only half-full when I was with Ryan. He was an incredible man, and I feel very blessed to have had him in my life and to have experienced a wonderful relationship. If I had known then what I know now, I would not only have been able to communicate with him but also to receive his love and love him in return. I have yet to meet another man like Ryan, but when I do, I know that I'll be able to give him a full package.

When I got my hearing aids several years after Ryan and I split up, I finally began to understand what my strengths and limitations were and that the limitations were not very serious at all. From that point on, I had a new identity. I started my journey of self-discovery and realized that many of the people who had crossed my path were like angels here on earth. By seeing how they lived their lives, I was able to choose how I wanted to live mine. I started counting my blessings, which are endless, and began living in the moment.

Nowadays I wake up each morning with a smile on my face. When-ever I stay at my mom's house, she can't get over it.

"How can you wake up so happy?" she asks.

" 'Cause I have your face to kiss this morning, Ma."

"You're happy about nothing!"

It drives her nuts, but she can't help but smile, too.

23

Ovation

LOTS OF PEOPLE go into comedy thinking it will be a good bridge into acting. They'll do stand-up, maybe get an HBO special, and then—at last!—a sitcom, the gold at the end of the rainbow. Once I got into stand-up, I thought the very same thing. I believed the comedy would help with my acting career, that it would break the ice about my hearing impairment. However, things didn't go quite as smoothly as I had hoped.

Acting was still my passion and I was determined to figure out some way to convince the industry that I was more than "the deaf comic." Unfortunately, I was out on the road nearly every week and never seemed to be home when it was casting time. With my comedy, motivational speaking, doing work for nonprofit organizations, and advocating for people with disabilities, my schedule was packed. The advocacy work was very rewarding and was part of the reason I wanted to continue being a performer. It's a known fact that when celebrities talk, people pay attention. I had always wanted a powerful voice to promote the causes I believed in, especially children's rights. Now I had one. Meanwhile, I had to figure out some way to move closer to my goal of acting, which would also raise my profile and allow my voice to reach more people.

I had heard about actors staging one-person showcases to display their talents for the industry. At least that was something I could do by myself, without having to wait for a casting director to call. As soon as this idea occurred to me, my mind was flooded with characters I could portray in a one-woman show. I would create six different women, each with her own monologue. Among my possible creations were a manic depressive, one of my old ladies, a washed-out star, a deaf teenager on her first date, and my favorite, a prostitute with an "I don't care" attitude. The only problem was that I knew nothing about prostitutes other than what my old ladies had taught me—the red light down the street and dyed "petunias."

The role called for some research. I was working in a San Jose comedy club when I met the perfect interview subject, a gay woman who had been madam of her own brothel. She had no qualms about talking to me and no inhibitions at all. For a few hours, I felt like I was back on the porch with my old ladies.

"What type of men came to you?" I asked her.

"The prime clientele was in their forties, fifties, and sixties, from all professions. I had a big cop from New York City break down and cry in my arms because he had to be such a son-of-a-bitch on the job. I had a man come in and, before he actually got into the act, he would say, 'I'm sorry, I made a mistake. I love my wife, I really don't want to do this. Keep the money.' As if I would give it back."

"So it wasn't always about sex?"

"No. Some guys just wanted someone to listen to them, just needed a hug. Then there are your guys who have some kind of fetish. I had a client who wanted to be a slave boy, and another who had a foot fetish. He wanted a hand job done by foot, a foot job. I can pick up a golf ball with my toes, but I ain't playing with someone's willie with my toes."

"What sold the most?"

"Phone sex and blow jobs, to put it bluntly. That's your biggest market, the things wives won't do."

"Well, that figures. Men always want to be in charge."

"Oh, that's where you're wrong," she told me, leaning closer to make her point. "You're in charge of him. Think about it: you have his family jewels in your hands. He's vulnerable. He leans back and can be as passive and gentle as he wants and feel strong at the same time. Out in the real world, men have to be macho, but lots of times they want to let down the walls and be gentler creatures. I see underneath the exterior. They just want to be themselves without being criticized and judged, without having to perform."

Who would have guessed I'd get such valuable insights from a madam? I had always assumed that men felt invincible and enjoyed lording it over women. The decent ones, such as my grandpa, Max Showalter, Ryan, and Jane's husband Jay, had seemed to be exceptions to the rule. If this woman was telling the truth, men resented society's labels and expectations just as I did. Maybe there were more decent guys out there than I had imagined.

After that conversation I had a different perspective about both prostitutes and men, and a different way of developing my character. But I never ended up using the information. Instead, I decided that my best shot would probably be to reenact the story of my life. For drama it couldn't be beat, even by a madam.

A director who worked with HBO Workplace signed on to help me. The Workplace was a theater where performers could put on a one-night showcase for HBO producers, casting directors, and so on. My director assured me that if I put my show up there, the people from HBO would see it. He and I worked together a couple of times a week trying to get the stage setting and stories just right. We didn't want the scenes to be too long, and Lord knows I can go on forever, so editing was a must. It felt weird reenacting my life. Telling it to motivational groups or using it as material for a stand-up routine was one thing, but to become who I had been and feel how I had felt all over again was bizarre. I re-experienced the pain, the fear, the despair, the joy, just as I had the first time. It was as though the muscles in my body had stored these emotions and all I had to do was call on them and they'd come alive.

The set was simple because I didn't want it to distract people from the performance. When I go to a show I'm always so busy trying to figure out how they're going to use the props that I tend to lose track of the dialogue. Of course, I probably pay more attention to the visual part of a play than most people do, but I still wasn't taking any chances. I wanted the audience to hear my stories and look at me. In the end, my props consisted of a small school desk, a bench, a bar stool, and a rocking chair. I also had my report card, audiogram, and the Jeep accident article blown up and mounted on foamboard.

The day of my showcase I got so sick to my stomach that I thought I was coming down with the flu. I was petrified. I never got like this when I did my comedy. In fact, I hadn't been this scared the night of the comedy contest. But the format for the showcase was completely new for me; I was going to be acting in front of lots of important people; and if I did well it might even lead to a sitcom. Suddenly the stakes seemed enormous.

Shortly before showtime the flu medicine I had taken kicked in. It numbed my nerves . . . and my arms and legs. Adrenaline helped me to shake it off, and I managed to get onstage appearing normal, I think. The theater held about 100 people, and it was packed. I walked on the stage and thought to myself, *I am going to show these people I am not just a comedian.* Then I launched right into my opening line, which happened to be the first joke I ever told onstage, complete with the plastic hand: "You would think with today's technology . . ." Well, that was a part of the show, I was reenacting being a comedian. Actually, I was probably wise to open with it because it was familiar territory and helped put me at ease. After a few minutes, everything fell into place. I was totally in the moment with the audience. When it ended, I received a standing ovation. Victory was mine!

The first thing I asked the director when I went backstage was, "How many HBO people where here?"

"None," he said sheepishly. "No one showed up."

"What? Who were all those people?"

"People who wanted to see your show."

"But this was supposed to be a showcase for the HBO people, they said they were going to come. Come on, you're kidding me. None of them came?"

"No."

"Why? Did they figure they had already seen my comedy stuff, so they didn't need to come? Did you tell them that this is different? What is it going to take to show people that there's more to me than jokes?" The director felt terrible, but I felt worse. I was so hurt that I was ready to hang my hat and say to hell with it all.

Completely discouraged, I loaded all my props up into my Jeep and went home. (Yes, I bought a Jeep. I figured it was safer to be in one than under it.) What a waste of time and money the whole thing had been. But after a few days, I reconsidered. I had learned by then that rejection is usually nothing more than God telling you you're on the wrong path. So what if the HBO people didn't come? I still had a show, and there were other industry people in Los Angeles. I could set up my own showcase, get my own theater. If I wanted this, I'd have to make it happen.

I knew nothing about the theater world and had no idea where to start, so for the next six months I researched every theater in L.A., questioning everyone I came into contact with. I met my publicist, Michael Sterling, at my health club, and my director, Sue Wolf, in a Dallas airport. A friend who had seen me speak at Tony Robbins's Life Mastery knew Tom Kendall, who ran the Tamarind Theatre in Hollywood and agreed to put the show on there despite having some initial doubts about it.

I had to come up with a name for the show, so on New Year's Eve, 1997, Jay, Jane, our friend John Secunda, and I got together to brainstorm. When John blurted out, "Don't Buck with Me," I knew we had it. The title was totally me—that was my attitude, that was how I had survived. I loved it.

Tom Kendall, Michael Sterling, and Sue Wolf became my new family. Sue had no problem with my hearing loss because she had lots of friends who were deaf. She expected nothing less than the best and worked my butt off. Meanwhile, in addition to all the rewriting and rehearsals, I was printing up flyers and invitations to send out to the industry people. My plan was to put the show up for four weeks so they could see my acting range.

My biggest fear on opening night was that I would need to go to the bathroom while I was up onstage. I had no one to cover for me, it was a one-woman show. I must have peed at least five times beforehand, trying to wring every last drop out of my bladder before hitting the stage.

Like it had been for the HBO showcase, the house was packed. I don't remember if any industry people were there, but I had a lot of friends in the audience. That night I felt like Cinderella with both glass slippers on. I knew I shined in that performance and I received a wondrous standing ovation that proved it to me. Michael and his friend Chad put on a reception after the show, and when I walked out into the lobby it was like a surprise party with everyone standing there waiting to greet me. The place was candlelit, and Michael had made some posters of me and put them up on the walls. The food was incredible; the whole evening was perfect.

Michael did an extraordinary job with the press. He had me in everything from local newspapers to *People* magazine, from local news to "Entertainment Tonight," and a lot of talk shows as well. I was busy with interviews left and right. Here I thought I would only be working at night doing my show, but Michael kept me busy in the day with all the publicity.

After every show I enjoyed going out into the lobby to meet my audience. At first I was hoping to meet directors, producers, and the like, but as I listened to audience members share their stories with me and tell me how mine had touched them, I began to wonder all over again about the purpose of the show. The industry people whom I had wanted to impress weren't coming, but everyone else seemed to be. My four-week show turned into four months. I would see the same people at two or three performances, often bringing their friends or family members along with them. I'd meet them after the show and it started to feel like a little community.

The day came when I finally had to close "Don't Buck with Me." The theater was promised to someone else, and I had to get back on the road. I had work lined up. But a few months later, in October, I got a big surprise. I was nominated for two Ovation Awards: Best Performer, and Best Writer of a World Premiere Play or Musical.

I had won a few awards by then, mostly for my work with organizations for people with disabilities. The American Comedy Awards had nominated me five times for Best Stand-Up Comedienne, but that was in my own profession, not theater. One of the biggest nights of my life was when my brother Bret flew out to California so that he and Mark, who lived south of L.A., could be my dates for one of the Comedy Award shows. I still thought of Bret as my baby, even though he was now married and the father of two girls. Mark and Debbie had two children as well. I knew it was a big deal for my brothers to get away for a whole weekend, and I was thrilled to have them to myself.

Bret and Mark had grown up to be tall, good-looking men, but award shows were not their usual stomping ground. Bret never wore anything but jeans and a flannel shirt. Watching the two of them try to figure out how to put on the tie, vest, cummerbund, and cufflinks was a comedy in itself. Once they wrestled their tuxes into submission, I had two gorgeous dates.

Mark has always been my biggest fan and supports my career more than anyone in my family. During the run of "Don't Buck with Me" he was in the audience almost every night. When I called to tell him about the Ovation Awards, he started whooping and hollering. I myself didn't realize how big the Ovations

were until I went to the brunch for the nominees. Then I understood that the Ovation Awards in L.A. were like the Tony Awards
in New York. I was surrounded by dozens of incredibly talented
theater people and felt quite honored to be among them. As I
considered the competition, my fantasies about winning started
to fade.

The awards ceremony took place in November, and I wanted
all the people who had got me there to come with me, especially
Tom, Michael, and Sue. It was just as much their show as mine. My
brother Mark was there that night along with his wife, Debbie,
Jane, John Secunda, and Roberta Kent, my biggest booster and
close friend. I would have invited the whole world if I had had
enough tickets. I even took a date with me, Matthew. Before the
show I told him, "If I don't receive this award tonight, would you
be willing to put out? 'Cause I hate the idea of getting all dressed
up for nothing."

I drove to the Schubert Theater with Mark and Debbie and met
everyone else there, including Matthew. That's how you date in
L.A. When I stepped out of the car it was just like I'd seen it in the
movies, with searchlights shooting up into the sky and people pos-
ing and schmoozing, all dressed up. I wore black pants and a short,
red, military type jacket with lots of gold trim. I looked like Michael
Jackson, only without the chimpanzee.

All along the red carpet leading up to the theater, photographers were shouting out my name: "Look over here, Miss Buckley!" "Miss Buckley, over here!" I couldn't tell which one was
where, there were so many. Matthew was kind enough to point in
the direction of the photographers calling my name; otherwise I
would have been looking into the disposable cameras.

I told myself there was no way I was going to win. It was reward
enough to be a nominee. But if I did win, just *if,* I wanted it to be
for Best Performer. That would show them I could act, once and
for all. My category came up, and the announcer called out the
nominees. He opened the envelope. And he said, "Winner for Best

Writing of a World Premiere Play or Musical: Kathy Buckley for 'Don't Buck with Me'!"

Never in my life have I felt such exhilaration, such a sense of accomplishment. I had wanted to win for Best Performer, but Best Writer? Me, a writer? I had a speeding flashback of all the teachers and school administrators who had told me *you can't, you won't, you will never be able to*. In that instant, they all exploded into bits of dust and disappeared. My smile was so big it nearly took over my whole face.

I don't know how I got up to the podium—somehow I just floated up there. The first thing that came out of my mouth was, "I am so excited! You just can't tell with this jacket on." They had told us we only had one minute to talk, but the mike was mine and I had to thank Sue Wolf, Michael Sterling, and Tom Kendall, my theater family. Without them, I don't think I would have ever known I could pull it off.

We opened the show again the following year at a different theater, the Tiffany in Hollywood. It was bigger than the Tamarind, and luckily for me Tom continued to produce the show with Sue and me. Michael kept up with the PR, so my family was intact. And the Tiffany's owner, Paula Holt, was a dream to work with.

During one of my performances all the lights went out in the theater, and we were left sitting there in pitch darkness. I didn't know what to do, so I just said "Hmmm, I could be playing with myself right now and nobody would know it." The lights came on and the audience was roaring with laughter. "Oh, that's right, you can hear in the dark."

This time around, lots of celebrities came to see the show. One night as I was performing my eyes kept being pulled to a familiar face. Was that Mick Jagger? It turned out to be Don Knotts. Before each performance, Tom would come backstage and tell me if any famous people were out there. Once, as I was getting ready, he poked his head in the door and said, "Guess who's here."

"I don't know."

"Monica Lewinsky."

The name didn't ring a bell with me.

"What did she play on?"

"Bill Clinton."

Okay, that rang a bell.

David Hyde Pierce, whose work I adored; Scott Hamilton, Linda Lavin, Sally Struthers, and so many people I had admired sat in my audience and allowed me to entertain them. Wow! Life couldn't get much better than this, but it did.

Every Thursday night we had agreed to comp a group of kids from different halfway houses around Los Angeles. The first Thursday we did this, my brother Mark was there. He came into the greenroom and said, "Kathy, I don't think you should go out there tonight."

"Why? What's wrong?"

"There's a group of about twenty tough-looking kids leaning up against the walls."

"Mark, I think I invited those kids."

I did my show, and the kids were told to stay in the theater while I said good-bye to the other people in the lobby. I wanted to spend some more time with them, asking and answering questions. I love talking with teenagers. One boy was sitting off to the side by himself, so naturally he was my target. He had tattoos all over, a pierced nose, a hoop through his eyebrow, and at least six earrings in each ear. In his black jeans and T-shirt, he almost blended into the walls.

"Hey, why don't you come over here and sit with the rest of us?"

"Nah, I like it over here."

"Don't they have any paper at your halfway house?"

"Yeah, why?"

" 'Cause you're drawing all over yourself. And you have more jewelry on your head than I do in my whole jewelry box."

"Yeah, well, I'm just making a statement. I'm just being an individual."

"You are, are you? Come on up here for minute, will you?"

I had him stand in front of me and I put my hands on his shoulders from behind him.

"I'm not going to hurt you. Are you okay with me touching you?"

"Yeah, I'm cool."

"Good. Now just watch and listen. How many of you kids own a big, baggy, black T-shirt?"

They all raised their hands.

"How many of you own a pair of black jeans twenty times bigger than your size?"

They all raised their hands.

"How many of you have a tattoo?"

Almost all of them raised their hands.

"Hey, where are you getting the money to do this? Okay, how many of you have more than two holes pierced in your body—and I don't want to know where!" Again, almost all of them raised their hands.

I was still holding the boy's shoulders from behind. "You see, honey, you're not making a statement, you're not being an individual. You're just looking for a place to fit, a place to belong. You want to make a statement and be an individual? Then wear your heart on your sleeve and let us see you for who you really are, pain and all." The young man started to cry, and I turned him around and hugged him. When I looked up, I saw that a few other kids were weeping, too. "Oh great," I said. "Now look what we've done! So let's talk about who we really are and what we really want as individuals." And we did, into the wee hours.

That was as good as it gets.

When I was a little girl, I used to watch TV with my family. I never really understood television because I couldn't hear what was going on. When my family would laugh I would laugh just to fit in, and if they cried, I cried. Then one day I saw Red Skelton. He was doing Freddie the Freeloader and I was laughing all by myself. It was the first time I actually related to television. When I turned around, my grandmother was standing behind me crying. It was confusing because I thought Red was funny, but of course she was weeping because she realized that I was relating to a performer who didn't use words. In a way, Red Skelton was the first one to teach me the value of communication—not of words, but of what the heart has to say.

At the first comedy awards show I ever went to, my hero Red Skelton was there being honored as a comedy legend. I was still in awe of him, and although I was dying to go to his table and introduce myself, I didn't want to impose. I hung back all night and then finally, when he started to leave, I approached him and said, "Red? Do you have a moment?" I told him about watching TV as a little girl and how he was the only one I could understand. Then I asked if I could hug him, so that our two hearts could meet as one. We stood there embracing for a moment or two, a little teary-eyed. When we let go we saw that everyone around us was choked up, too. About a week later I received a photo of Red and me hugging that night. I don't even know how I got it, it was taken by a stranger. All I know is that I have it and treasure it.

In the years since I first laughed at Red, I've come to understand that communication makes all the difference in life. Communication leads to friendship, knowledge, love, self-confidence, and acceptance. Failing to communicate leads to isolation, suspicion, intolerance, and fear. Wherever I perform and whomever I talk to, it's always about communicating and breaking down walls.

When I look back on my past, I can see that I was a victim of ignorance. Not only the ignorance of the adults around me, but of my own ignorance as well. I didn't know how to communicate or ask questions. I believed what I was told and accepted the labels adults placed on me, not realizing I had a choice. Now I have created a new set of labels—actress, comedienne, playwright, motivational speaker, and author. I like to call them my designer labels because I chose who I wanted to be instead of accepting who I was taught to be.

I have learned that it takes courage to receive love. When you accept love, you accept yourself. In the old days, I didn't want people to know who I really was in case it wasn't good enough. I used to feel as if I had to keep part of myself hidden. After being in front of audiences for a while, I realized that everyone feels this way. We all have the same basic needs. We want to be loved, accepted, and treated with respect. We want to feel part of something. We all have the same fears of rejection and abandonment. Why bother to hide those feelings, when it gets in the way of living your life? Let go, be yourself, tell people how you feel. Communicate.

That's what I've learned to do. I confronted the man who molested me and gave him back the sadness and sickness that belonged to him. I confronted my mother and told her, "I'm sorry we had a difficult relationship when I was young, but I'm not going to relive it any more. Don't let guilt spoil everything today. Let's be friends." I even confronted my brother Mark about the way he used to taunt me in high school. Actually, he brought it up himself one day by asking, "Are you reluctant to date guys because of the things I said, Kathy?"

I couldn't lie to him. "I'm sure that's part of it, Mark. You helped program me about how ugly I was, and it did affect me."

"From this day on I will never put you down again or make another joke about you," he vowed.

For a split second I hesitated. His jokes were pretty good, and in a way I hated to see them go. I was making money off those! But I did accept his offer, and Mark kept his promise. It's been four years, and he hasn't made a single wisecrack about my looks.

I've learned that you don't have to wallow in hurt. When I first began doing motivational speaking, I used to try to fix all the people who approached me after the show, needing to share their stories with me. I soon discovered that I couldn't fix them, they had to want to do it themselves. What came naturally to me was to break into their sad stories and try to change their pattern. That's what I was aiming for when I spoke to the blue-eyed woman who had been molested by her father and borne his son, been gang-raped by thirteen men, and hadn't looked in a mirror for fourteen years. I knew she had told that story dozens of times before. Now she'll never be able to tell it again without hearing me ask, "Have you always had big boobs?" She's going to have to stop and giggle when she thinks of that, and it may change the way she tells the story or even break her pattern.

From my own experience and from listening to thousands of people who come to hear me speak, I've learned that the darkness in our life is darkness we have created or held on to. Whether it's an accident, an illness, a failed marriage, or a tragedy with a loved one, we control how long the hurt lasts and how deep it goes. We decide how long to sit in the darkness and when to turn on the light.

I made a choice: I want to carry the light I found in God the day I had the Jeep accident, and I want to share it. I never could have dreamed the life I have today. I spent my childhood struggling to communicate and my adulthood searching for a way to fit in. Now I make my living communicating, using the very mouth I was once told would never work properly. I have my own theory about how all this came to be. I believe I became deaf so I wouldn't have to listen to half the nonsense that goes on down here, and so I could hear the One upstairs more clearly. One of my favorite sayings is, "What you are is God's gift to you. What you make of yourself is your gift to God." God gave us life so that we would live it, not just exist. I want to respect the gift as He intended. I never lay my head on the pillow at night until I know I have put at least one smile on His face that day.

Looking back at my life, I realize I was never really alone. There is no way I could have found this happiness without God's guidance, because it was He who put so many extraordinary people in my path. I have learned that faith is having the patience to wait, knowing that all things will be done in His time. I only wish I owned one of his watches.